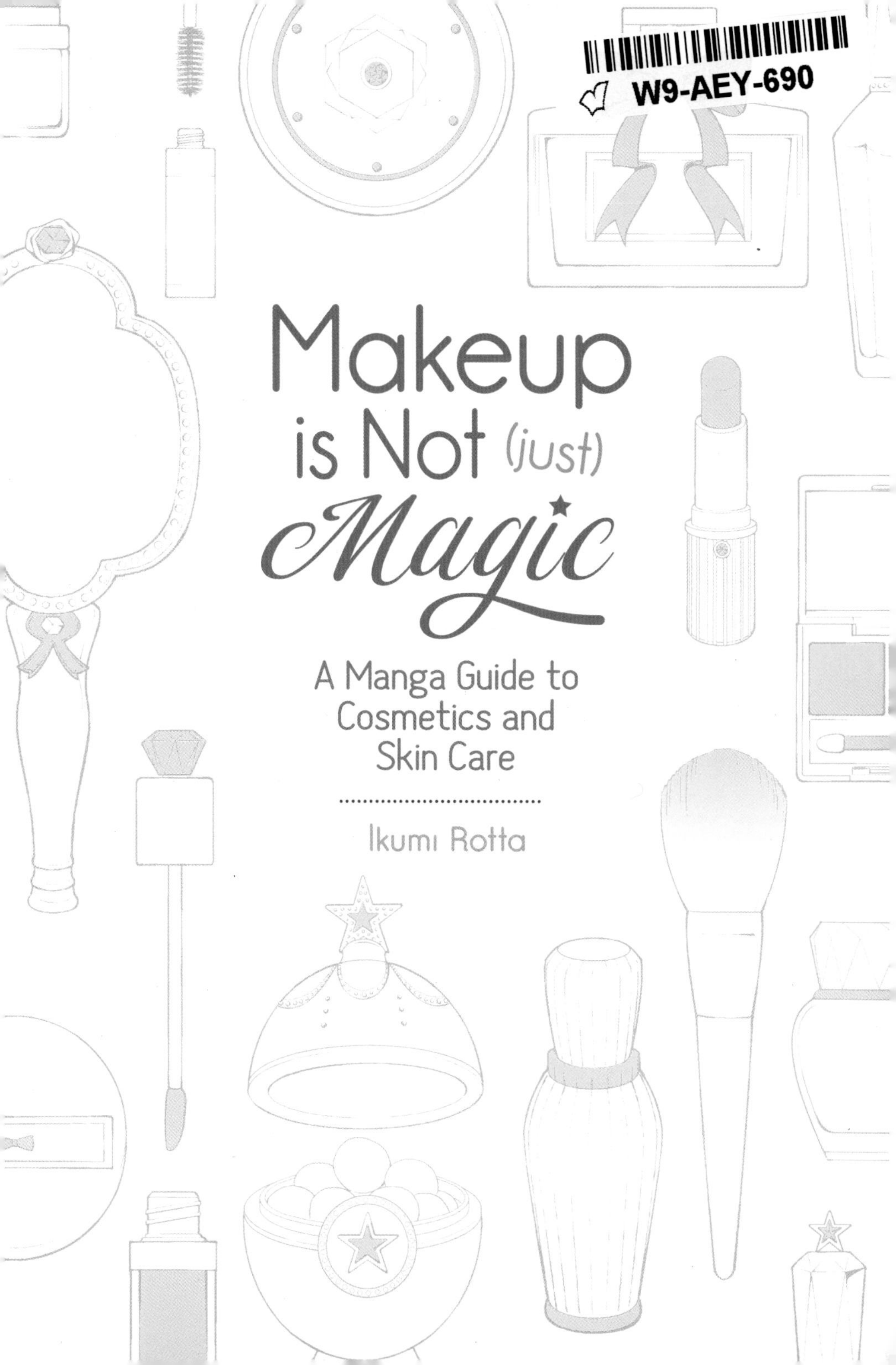

Makeup is Not (just) Magic

A Manga Guide to Cosmetics and Skin Care

Ikumi Rotta

Contents

Prologue

[redacted]

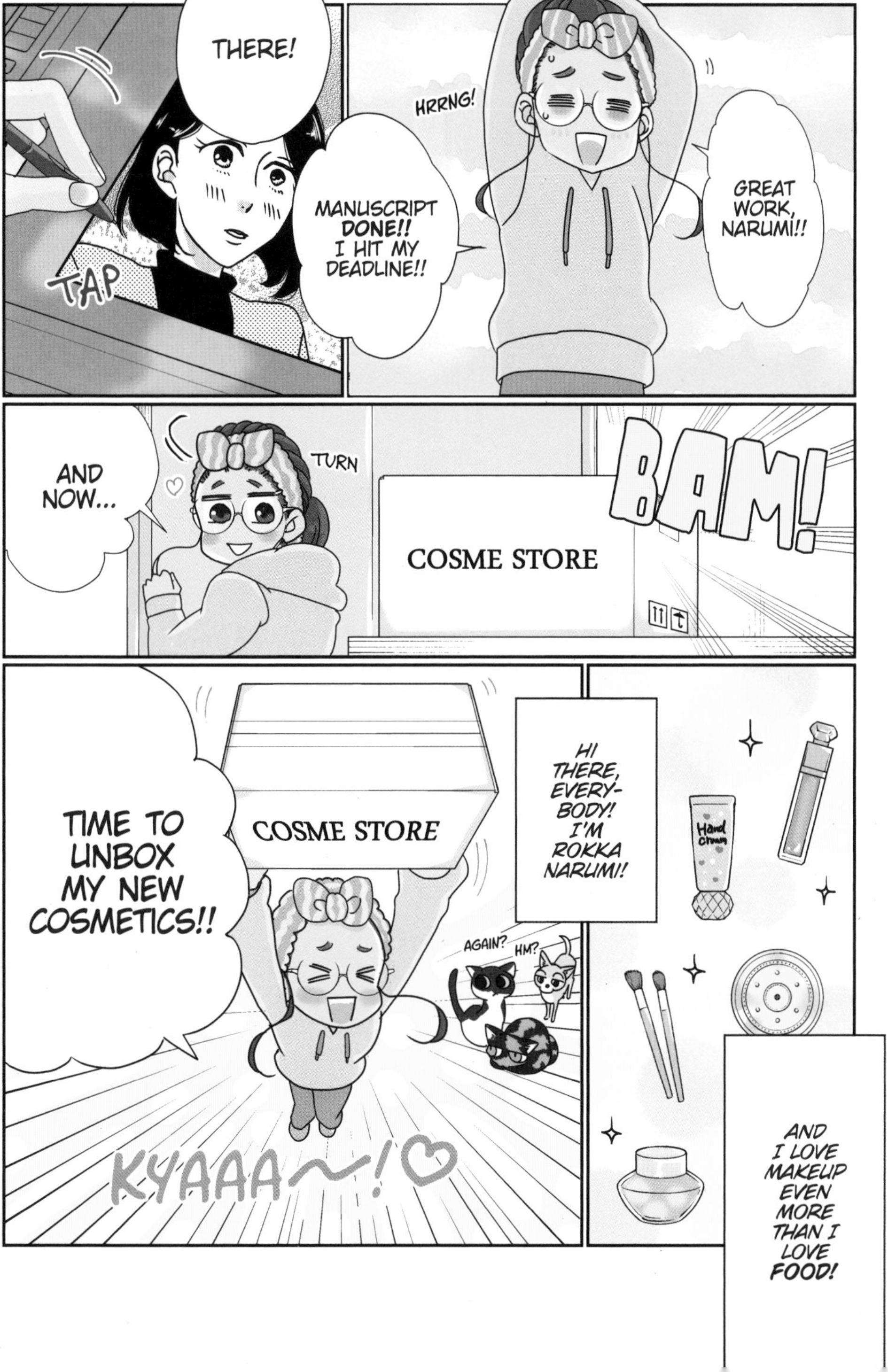

THERE!
MANUSCRIPT DONE!! I HIT MY DEADLINE!!
TAP
HRRNG!
GREAT WORK, NARUMI!!
AND NOW...
TURN
BAM!
COSME STORE
TIME TO UNBOX MY NEW COSMETICS!!
COSME STORE
AGAIN?
HM?
KYAAA~!
HI THERE, EVERY-BODY! I'M ROKKA NARUMI!
Hand Cream
AND I LOVE MAKEUP EVEN MORE THAN I LOVE FOOD!

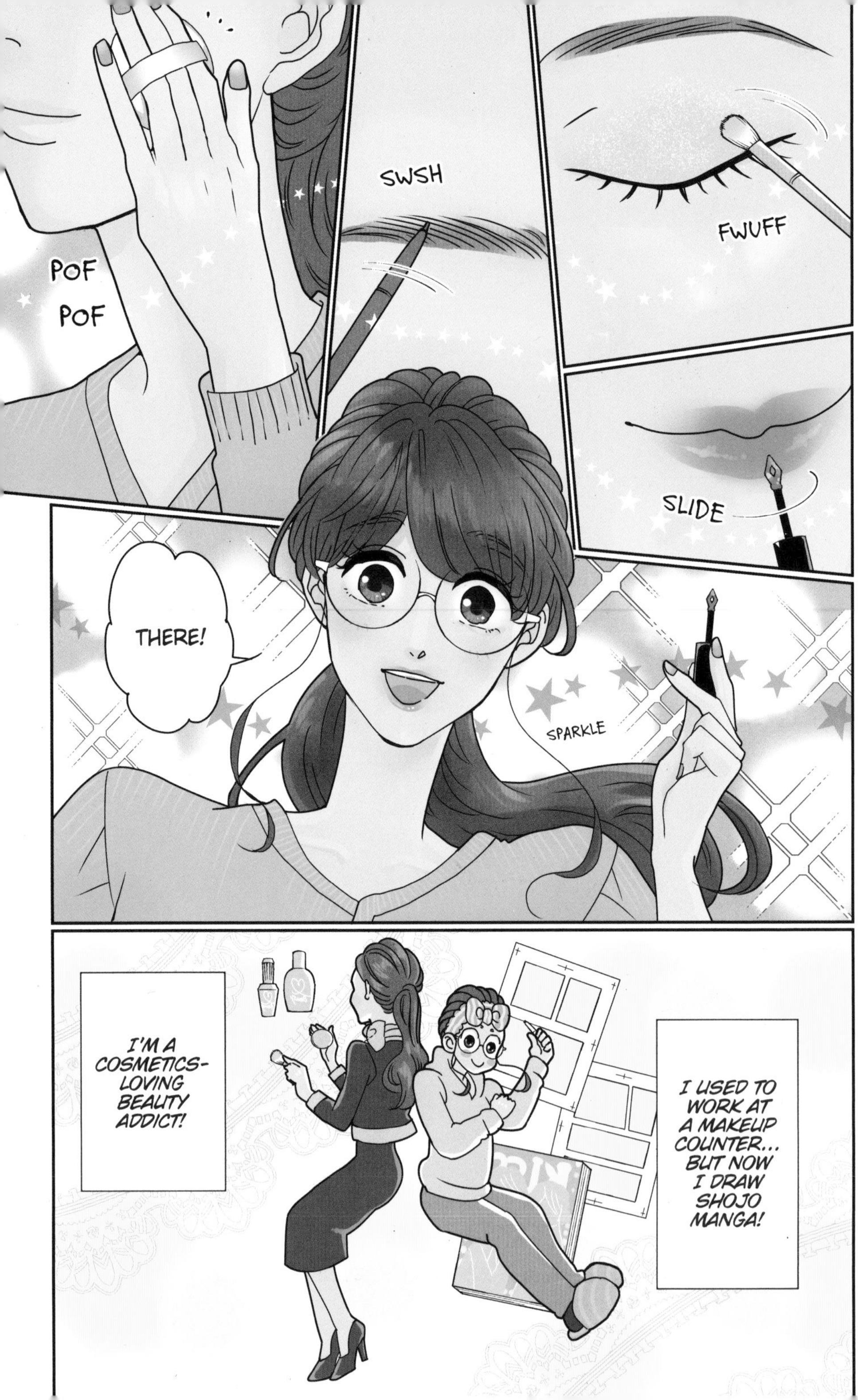

...
FWUFF
SWSH
POF
POF
SLIDE
THERE!
SPARKLE
I USED TO WORK AT A MAKEUP COUNTER... BUT NOW I DRAW SHOJO MANGA!
I'M A COSMETICS-LOVING BEAUTY ADDICT!

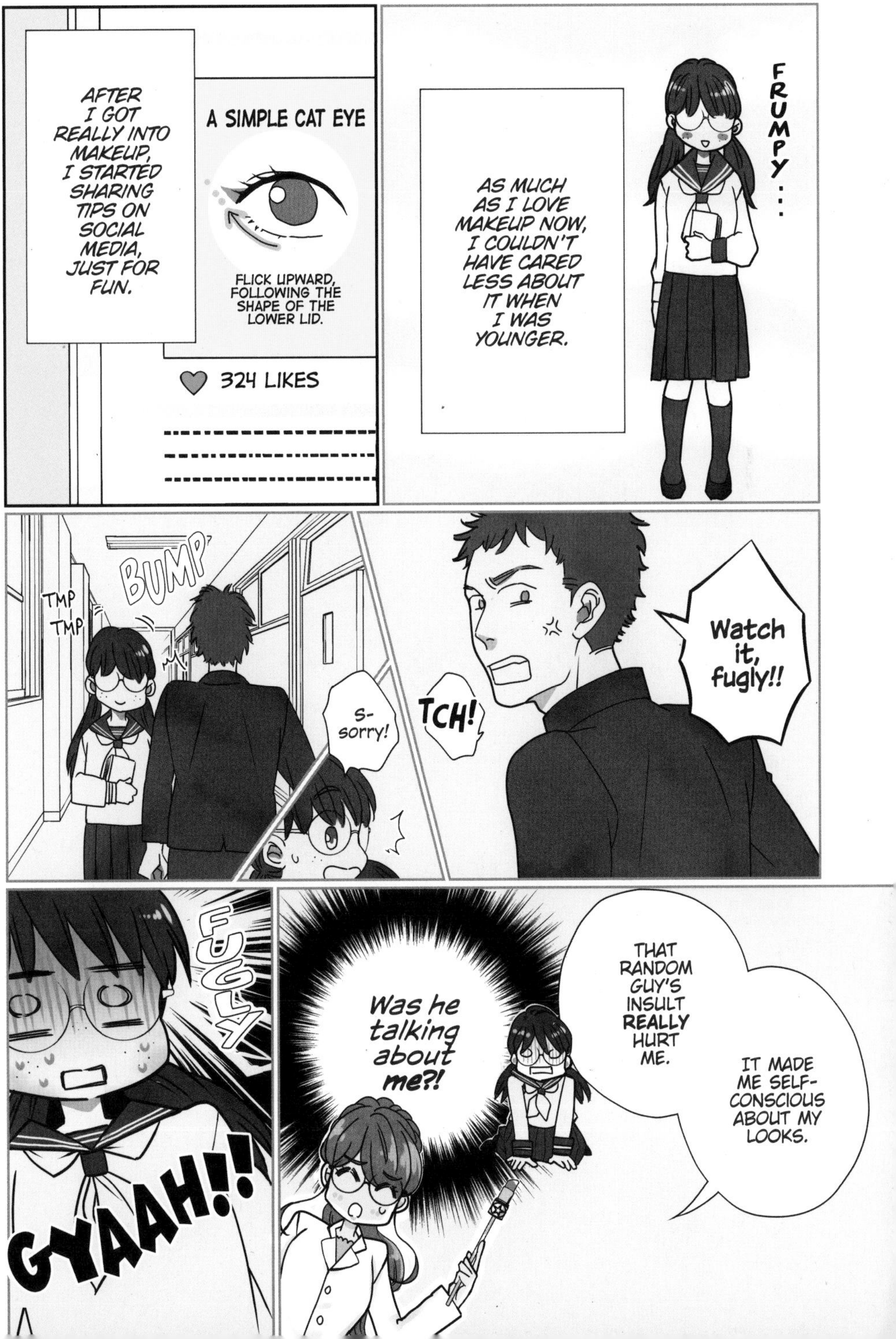
AFTER I GOT REALLY INTO MAKEUP, I STARTED SHARING TIPS ON SOCIAL MEDIA, JUST FOR FUN.
A SIMPLE CAT EYE
FLICK UPWARD, FOLLOWING THE SHAPE OF THE LOWER LID.
324 LIKES
AS MUCH AS I LOVE MAKEUP NOW, I COULDN'T HAVE CARED LESS ABOUT IT WHEN I WAS YOUNGER.
FRUMPY...
TMP TMP
BUMP
S-sorry!
TCH!
Watch it, fugly!!
FUGLY
GYAAH!!
Was he talking about me?!
THAT RANDOM GUY'S INSULT REALLY HURT ME.
IT MADE ME SELF-CONSCIOUS ABOUT MY LOOKS.

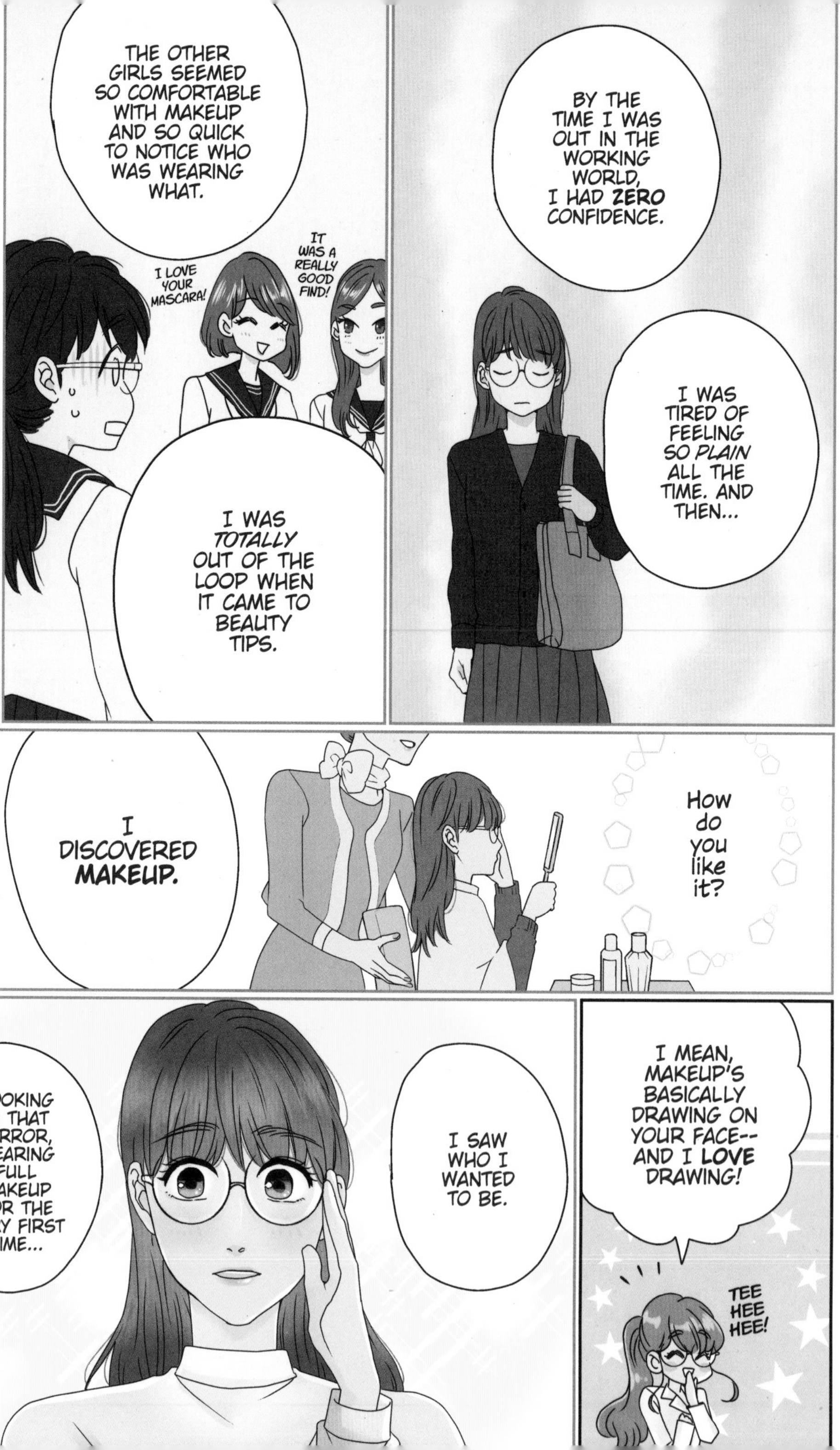
THE OTHER GIRLS SEEMED SO COMFORTABLE WITH MAKEUP AND SO QUICK TO NOTICE WHO WAS WEARING WHAT.
I LOVE YOUR MASCARA!
IT WAS A REALLY GOOD FIND!
I WAS *TOTALLY* OUT OF THE LOOP WHEN IT CAME TO BEAUTY TIPS.
BY THE TIME I WAS OUT IN THE WORKING WORLD, I HAD **ZERO** CONFIDENCE.
I WAS TIRED OF FEELING SO *PLAIN* ALL THE TIME. AND THEN...
I DISCOVERED **MAKEUP.**
How do you like it?
LOOKING IN THAT MIRROR, WEARING FULL MAKEUP FOR THE VERY FIRST TIME...
I SAW WHO I WANTED TO BE.
I MEAN, MAKEUP'S BASICALLY DRAWING ON YOUR FACE--AND I **LOVE** DRAWING!
TEE HEE HEE!

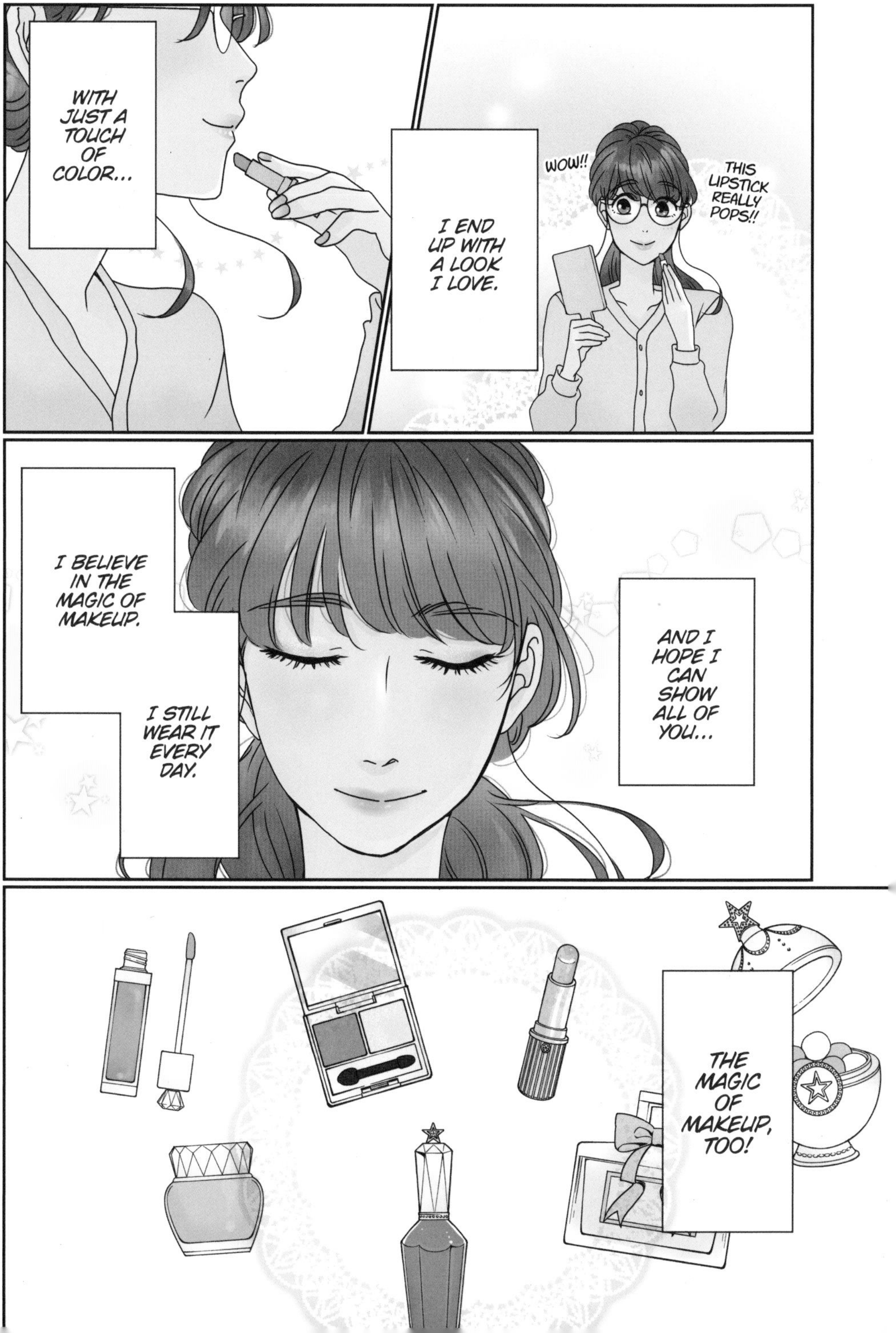
WITH JUST A TOUCH OF COLOR...
I END UP WITH A LOOK I LOVE.
WOW!!
THIS LIPSTICK REALLY POPS!!
I BELIEVE IN THE MAGIC OF MAKEUP.
I STILL WEAR IT EVERY DAY.
AND I HOPE I CAN SHOW ALL OF YOU...
THE MAGIC OF MAKEUP, TOO!

MY ON-THE-GO MAKEUP BAG ♡

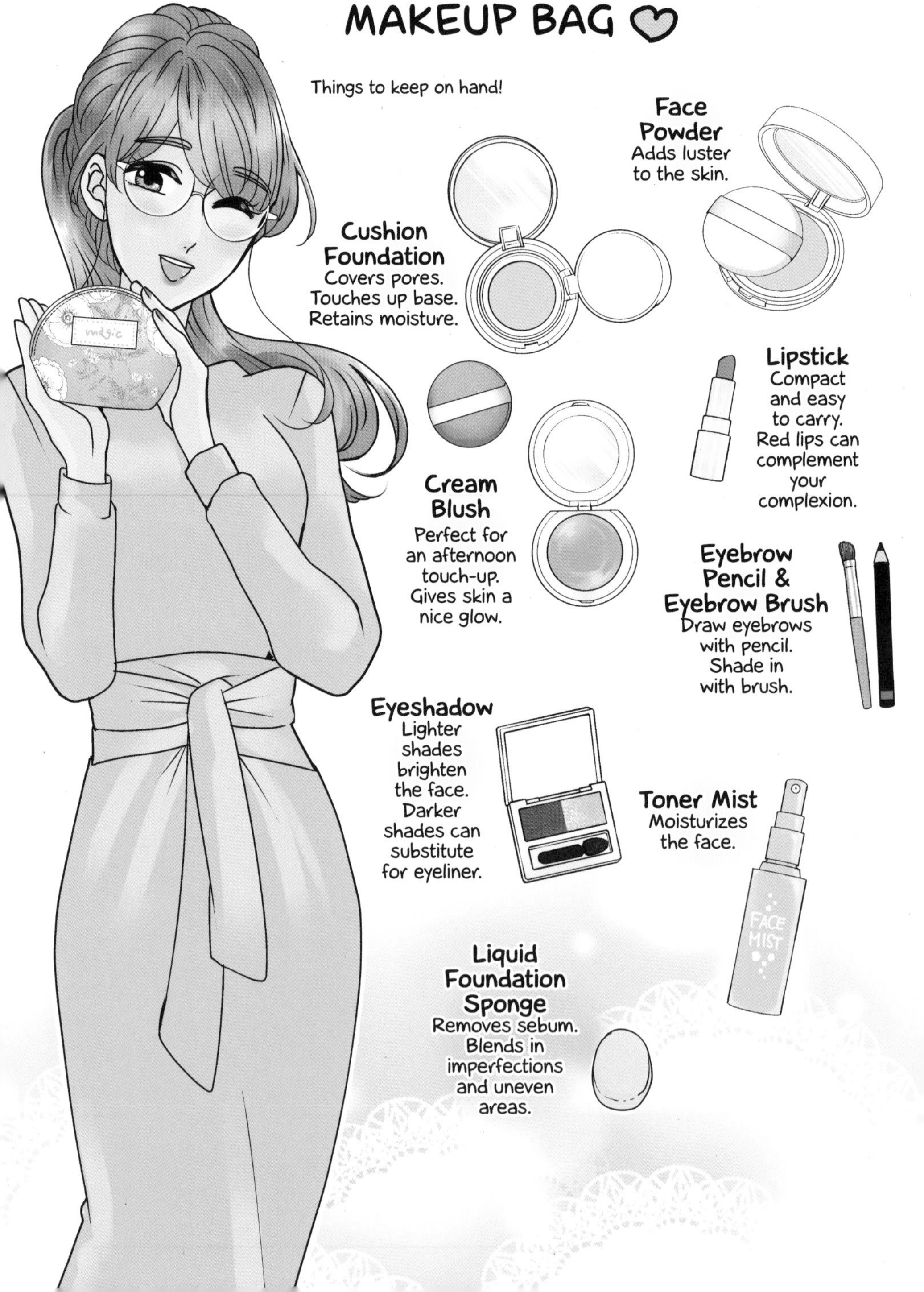
Things to keep on hand!
Face Powder
Adds luster to the skin.
Cushion Foundation
Covers pores. Touches up base. Retains moisture.
magic
Lipstick
Compact and easy to carry. Red lips can complement your complexion.
Cream Blush
Perfect for an afternoon touch-up. Gives skin a nice glow.
Eyebrow Pencil & Eyebrow Brush
Draw eyebrows with pencil. Shade in with brush.
Eyeshadow
Lighter shades brighten the face. Darker shades can substitute for eyeliner.
Toner Mist
Moisturizes the face.
FACE MIST
Liquid Foundation Sponge
Removes sebum. Blends in imperfections and uneven areas.

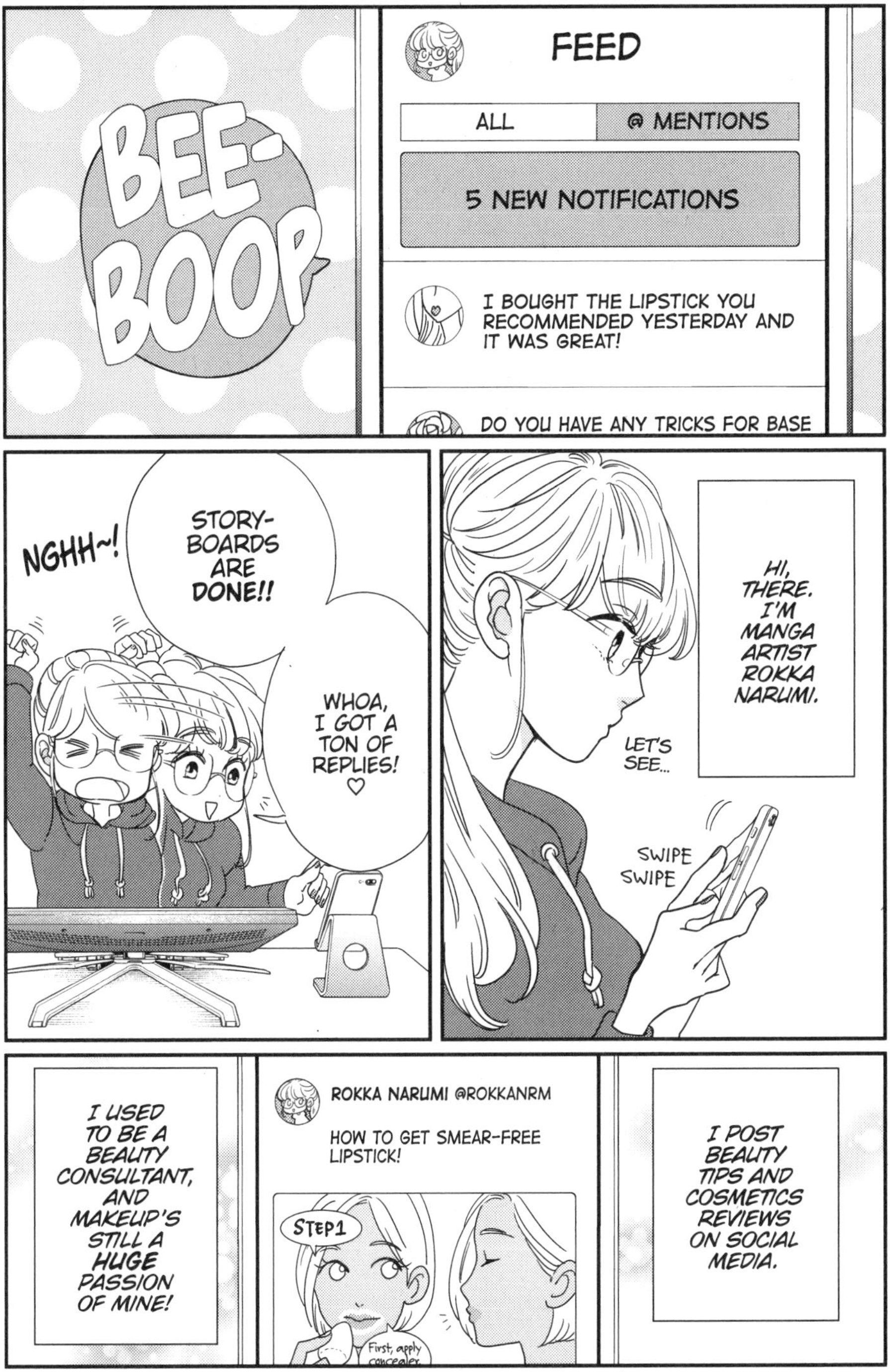
BEE-BOOP
FEED
ALL
@ MENTIONS
5 NEW NOTIFICATIONS
I BOUGHT THE LIPSTICK YOU RECOMMENDED YESTERDAY AND IT WAS GREAT!
DO YOU HAVE ANY TRICKS FOR BASE
NGHH~!
STORY-BOARDS ARE DONE!!
WHOA, I GOT A TON OF REPLIES! ♡
HI, THERE. I'M MANGA ARTIST ROKKA NARUMI.
LET'S SEE...
SWIPE SWIPE
I USED TO BE A BEAUTY CONSULTANT, AND MAKEUP'S STILL A HUGE PASSION OF MINE!
ROKKA NARUMI @ROKKANRM
HOW TO GET SMEAR-FREE LIPSTICK!
STEP1
First, apply concealer.
I POST BEAUTY TIPS AND COSMETICS REVIEWS ON SOCIAL MEDIA.

※ Not a real account!

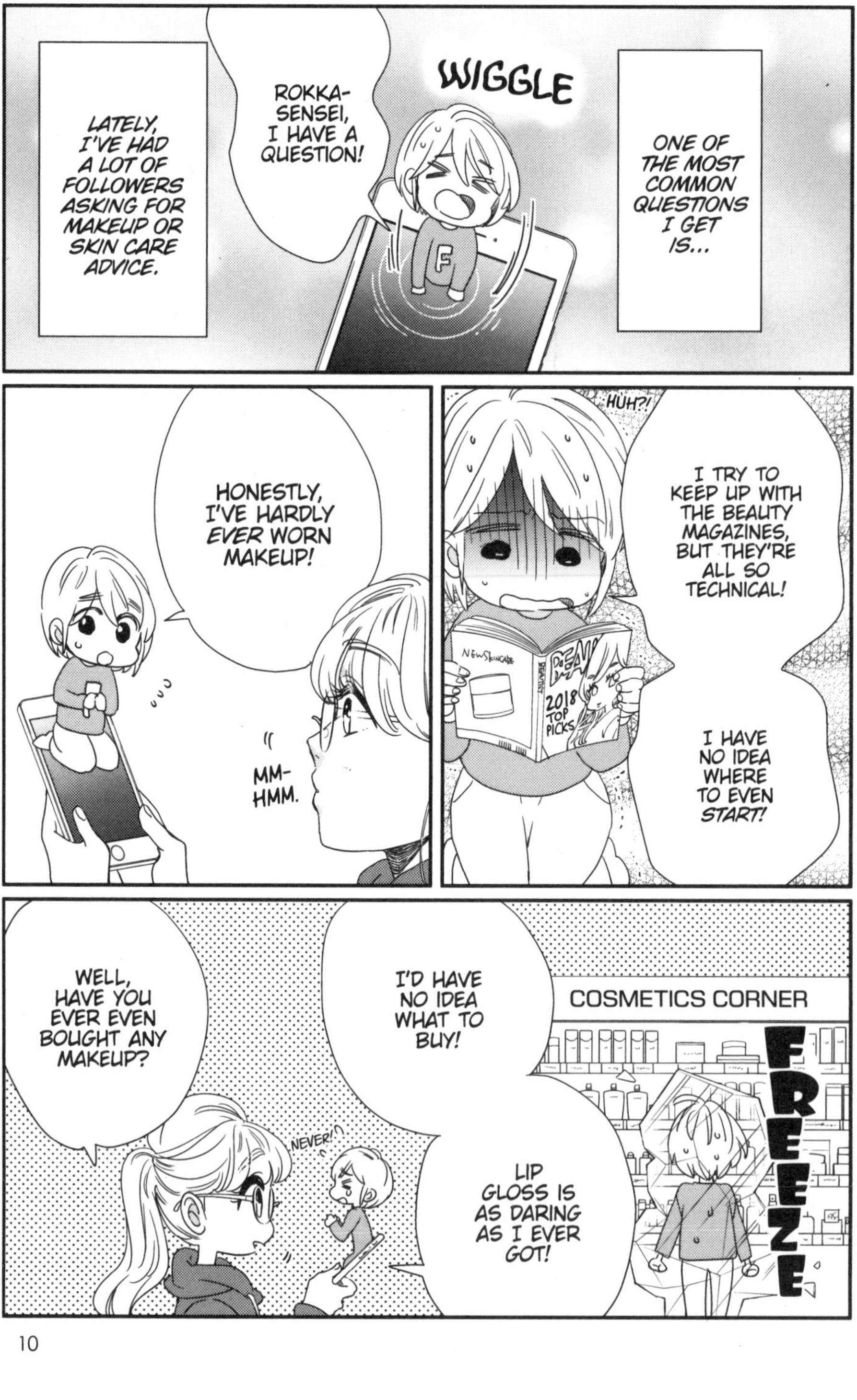
LATELY, I'VE HAD A LOT OF FOLLOWERS ASKING FOR MAKEUP OR SKIN CARE ADVICE.
ROKKA-SENSEI, I HAVE A QUESTION!
WIGGLE
ONE OF THE MOST COMMON QUESTIONS I GET IS...
HONESTLY, I'VE HARDLY EVER WORN MAKEUP!
MM-HMM.
HUH?!
I TRY TO KEEP UP WITH THE BEAUTY MAGAZINES, BUT THEY'RE ALL SO TECHNICAL!
I HAVE NO IDEA WHERE TO EVEN START!
2018 TOP PICKS
WELL, HAVE YOU EVER EVEN BOUGHT ANY MAKEUP?
NEVER!
I'D HAVE NO IDEA WHAT TO BUY!
LIP GLOSS IS AS DARING AS I EVER GOT!
COSMETICS CORNER
FREEZE

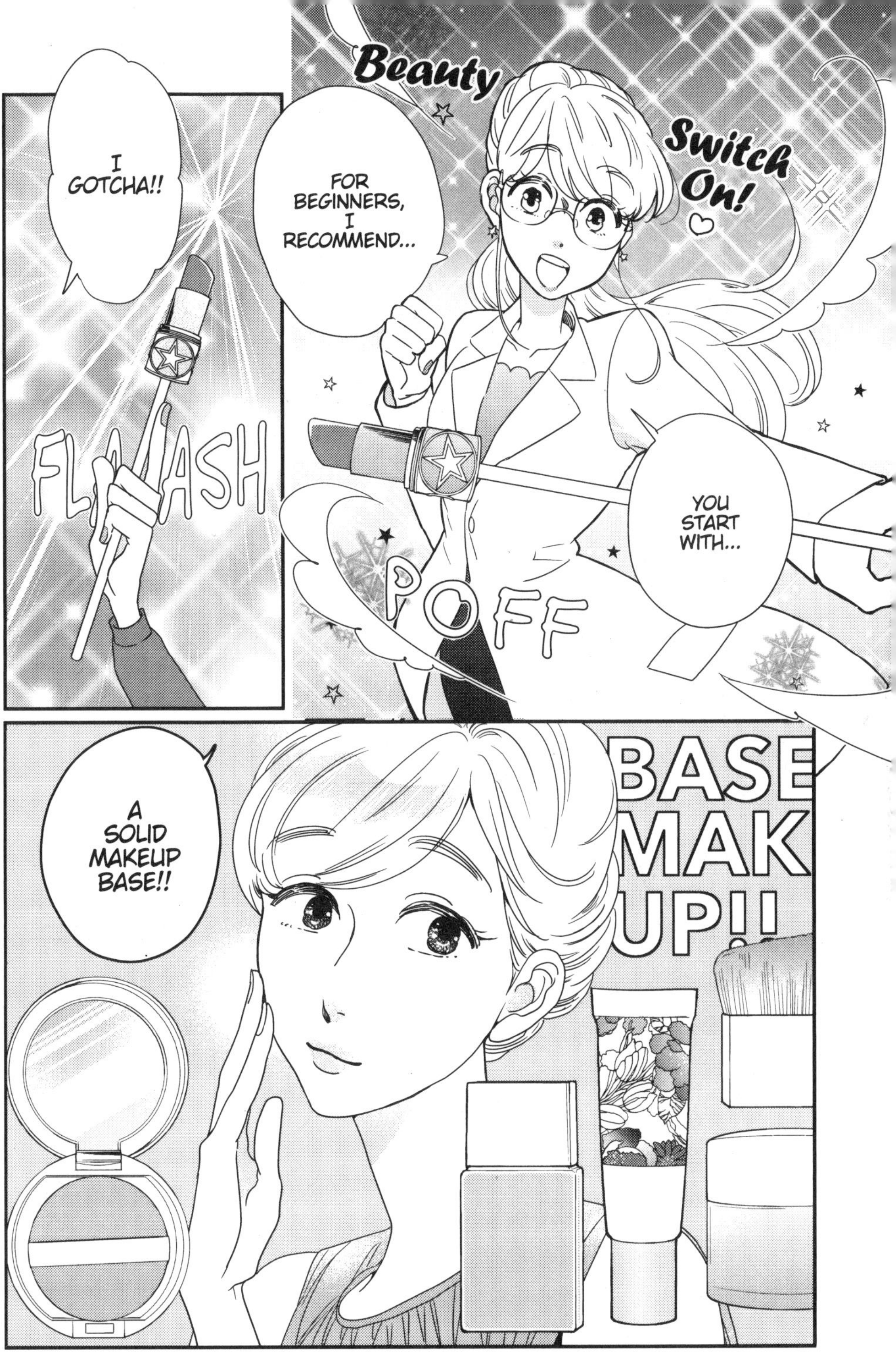
I GOTCHA!!
FLAASH
Beauty Switch On!
FOR BEGINNERS, I RECOMMEND...
YOU START WITH...
POFF
A SOLID MAKEUP BASE!!
BASE MAKEUP!!

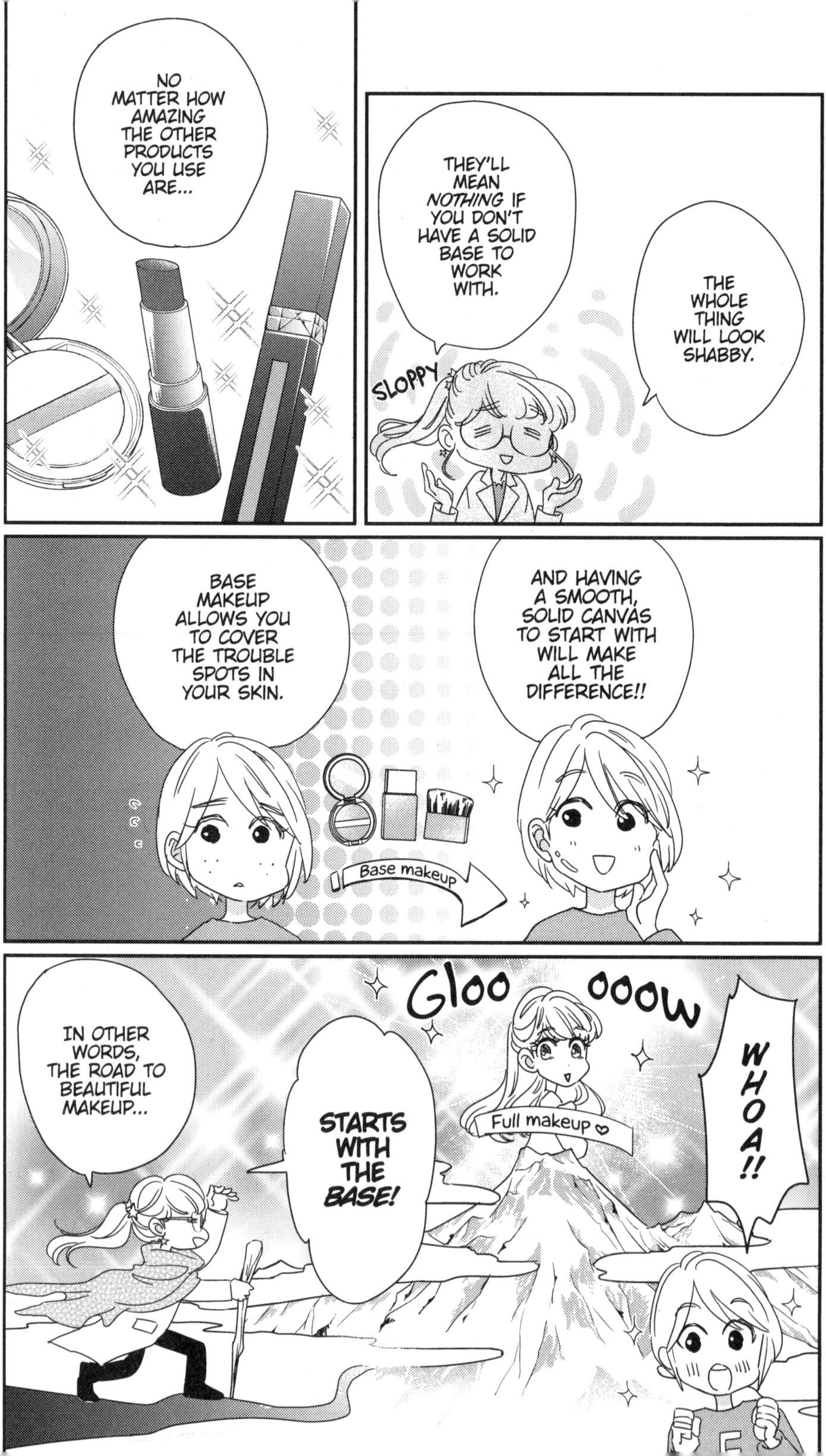
NO MATTER HOW AMAZING THE OTHER PRODUCTS YOU USE ARE...
THEY'LL MEAN *NOTHING* IF YOU DON'T HAVE A SOLID BASE TO WORK WITH.
THE WHOLE THING WILL LOOK SHABBY.
SLOPPY
BASE MAKEUP ALLOWS YOU TO COVER THE TROUBLE SPOTS IN YOUR SKIN.
AND HAVING A SMOOTH, SOLID CANVAS TO START WITH WILL MAKE ALL THE DIFFERENCE!!
Base makeup
IN OTHER WORDS, THE ROAD TO BEAUTIFUL MAKEUP...
STARTS WITH THE *BASE*!
Gloo oooow
Full makeup ♡
WHOA!!

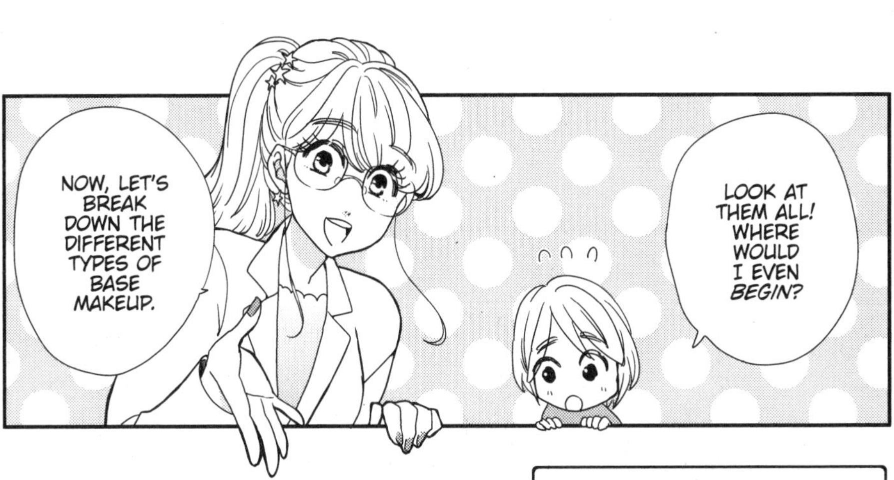
LOOK AT THEM ALL! WHERE WOULD I EVEN *BEGIN?*
NOW, LET'S BREAK DOWN THE DIFFERENT TYPES OF BASE MAKEUP.

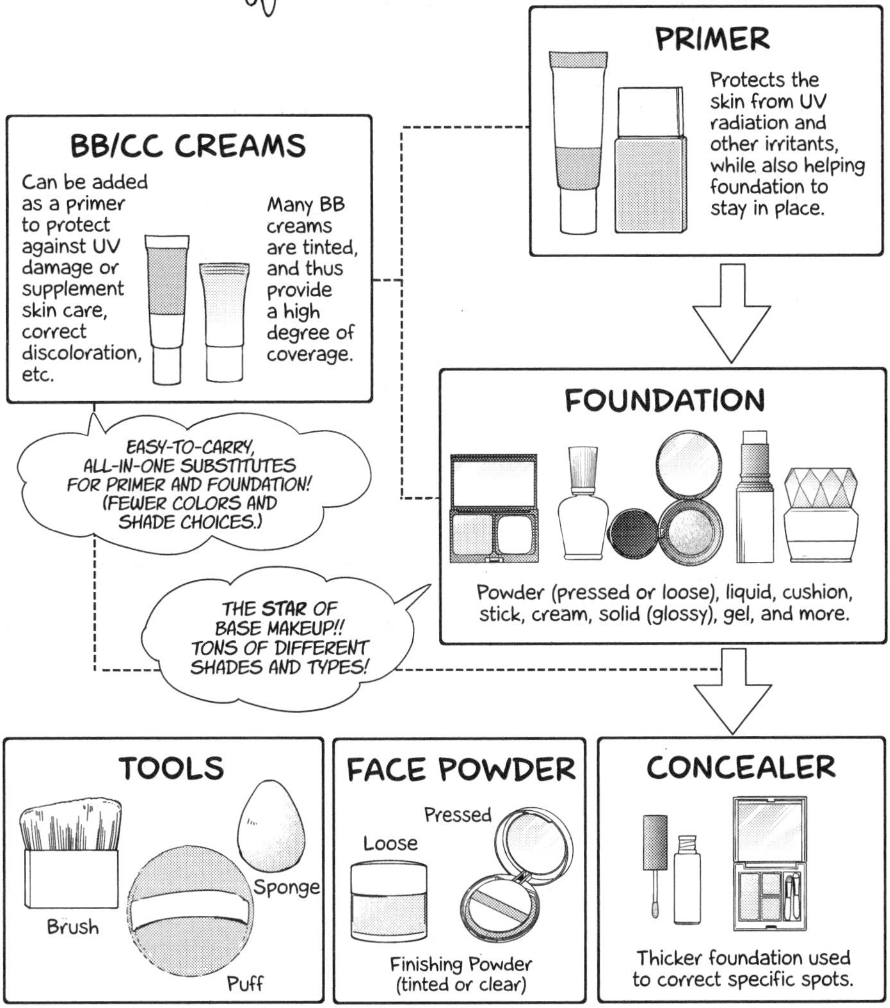
PRIMER
Protects the skin from UV radiation and other irritants, while also helping foundation to stay in place.
BB/CC CREAMS
Can be added as a primer to protect against UV damage or supplement skin care, correct discoloration, etc.
Many BB creams are tinted, and thus provide a high degree of coverage.
EASY-TO-CARRY, ALL-IN-ONE SUBSTITUTES FOR PRIMER AND FOUNDATION! (FEWER COLORS AND SHADE CHOICES.)
FOUNDATION
Powder (pressed or loose), liquid, cushion, stick, cream, solid (glossy), gel, and more.
THE **STAR** OF BASE MAKEUP!! TONS OF DIFFERENT SHADES AND TYPES!
TOOLS
Brush
Puff
Sponge
FACE POWDER
Loose
Pressed
Finishing Powder (tinted or clear)
CONCEALER
Thicker foundation used to correct specific spots.

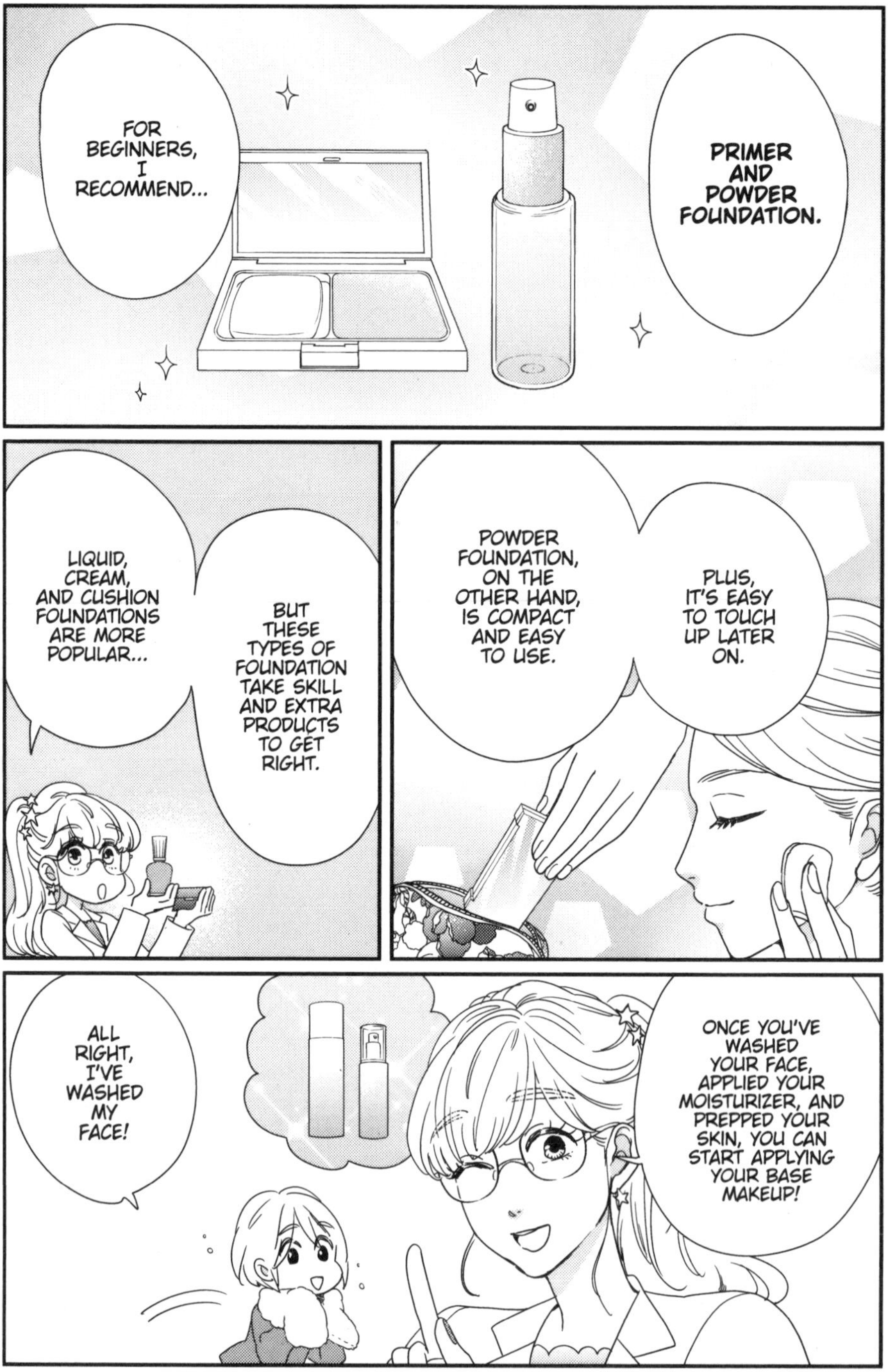
FOR BEGINNERS, I RECOMMEND...
PRIMER AND POWDER FOUNDATION.
LIQUID, CREAM, AND CUSHION FOUNDATIONS ARE MORE POPULAR...
BUT THESE TYPES OF FOUNDATION TAKE SKILL AND EXTRA PRODUCTS TO GET RIGHT.
POWDER FOUNDATION, ON THE OTHER HAND, IS COMPACT AND EASY TO USE.
PLUS, IT'S EASY TO TOUCH UP LATER ON.
ALL RIGHT, I'VE WASHED MY FACE!
ONCE YOU'VE WASHED YOUR FACE, APPLIED YOUR MOISTURIZER, AND PREPPED YOUR SKIN, YOU CAN START APPLYING YOUR BASE MAKEUP!

THERE ARE DOZENS OF DIFFERENT TYPES AND COLORS OF PRIMER.

BUT WHAT *REALLY* MATTERS WHEN YOU'RE CHOOSING ONE IS YOUR SKIN TYPE AND HOW YOU WANT YOUR SKIN TO LOOK.

Glossy

FOR DRY SKIN
I recommend a glossy, moisturizing finish.

WE'LL GO OVER HOW TO IDENTIFY YOUR SKIN TYPE ANOTHER TIME. ☆

Matte

FOR OILY SKIN
I recommend a grainier, more matte finish that suppresses sebum.

※ For combination skin, pick a primer that targets your specific areas of concern.

With Microbeads

FEEL

→ Shiny

Gives skin moisture. Leaves a glossy finish.

*Microbeads are tiny pieces of plastic often used in beauty products. For environmental reasons, they have been banned in many countries, including the U.S.

Without Microbeads

→ Semi-Matte
Matte

Removes shine from sebum. Leaves skin with a powdery finish.

Color	
Pink	Accentuates a great complexion. Perfect for fair skin.
Yellow	Covers acne or uneven skin. Gives skin a healthy color.
Purple	Removes dull yellow spots. Makes skin more translucent.
Green	Hides pimples and obscures redness.
Clear	Goes on light. Best for clear skin with no concerns.

YOU ALSO WANT TO CHECK HOW MUCH, IF ANY, SUN PROTECTION YOUR PRIMER HAS.

SPF32 PA++

SPF10~30
For normal, everyday use, especially if you spend all day inside.

SPF50 PA++++

SPF40~50
Good when playing sports, going outdoors, or spending a day at the beach. **Essential** if you burn easily.

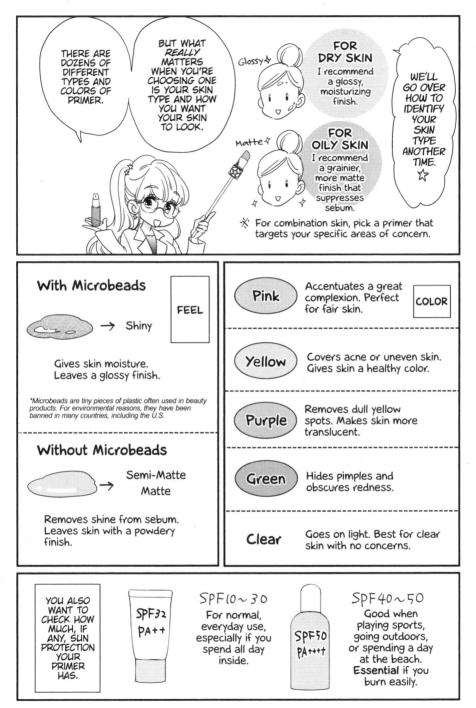

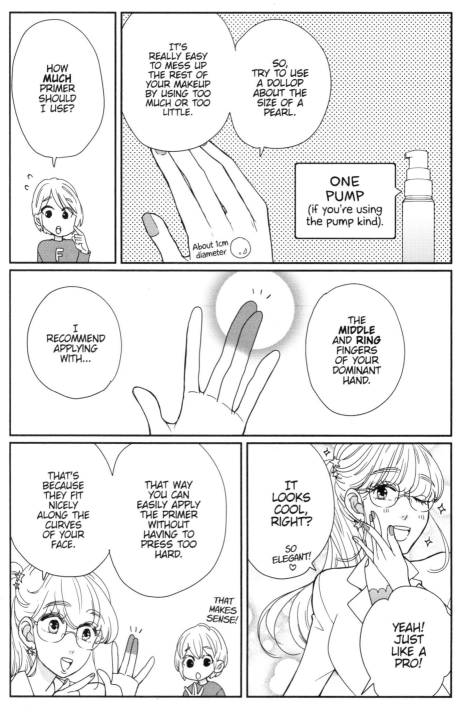

HOW **MUCH** PRIMER SHOULD I USE?

IT'S REALLY EASY TO MESS UP THE REST OF YOUR MAKEUP BY USING TOO MUCH OR TOO LITTLE.

SO, TRY TO USE A DOLLOP ABOUT THE SIZE OF A PEARL.

ONE PUMP (if you're using the pump kind).

About 1cm diameter

I RECOMMEND APPLYING WITH...

THE **MIDDLE** AND **RING** FINGERS OF YOUR DOMINANT HAND.

THAT'S BECAUSE THEY FIT NICELY ALONG THE CURVES OF YOUR FACE.

THAT WAY YOU CAN EASILY APPLY THE PRIMER WITHOUT HAVING TO PRESS TOO HARD.

THAT MAKES SENSE!

IT LOOKS COOL, RIGHT?

SO ELEGANT! ♡

YEAH! JUST LIKE A PRO!

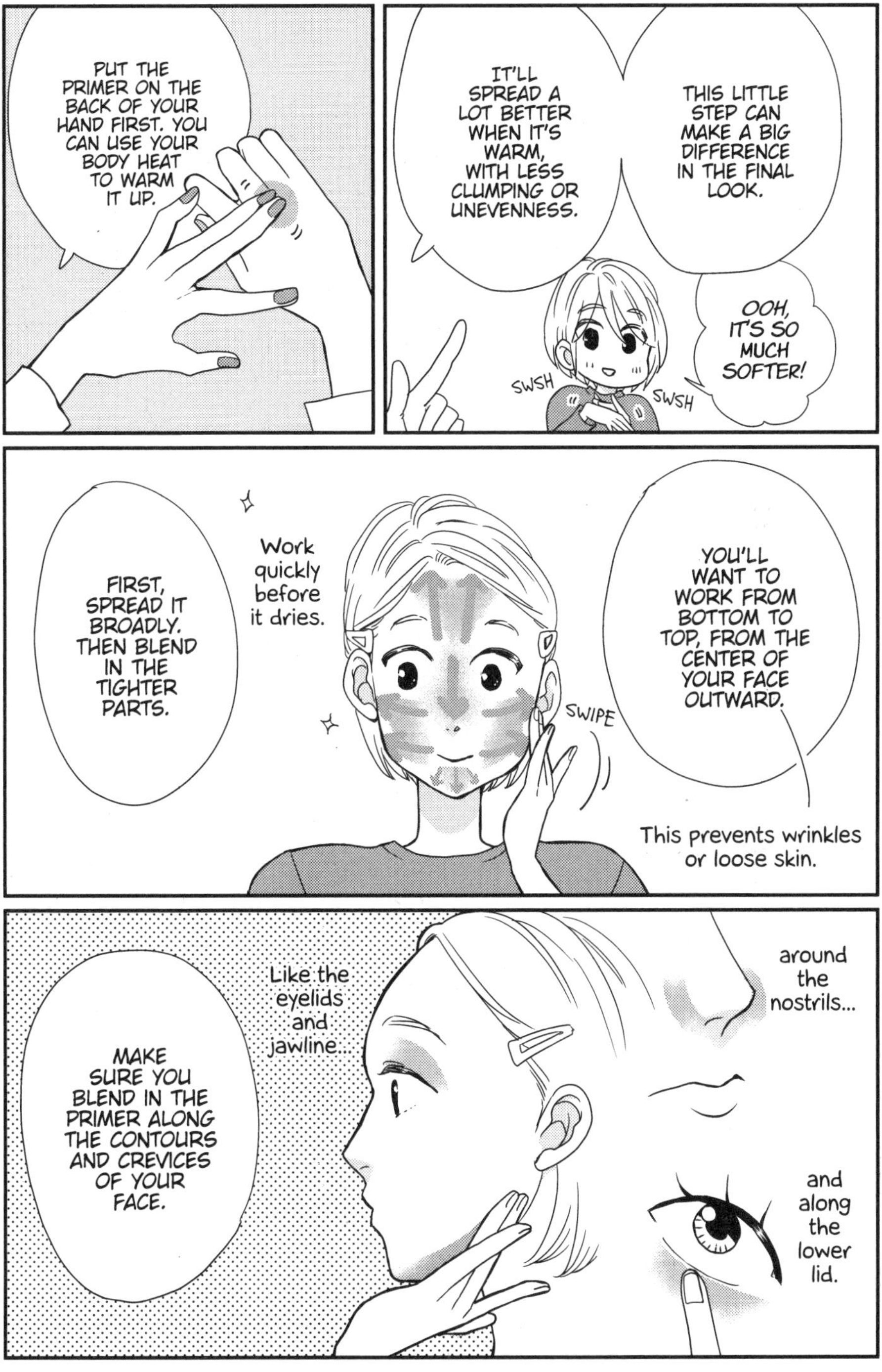
PUT THE PRIMER ON THE BACK OF YOUR HAND FIRST. YOU CAN USE YOUR BODY HEAT TO WARM IT UP.
IT'LL SPREAD A LOT BETTER WHEN IT'S WARM, WITH LESS CLUMPING OR UNEVENNESS.
THIS LITTLE STEP CAN MAKE A BIG DIFFERENCE IN THE FINAL LOOK.
OOH, IT'S SO MUCH SOFTER!
SWSH
SWSH
YOU'LL WANT TO WORK FROM BOTTOM TO TOP, FROM THE CENTER OF YOUR FACE OUTWARD.
This prevents wrinkles or loose skin.
Work quickly before it dries.
FIRST, SPREAD IT BROADLY. THEN BLEND IN THE TIGHTER PARTS.
SWIPE
around the nostrils...
Like the eyelids and jawline...
MAKE SURE YOU BLEND IN THE PRIMER ALONG THE CONTOURS AND CREVICES OF YOUR FACE.
and along the lower lid.

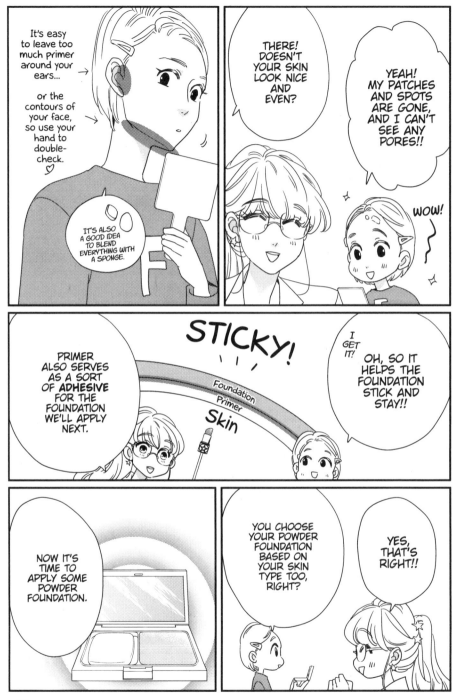

It's easy to leave too much primer around your ears...

or the contours of your face, so use your hand to double-check. ♡

IT'S ALSO A GOOD IDEA TO BLEND EVERYTHING WITH A SPONGE.

THERE! DOESN'T YOUR SKIN LOOK NICE AND EVEN?

YEAH! MY PATCHES AND SPOTS ARE GONE, AND I CAN'T SEE ANY PORES!!

WOW!

STICKY!

PRIMER ALSO SERVES AS A SORT OF **ADHESIVE** FOR THE FOUNDATION WE'LL APPLY NEXT.

Foundation

Primer

Skin

I GET IT! OH, SO IT HELPS THE FOUNDATION STICK AND STAY!!

NOW IT'S TIME TO APPLY SOME POWDER FOUNDATION.

YOU CHOOSE YOUR POWDER FOUNDATION BASED ON YOUR SKIN TYPE TOO, RIGHT?

YES, THAT'S RIGHT!!

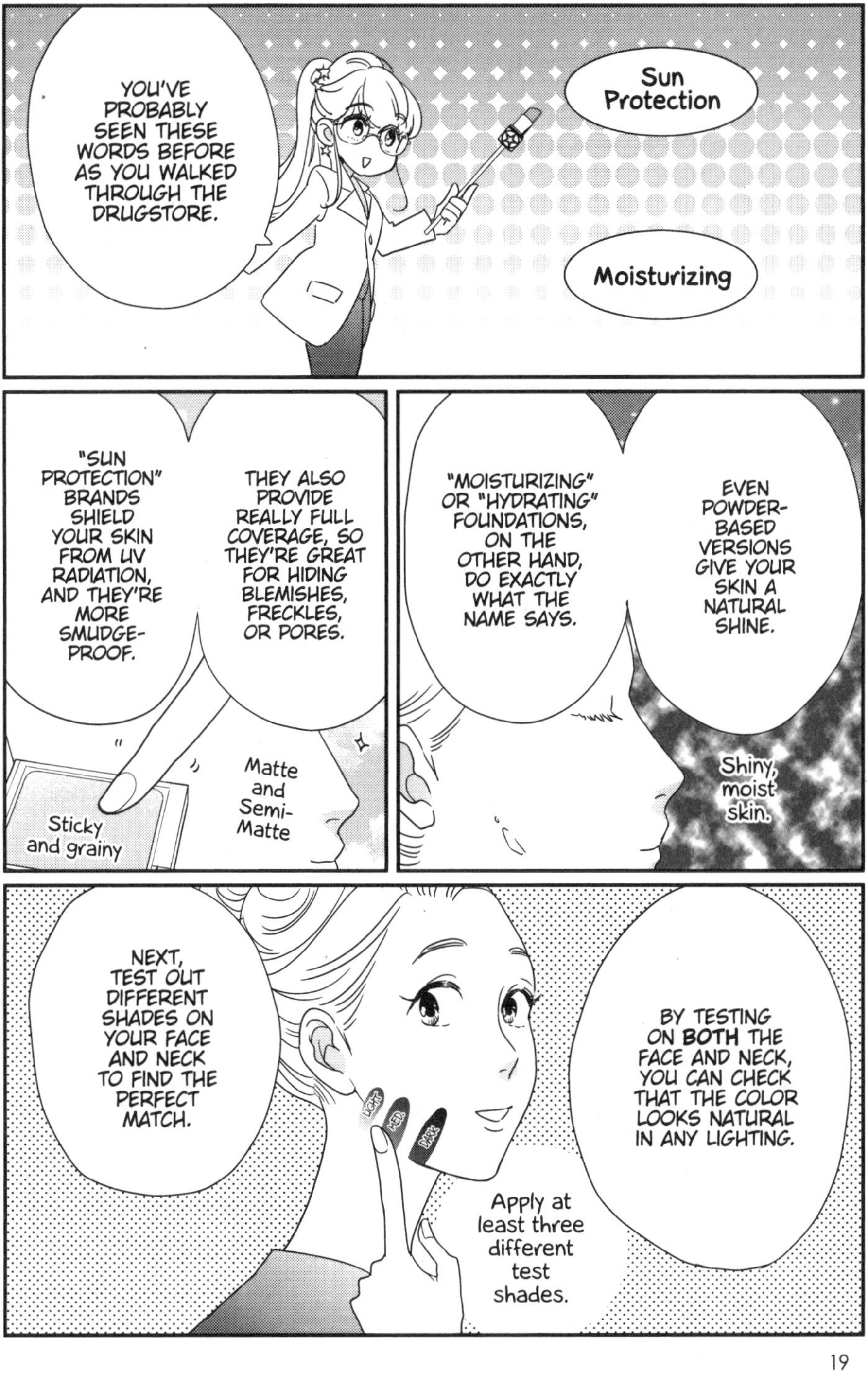

YOU'VE PROBABLY SEEN THESE WORDS BEFORE AS YOU WALKED THROUGH THE DRUGSTORE.
Sun Protection
Moisturizing
"SUN PROTECTION" BRANDS SHIELD YOUR SKIN FROM UV RADIATION, AND THEY'RE MORE SMUDGE-PROOF.
THEY ALSO PROVIDE REALLY FULL COVERAGE, SO THEY'RE GREAT FOR HIDING BLEMISHES, FRECKLES, OR PORES.
Matte and Semi-Matte
Sticky and grainy
"MOISTURIZING" OR "HYDRATING" FOUNDATIONS, ON THE OTHER HAND, DO EXACTLY WHAT THE NAME SAYS.
EVEN POWDER-BASED VERSIONS GIVE YOUR SKIN A NATURAL SHINE.
Shiny, moist skin.
NEXT, TEST OUT DIFFERENT SHADES ON YOUR FACE AND NECK TO FIND THE PERFECT MATCH.
LIGHT
MED.
DARK
BY TESTING ON **BOTH** THE FACE AND NECK, YOU CAN CHECK THAT THE COLOR LOOKS NATURAL IN ANY LIGHTING.
Apply at least three different test shades.

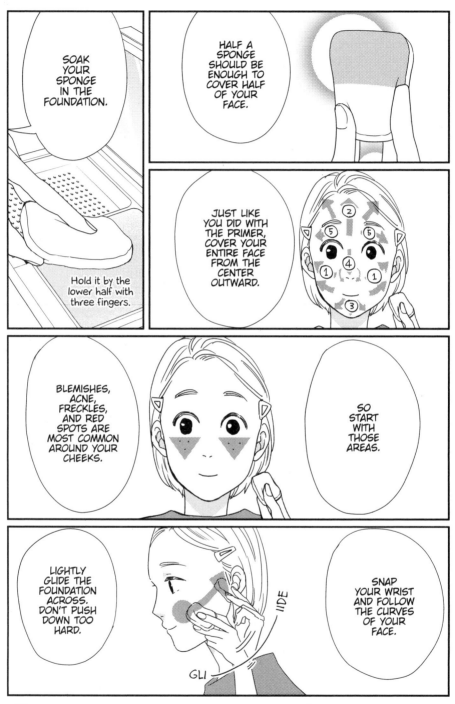

SOAK YOUR SPONGE IN THE FOUNDATION.

Hold it by the lower half with three fingers.

HALF A SPONGE SHOULD BE ENOUGH TO COVER HALF OF YOUR FACE.

JUST LIKE YOU DID WITH THE PRIMER, COVER YOUR ENTIRE FACE FROM THE CENTER OUTWARD.

BLEMISHES, ACNE, FRECKLES, AND RED SPOTS ARE MOST COMMON AROUND YOUR CHEEKS.

SO START WITH THOSE AREAS.

LIGHTLY GLIDE THE FOUNDATION ACROSS. DON'T PUSH DOWN TOO HARD.

SNAP YOUR WRIST AND FOLLOW THE CURVES OF YOUR FACE.

IIDE

GLI

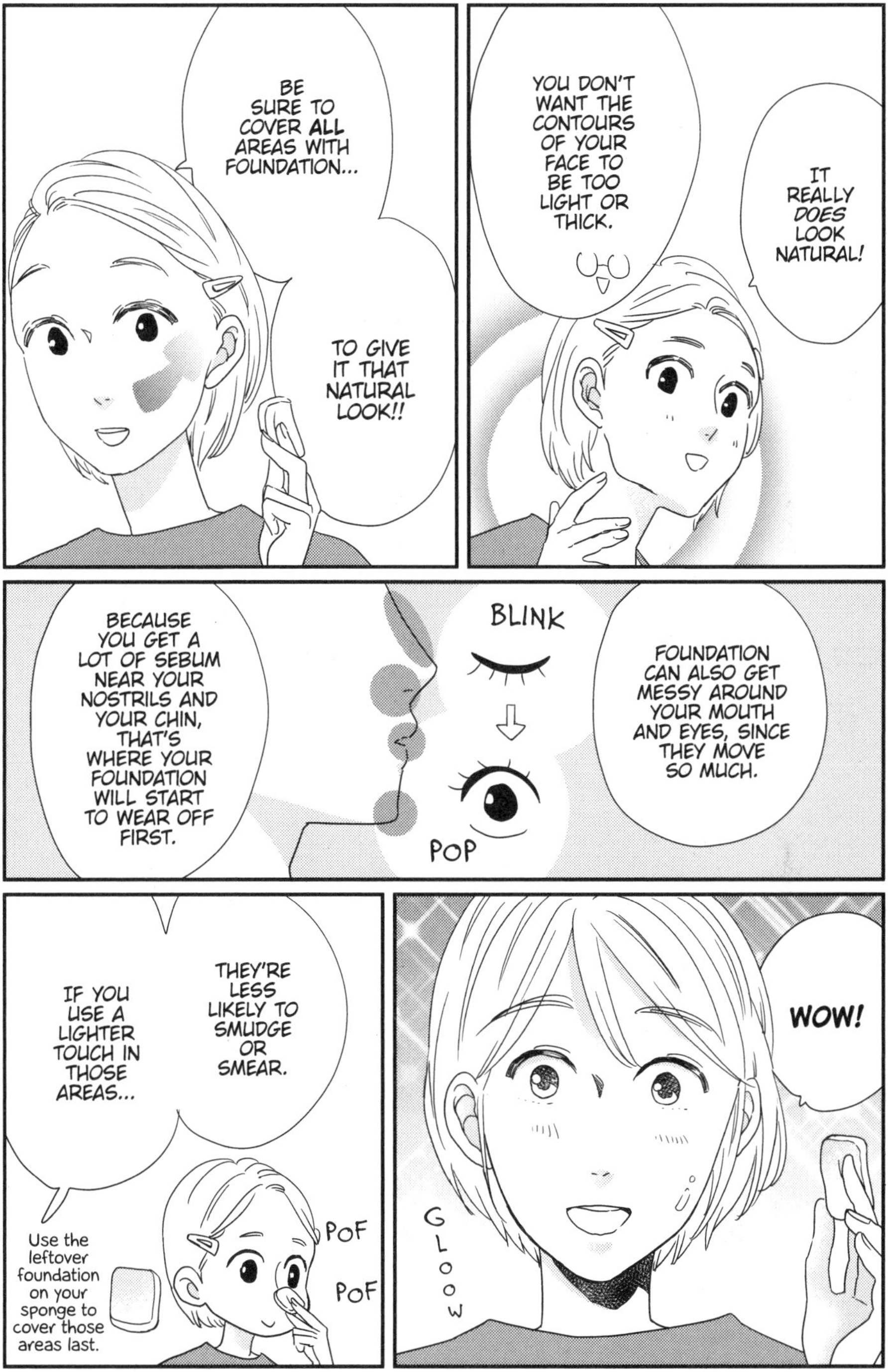
BE SURE TO COVER **ALL** AREAS WITH FOUNDATION...
TO GIVE IT THAT NATURAL LOOK!!
YOU DON'T WANT THE CONTOURS OF YOUR FACE TO BE TOO LIGHT OR THICK.
IT REALLY *DOES* LOOK NATURAL!
BECAUSE YOU GET A LOT OF SEBUM NEAR YOUR NOSTRILS AND YOUR CHIN, THAT'S WHERE YOUR FOUNDATION WILL START TO WEAR OFF FIRST.
BLINK
POP
FOUNDATION CAN ALSO GET MESSY AROUND YOUR MOUTH AND EYES, SINCE THEY MOVE SO MUCH.
IF YOU USE A LIGHTER TOUCH IN THOSE AREAS...
THEY'RE LESS LIKELY TO SMUDGE OR SMEAR.
Use the leftover foundation on your sponge to cover those areas last.
POF
POF
WOW!
GLOOW

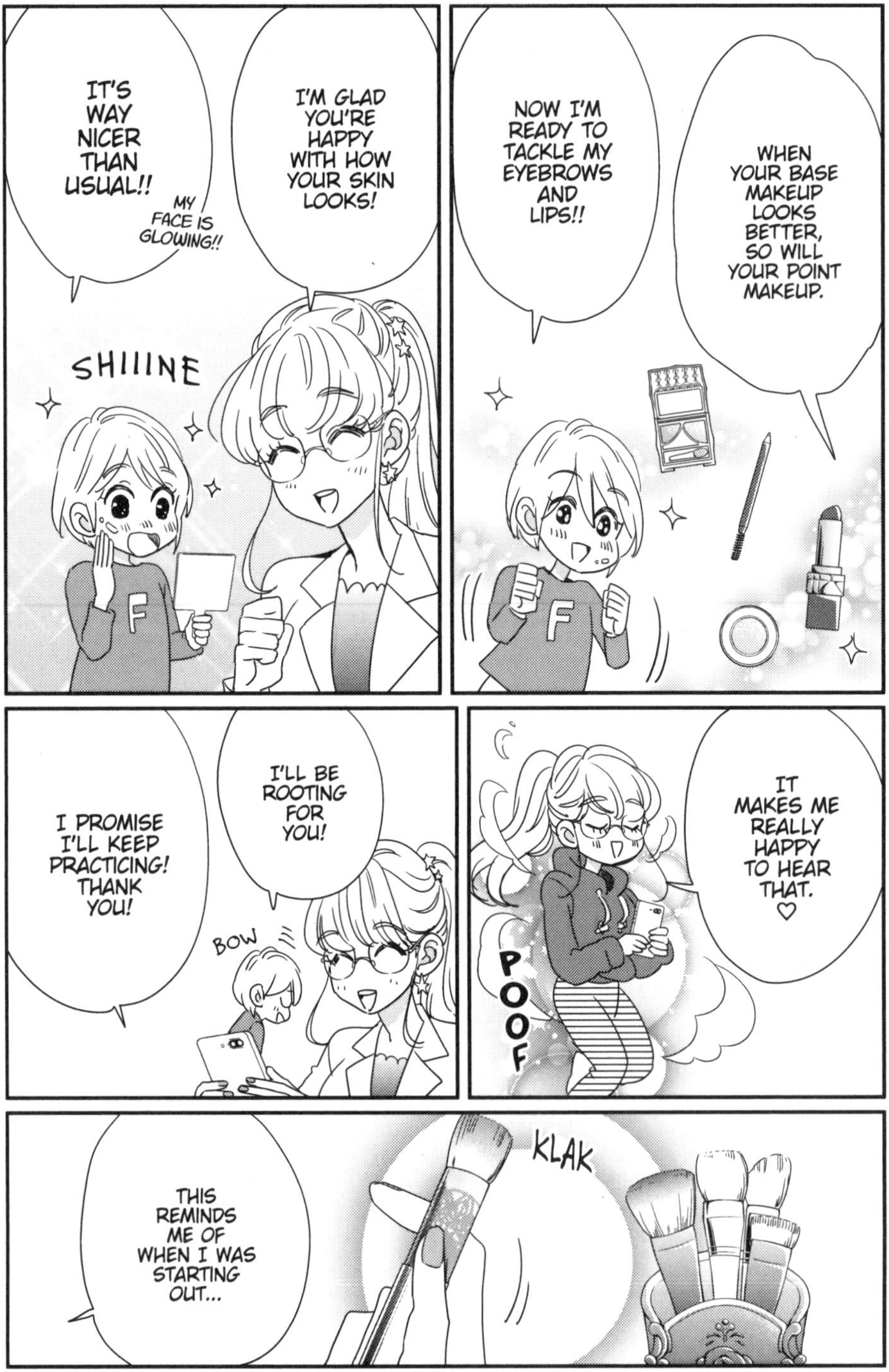
I'M GLAD YOU'RE HAPPY WITH HOW YOUR SKIN LOOKS!
IT'S WAY NICER THAN USUAL!!
MY FACE IS GLOWING!!
SHIIINE
WHEN YOUR BASE MAKEUP LOOKS BETTER, SO WILL YOUR POINT MAKEUP.
NOW I'M READY TO TACKLE MY EYEBROWS AND LIPS!!
I'LL BE ROOTING FOR YOU!
I PROMISE I'LL KEEP PRACTICING! THANK YOU!
BOW
IT MAKES ME REALLY HAPPY TO HEAR THAT. ♡
POOF
KLAK
THIS REMINDS ME OF WHEN I WAS STARTING OUT...

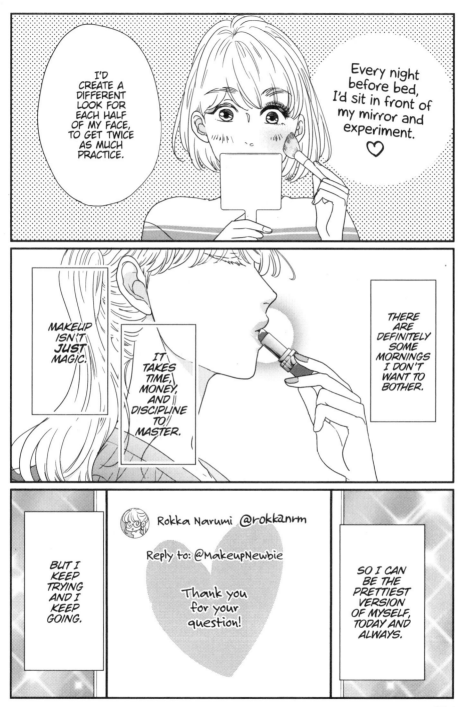

I'D CREATE A DIFFERENT LOOK FOR EACH HALF OF MY FACE, TO GET TWICE AS MUCH PRACTICE.

Every night before bed, I'd sit in front of my mirror and experiment. ♡

MAKEUP ISN'T JUST MAGIC.

IT TAKES TIME, MONEY, AND DISCIPLINE TO MASTER.

THERE ARE DEFINITELY SOME MORNINGS I DON'T WANT TO BOTHER.

BUT I KEEP TRYING AND I KEEP GOING.

Rokka Narumi @rokkanrm

Reply to: @MakeupNewbie

Thank you for your question!

SO I CAN BE THE PRETTIEST VERSION OF MYSELF, TODAY AND ALWAYS.

Let's Ask Rokka-Sensei!

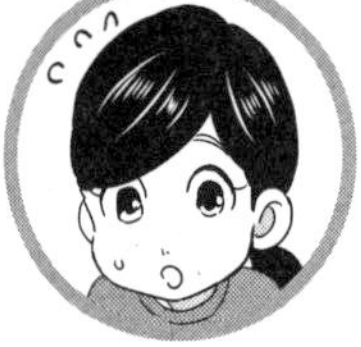

Q. I want to get my friend some makeup as a present.
What would you recommend, Rokka-sensei?

A. For special occasions, I'd get them a lipstick with a name that matches their personality. For friends who work a lot, I'd get a beauty drink. If they've got sensitive skin, I'd recommend blush brushes made from animal hair. Really, though, just match the gift to the person and you'll be fine!

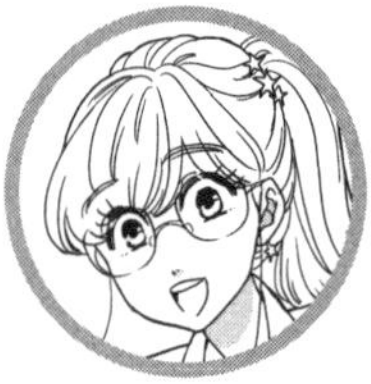

Lesson 2: Check Your Skin Type!

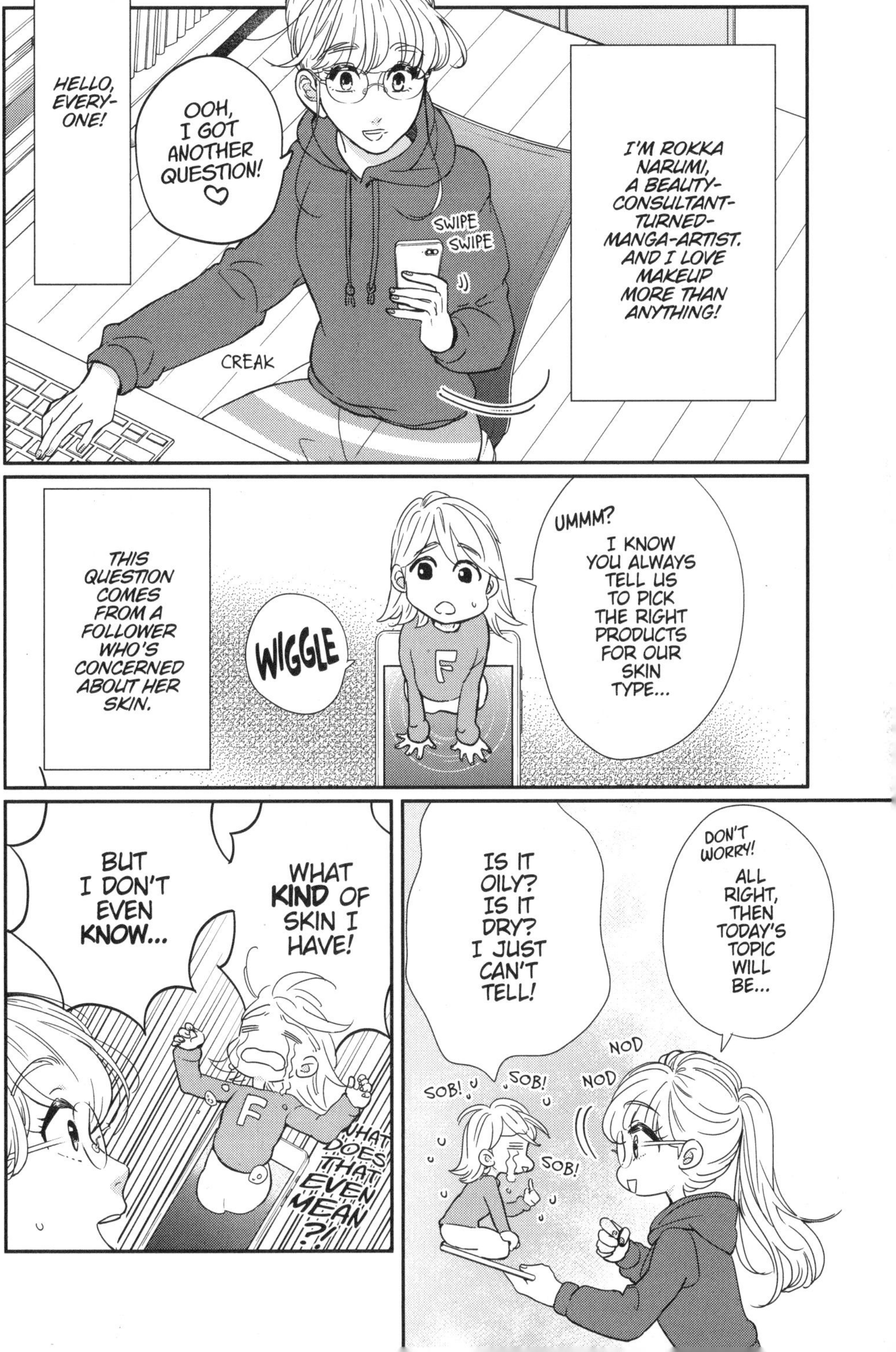
HELLO, EVERYONE!
I'M ROKKA NARUMI, A BEAUTY-CONSULTANT-TURNED-MANGA-ARTIST. AND I LOVE MAKEUP MORE THAN ANYTHING!
OOH, I GOT ANOTHER QUESTION! ♡
SWIPE SWIPE
CREAK
THIS QUESTION COMES FROM A FOLLOWER WHO'S CONCERNED ABOUT HER SKIN.
WIGGLE
UMMM?
I KNOW YOU ALWAYS TELL US TO PICK THE RIGHT PRODUCTS FOR OUR SKIN TYPE...
BUT I DON'T EVEN KNOW...
WHAT KIND OF SKIN I HAVE!
WHAT DOES THAT EVEN MEAN?!
IS IT OILY? IS IT DRY? I JUST CAN'T TELL!
SOB! SOB! SOB!
NOD NOD
DON'T WORRY!
ALL RIGHT, THEN TODAY'S TOPIC WILL BE...

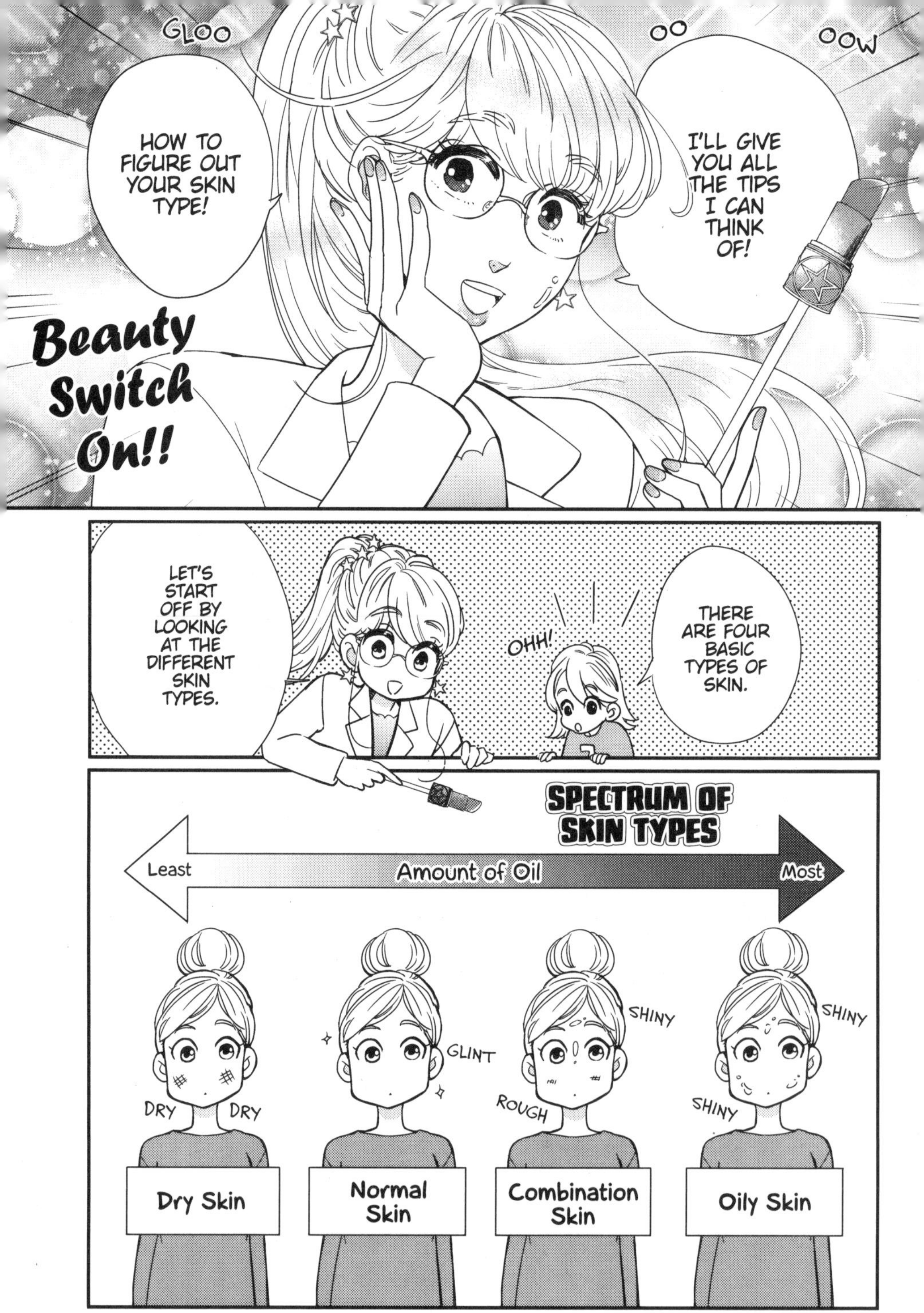
GLOO
OO
OOW
HOW TO FIGURE OUT YOUR SKIN TYPE!
I'LL GIVE YOU ALL THE TIPS I CAN THINK OF!
Beauty Switch On!!
LET'S START OFF BY LOOKING AT THE DIFFERENT SKIN TYPES.
OHH!
THERE ARE FOUR BASIC TYPES OF SKIN.
SPECTRUM OF SKIN TYPES
Least
Amount of Oil
Most
DRY
DRY
GLINT
SHINY
ROUGH
SHINY
SHINY
Dry Skin
Normal Skin
Combination Skin
Oily Skin

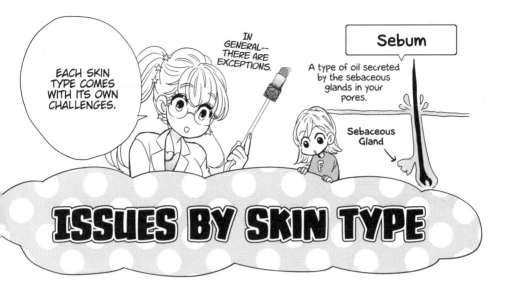

EACH SKIN TYPE COMES WITH ITS OWN CHALLENGES.

IN GENERAL-- THERE ARE EXCEPTIONS.

Sebum

A type of oil secreted by the sebaceous glands in your pores.

Sebaceous Gland

ISSUES BY SKIN TYPE

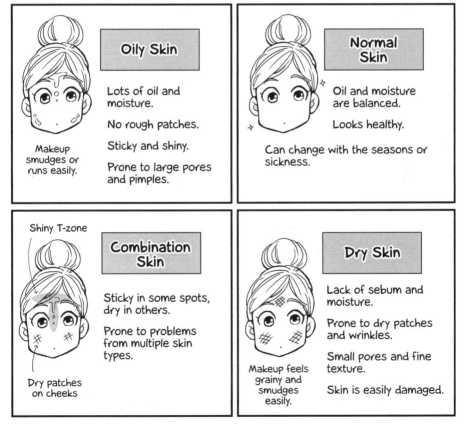

Oily Skin

Lots of oil and moisture.

No rough patches.

Sticky and shiny.

Prone to large pores and pimples.

Makeup smudges or runs easily.

Normal Skin

Oil and moisture are balanced.

Looks healthy.

Can change with the seasons or sickness.

Combination Skin

Shiny T-zone

Sticky in some spots, dry in others.

Prone to problems from multiple skin types.

Dry patches on cheeks

Dry Skin

Lack of sebum and moisture.

Prone to dry patches and wrinkles.

Small pores and fine texture.

Skin is easily damaged.

Makeup feels grainy and smudges easily.

27

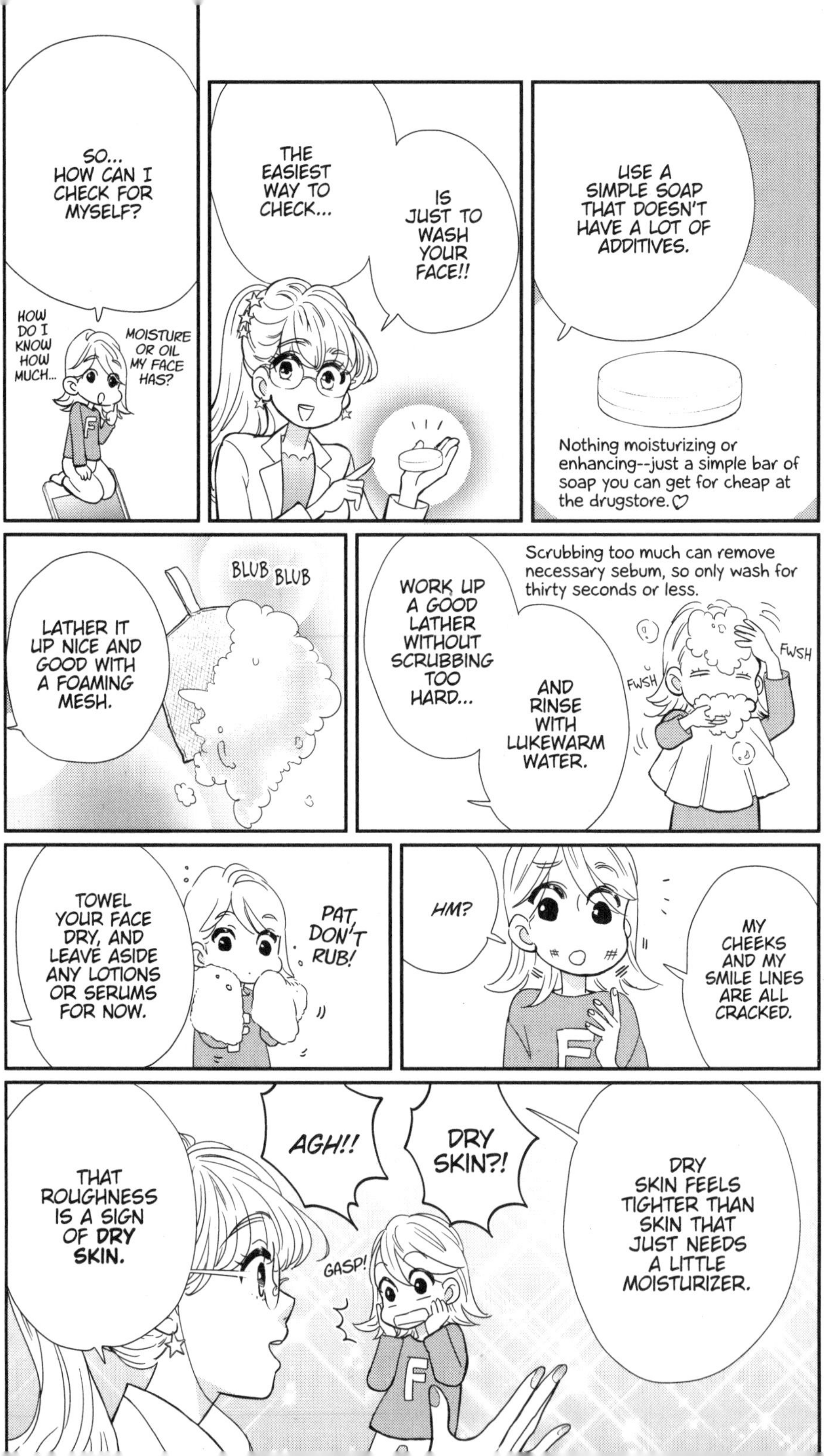
SO... HOW CAN I CHECK FOR MYSELF?
HOW DO I KNOW HOW MUCH...
MOISTURE OR OIL MY FACE HAS?
THE EASIEST WAY TO CHECK...
IS JUST TO WASH YOUR FACE!!
USE A SIMPLE SOAP THAT DOESN'T HAVE A LOT OF ADDITIVES.
Nothing moisturizing or enhancing--just a simple bar of soap you can get for cheap at the drugstore.♡
BLUB BLUB
LATHER IT UP NICE AND GOOD WITH A FOAMING MESH.
Scrubbing too much can remove necessary sebum, so only wash for thirty seconds or less.
WORK UP A GOOD LATHER WITHOUT SCRUBBING TOO HARD...
AND RINSE WITH LUKEWARM WATER.
FWSH
FWSH
TOWEL YOUR FACE DRY, AND LEAVE ASIDE ANY LOTIONS OR SERUMS FOR NOW.
PAT, DON'T RUB!
HM?
MY CHEEKS AND MY SMILE LINES ARE ALL CRACKED.
THAT ROUGHNESS IS A SIGN OF **DRY SKIN.**
AGH!!
DRY SKIN?!
GASP!
DRY SKIN FEELS TIGHTER THAN SKIN THAT JUST NEEDS A LITTLE MOISTURIZER.

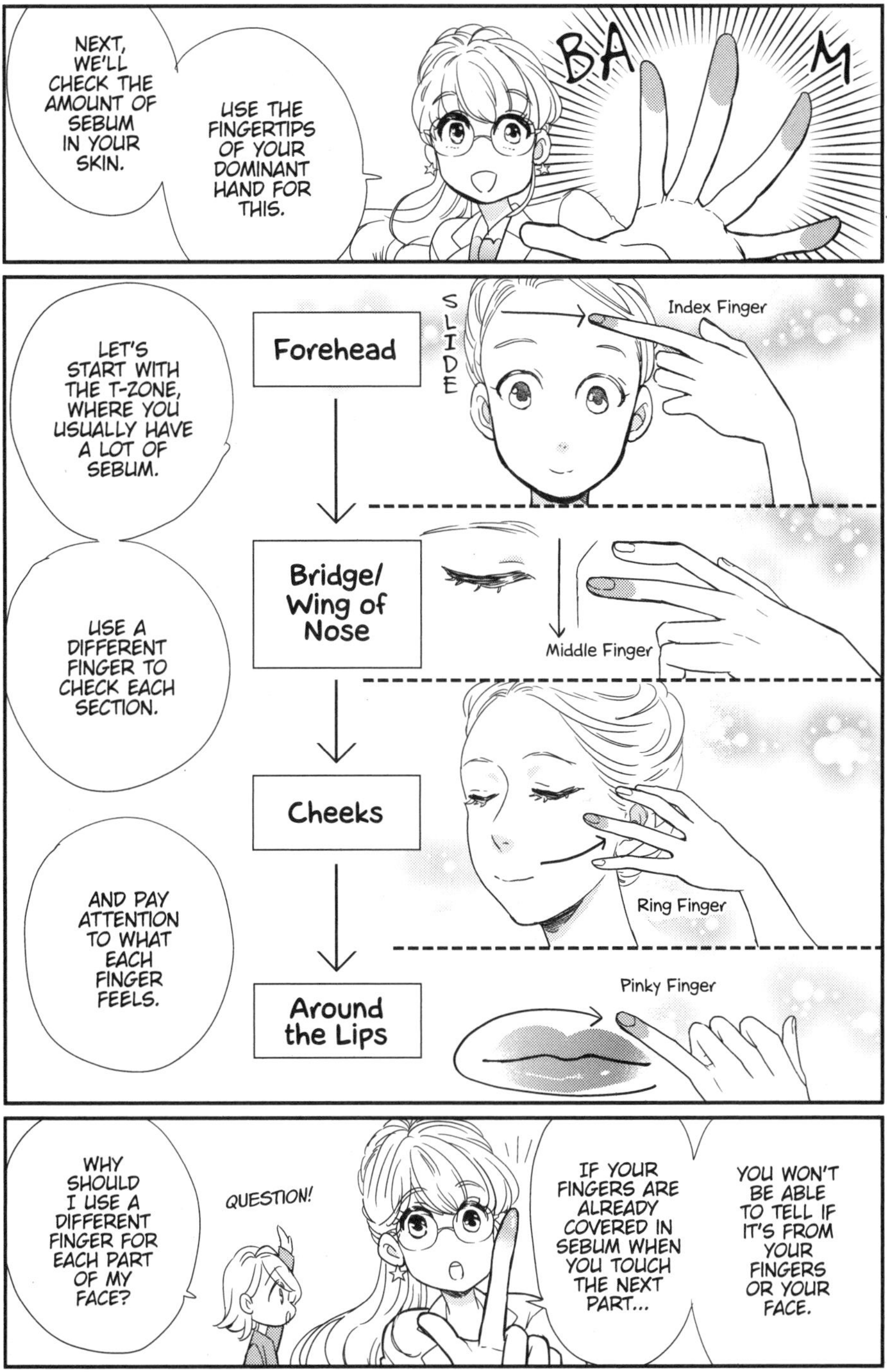

NEXT, WE'LL CHECK THE AMOUNT OF SEBUM IN YOUR SKIN.
USE THE FINGERTIPS OF YOUR DOMINANT HAND FOR THIS.
BAM
LET'S START WITH THE T-ZONE, WHERE YOU USUALLY HAVE A LOT OF SEBUM.
USE A DIFFERENT FINGER TO CHECK EACH SECTION.
AND PAY ATTENTION TO WHAT EACH FINGER FEELS.
Forehead
SLIDE
Index Finger
Bridge/ Wing of Nose
Middle Finger
Cheeks
Ring Finger
Around the Lips
Pinky Finger
WHY SHOULD I USE A DIFFERENT FINGER FOR EACH PART OF MY FACE?
QUESTION!
IF YOUR FINGERS ARE ALREADY COVERED IN SEBUM WHEN YOU TOUCH THE NEXT PART...
YOU WON'T BE ABLE TO TELL IF IT'S FROM YOUR FINGERS OR YOUR FACE.

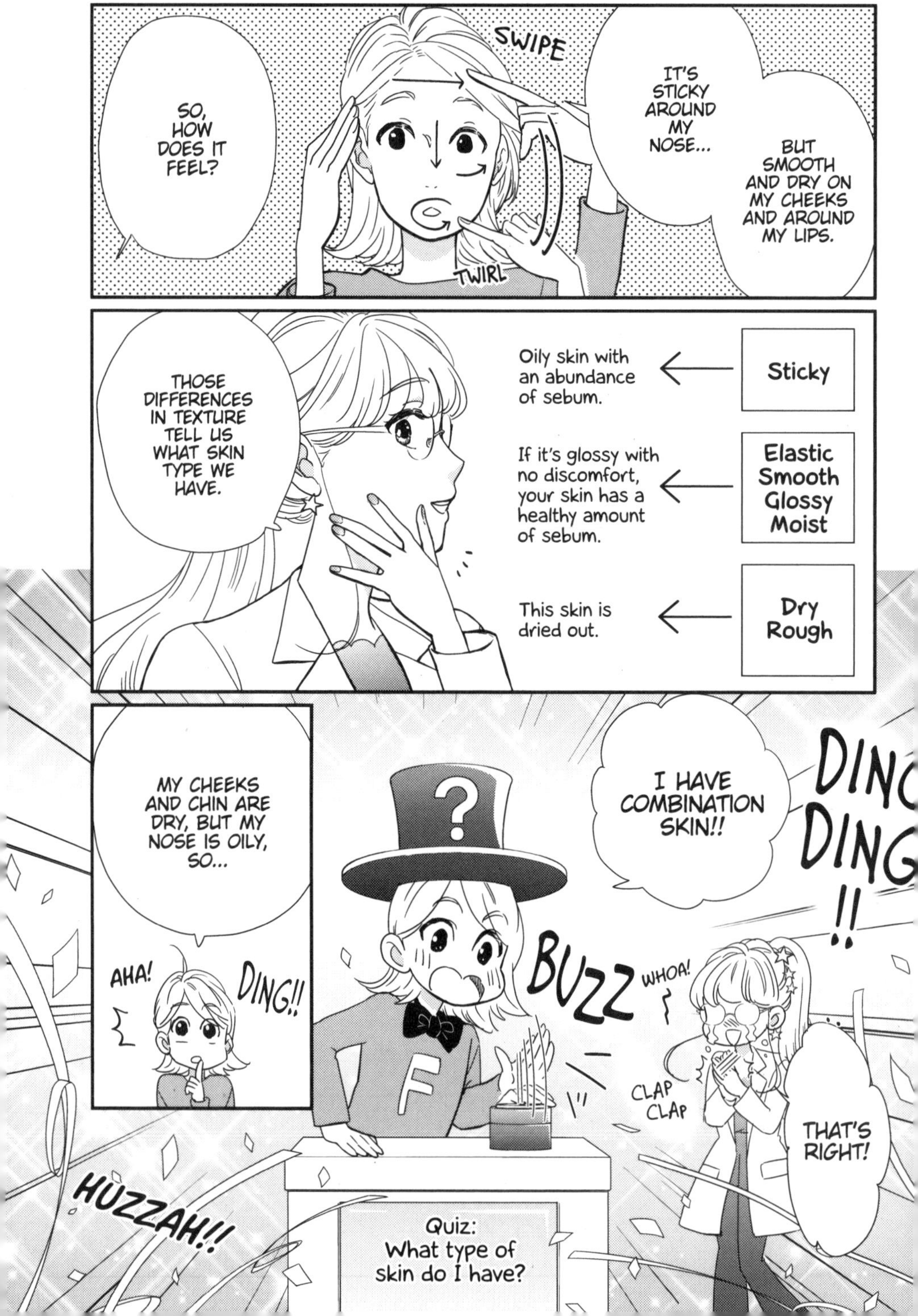
SO, HOW DOES IT FEEL?
SWIPE
IT'S STICKY AROUND MY NOSE...
BUT SMOOTH AND DRY ON MY CHEEKS AND AROUND MY LIPS.
TWIRL
THOSE DIFFERENCES IN TEXTURE TELL US WHAT SKIN TYPE WE HAVE.
Sticky
Oily skin with an abundance of sebum.
Elastic Smooth Glossy Moist
If it's glossy with no discomfort, your skin has a healthy amount of sebum.
Dry Rough
This skin is dried out.
MY CHEEKS AND CHIN ARE DRY, BUT MY NOSE IS OILY, SO...
AHA!
DING!!
I HAVE COMBINATION SKIN!!
BUZZ
WHOA!
CLAP CLAP
THAT'S RIGHT!
HUZZAH!!
Quiz: What type of skin do I have?

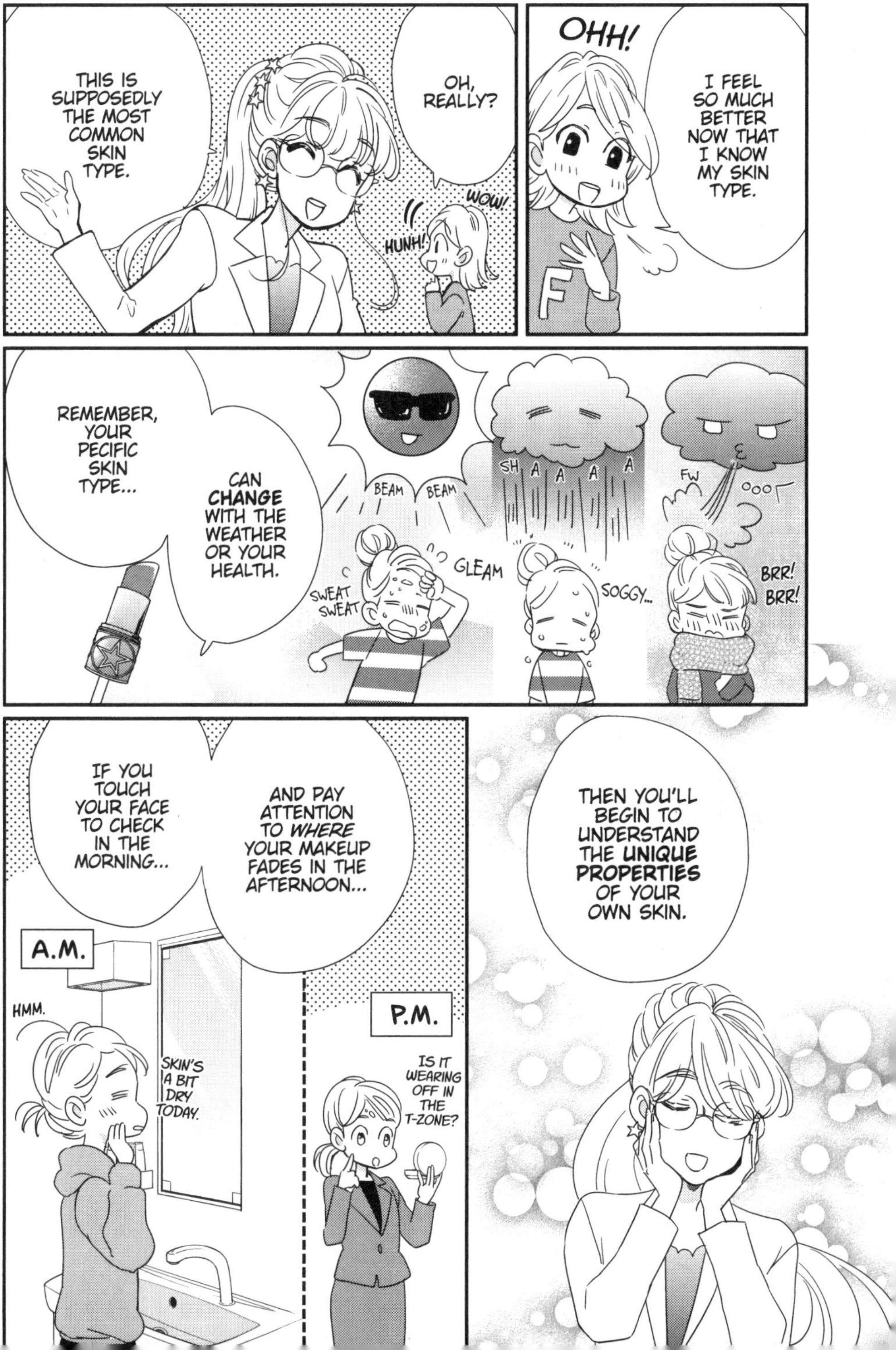
THIS IS SUPPOSEDLY THE MOST COMMON SKIN TYPE.
OH, REALLY?
HUNH!
WOW!
OHH!
I FEEL SO MUCH BETTER NOW THAT I KNOW MY SKIN TYPE.
F
REMEMBER, YOUR PECIFIC SKIN TYPE...
CAN **CHANGE** WITH THE WEATHER OR YOUR HEALTH.
BEAM
BEAM
GLEAM
SWEAT SWEAT
SHAAAAA
SOGGY...
FW
BRR! BRR!
IF YOU TOUCH YOUR FACE TO CHECK IN THE MORNING...
AND PAY ATTENTION TO *WHERE* YOUR MAKEUP FADES IN THE AFTERNOON...
A.M.
HMM.
SKIN'S A BIT DRY TODAY.
P.M.
IS IT WEARING OFF IN THE T-ZONE?
THEN YOU'LL BEGIN TO UNDERSTAND THE **UNIQUE PROPERTIES** OF YOUR OWN SKIN.

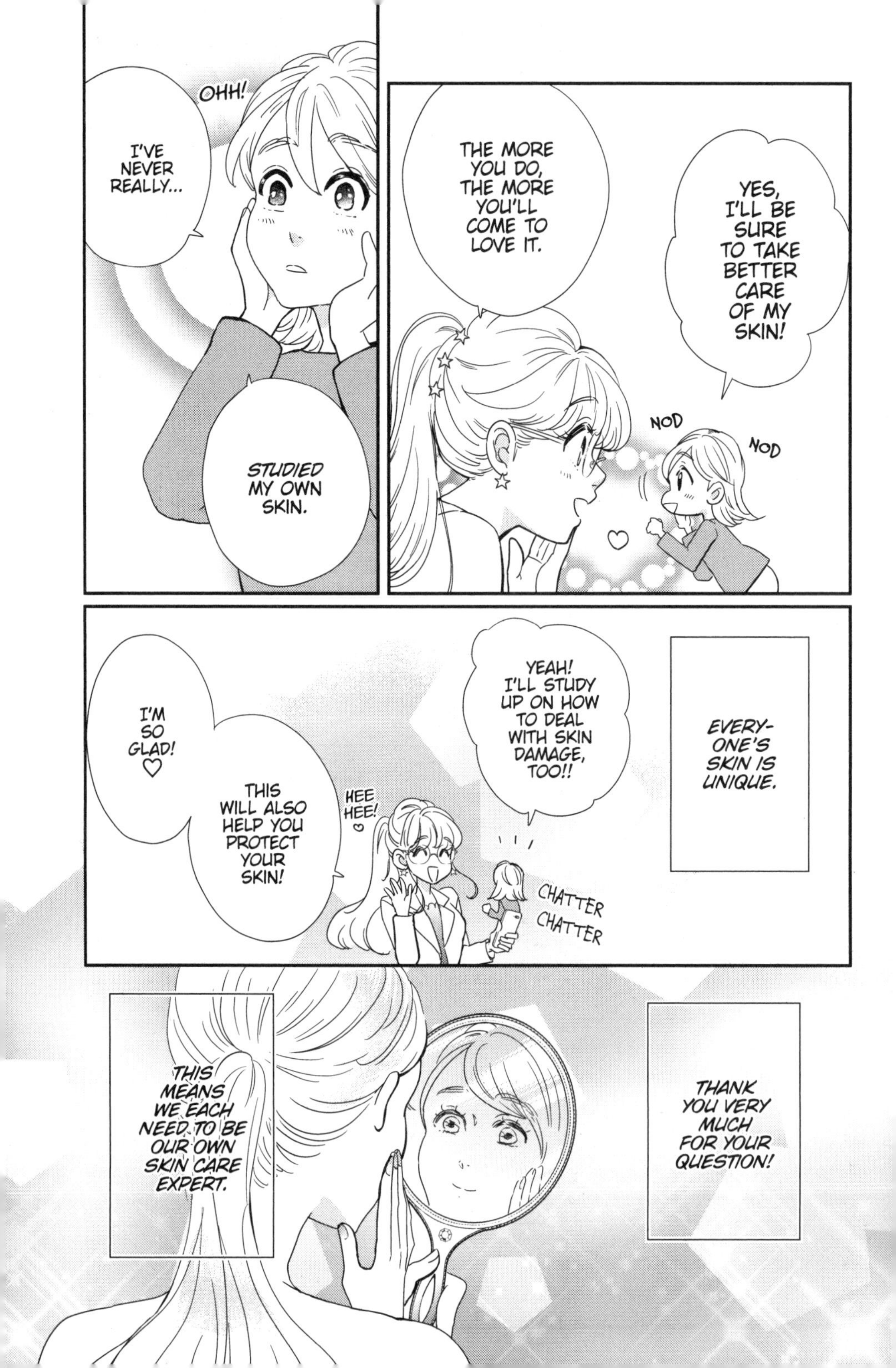
OHH!
I'VE NEVER REALLY...
STUDIED MY OWN SKIN.
THE MORE YOU DO, THE MORE YOU'LL COME TO LOVE IT.
YES, I'LL BE SURE TO TAKE BETTER CARE OF MY SKIN!
NOD
NOD
I'M SO GLAD! ♡
THIS WILL ALSO HELP YOU PROTECT YOUR SKIN!
HEE HEE! ♡
YEAH! I'LL STUDY UP ON HOW TO DEAL WITH SKIN DAMAGE, TOO!!
CHATTER CHATTER
EVERY-ONE'S SKIN IS UNIQUE.
THIS MEANS WE EACH NEED TO BE OUR OWN SKIN CARE EXPERT.
THANK YOU VERY MUCH FOR YOUR QUESTION!

Lesson 3: A Lesson on Buying from the Makeup Counter

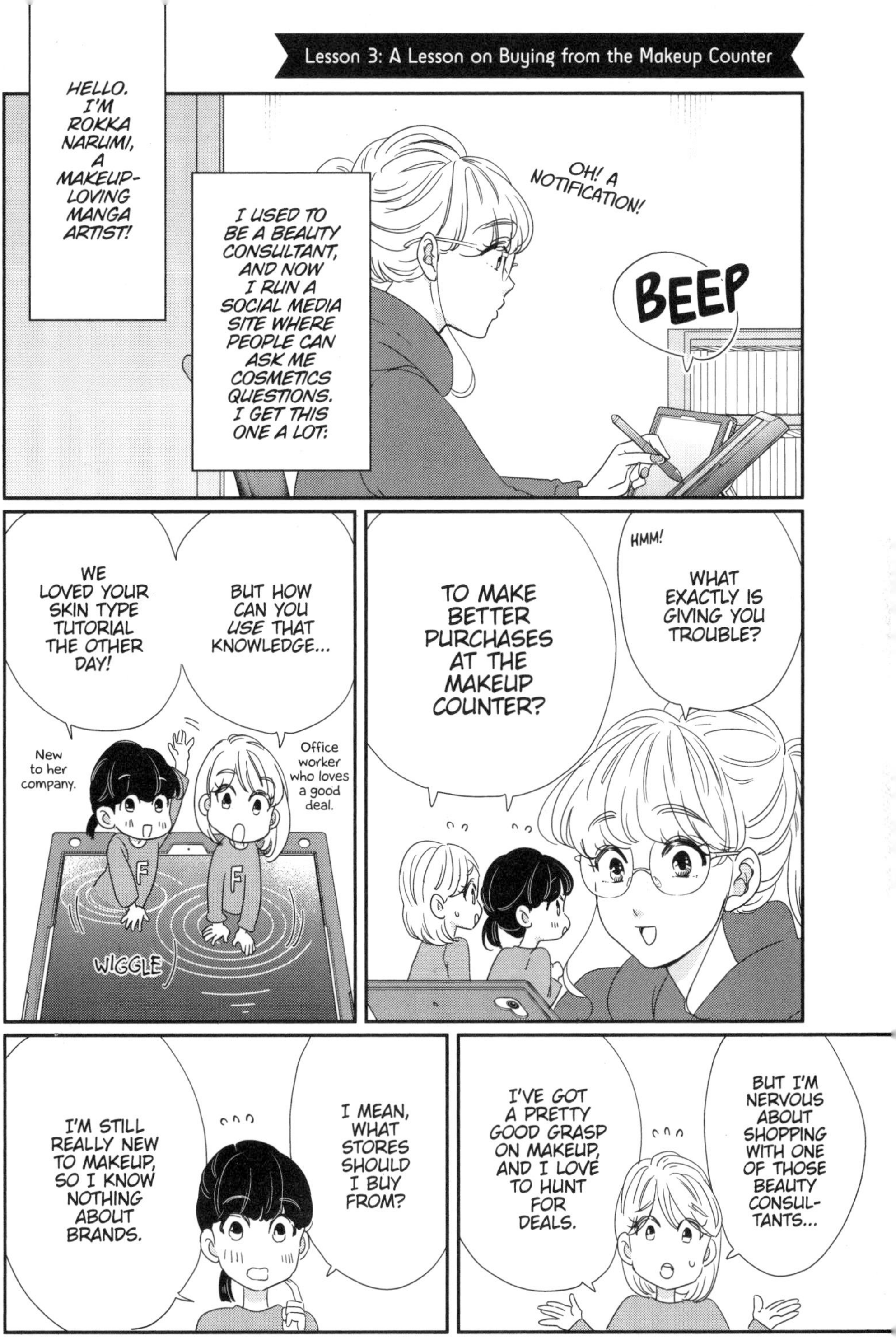

HELLO. I'M ROKKA NARUMI, A MAKEUP-LOVING MANGA ARTIST!
I USED TO BE A BEAUTY CONSULTANT, AND NOW I RUN A SOCIAL MEDIA SITE WHERE PEOPLE CAN ASK ME COSMETICS QUESTIONS. I GET THIS ONE A LOT:
OH! A NOTIFICATION!
BEEP
WE LOVED YOUR SKIN TYPE TUTORIAL THE OTHER DAY!
BUT HOW CAN YOU USE THAT KNOWLEDGE...
New to her company.
Office worker who loves a good deal.
WIGGLE
TO MAKE BETTER PURCHASES AT THE MAKEUP COUNTER?
HMM!
WHAT EXACTLY IS GIVING YOU TROUBLE?
I'M STILL REALLY NEW TO MAKEUP, SO I KNOW NOTHING ABOUT BRANDS.
I MEAN, WHAT STORES SHOULD I BUY FROM?
I'VE GOT A PRETTY GOOD GRASP ON MAKEUP, AND I LOVE TO HUNT FOR DEALS.
BUT I'M NERVOUS ABOUT SHOPPING WITH ONE OF THOSE BEAUTY CONSUL-TANTS...

※Cosmetic Counseling refers to sitting down with a consultant at a makeup counter and having them recommend or test makeup for you.

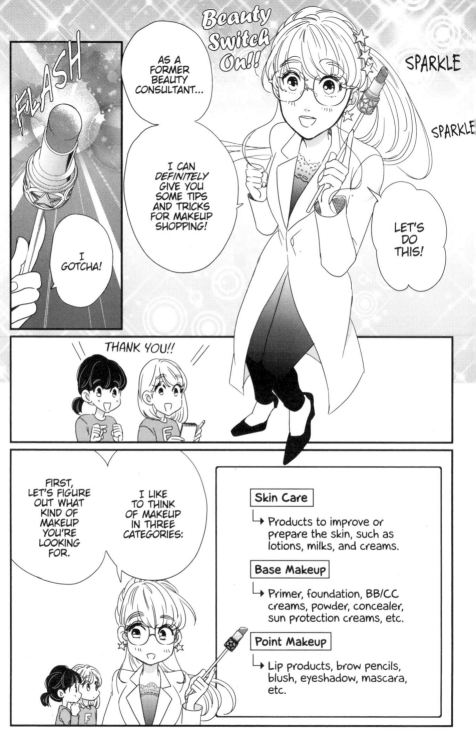

Beauty Switch On!!

SPARKLE

SPARKLE

AS A FORMER BEAUTY CONSULTANT...

FLASH

I CAN *DEFINITELY* GIVE YOU SOME TIPS AND TRICKS FOR MAKEUP SHOPPING!

LET'S DO THIS!

I GOTCHA!

THANK YOU!!

FIRST, LET'S FIGURE OUT WHAT KIND OF MAKEUP YOU'RE LOOKING FOR.

I LIKE TO THINK OF MAKEUP IN THREE CATEGORIES:

Skin Care
↳ Products to improve or prepare the skin, such as lotions, milks, and creams.

Base Makeup
↳ Primer, foundation, BB/CC creams, powder, concealer, sun protection creams, etc.

Point Makeup
↳ Lip products, brow pencils, blush, eyeshadow, mascara, etc.

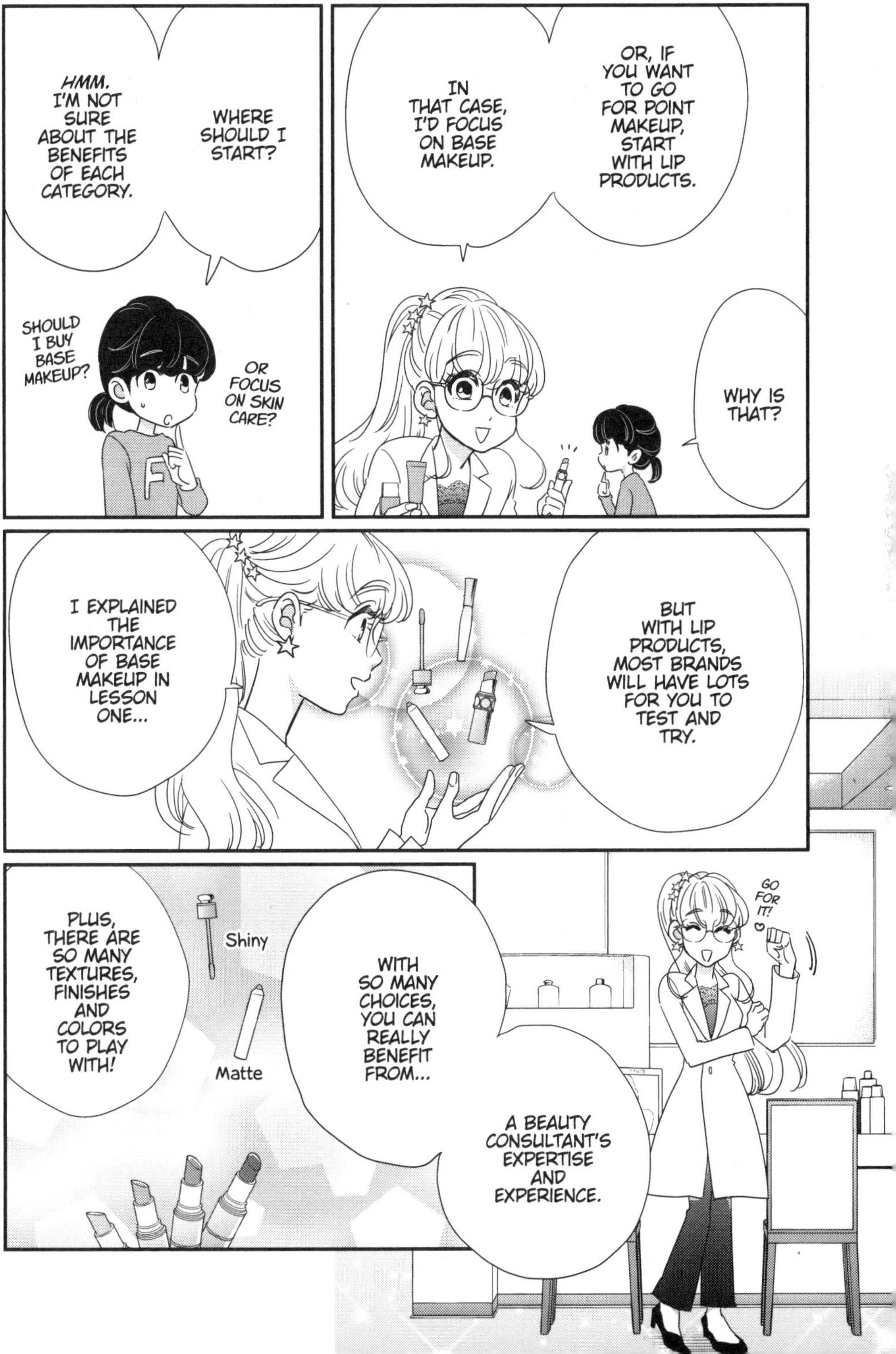

HMM. I'M NOT SURE ABOUT THE BENEFITS OF EACH CATEGORY.
WHERE SHOULD I START?
SHOULD I BUY BASE MAKEUP?
OR FOCUS ON SKIN CARE?
IN THAT CASE, I'D FOCUS ON BASE MAKEUP.
OR, IF YOU WANT TO GO FOR POINT MAKEUP, START WITH LIP PRODUCTS.
WHY IS THAT?
I EXPLAINED THE IMPORTANCE OF BASE MAKEUP IN LESSON ONE...
BUT WITH LIP PRODUCTS, MOST BRANDS WILL HAVE LOTS FOR YOU TO TEST AND TRY.
PLUS, THERE ARE SO MANY TEXTURES, FINISHES AND COLORS TO PLAY WITH!
Shiny
Matte
WITH SO MANY CHOICES, YOU CAN REALLY BENEFIT FROM...
A BEAUTY CONSULTANT'S EXPERTISE AND EXPERIENCE.
GO FOR IT!

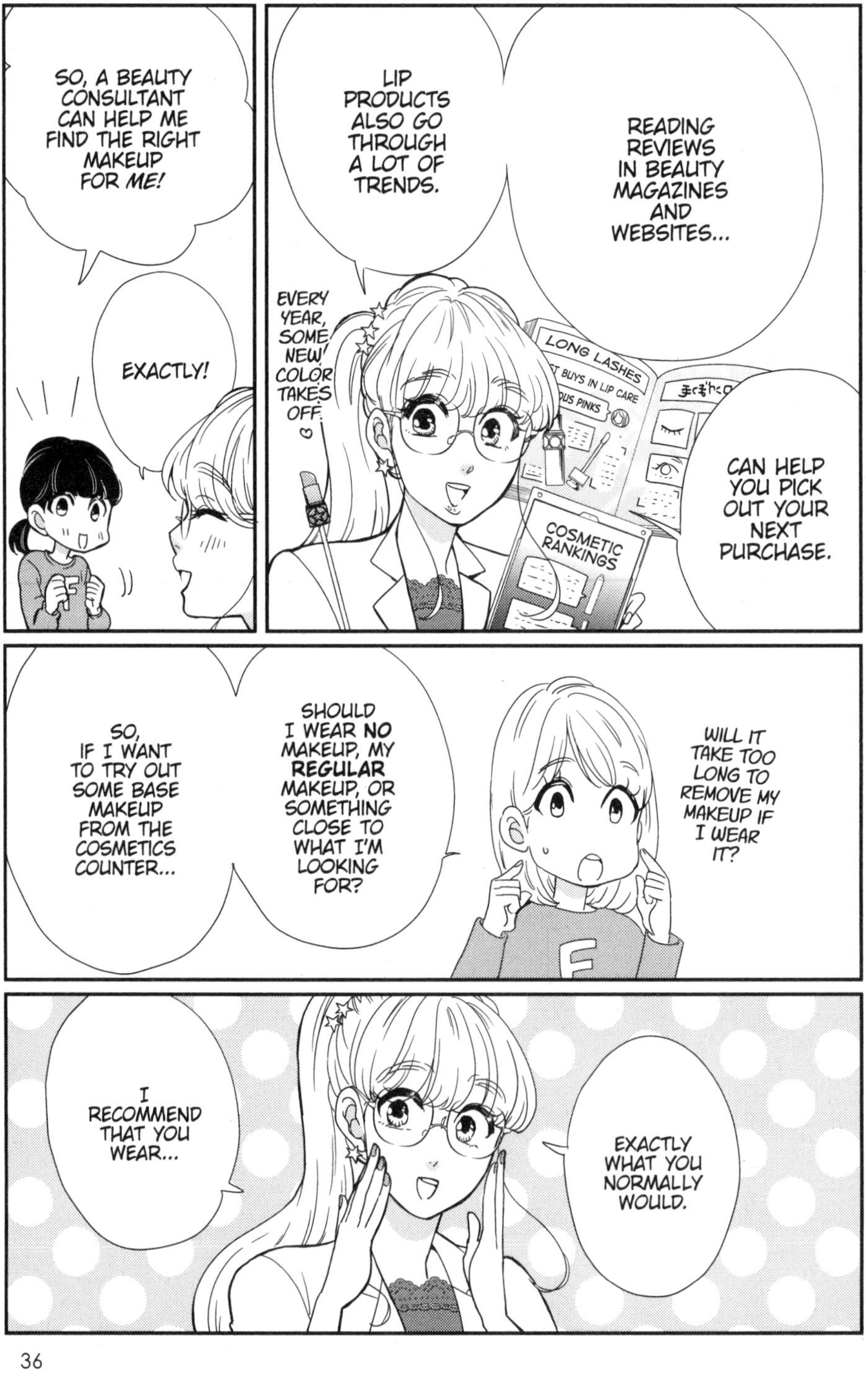

READING REVIEWS IN BEAUTY MAGAZINES AND WEBSITES...
CAN HELP YOU PICK OUT YOUR NEXT PURCHASE.
LONG LASHES
COSMETIC RANKINGS
LIP PRODUCTS ALSO GO THROUGH A LOT OF TRENDS.
EVERY YEAR, SOME NEW COLOR TAKES OFF.
SO, A BEAUTY CONSULTANT CAN HELP ME FIND THE RIGHT MAKEUP FOR *ME*!
EXACTLY!
WILL IT TAKE TOO LONG TO REMOVE MY MAKEUP IF I WEAR IT?
SO, IF I WANT TO TRY OUT SOME BASE MAKEUP FROM THE COSMETICS COUNTER...
SHOULD I WEAR **NO** MAKEUP, MY **REGULAR** MAKEUP, OR SOMETHING CLOSE TO WHAT I'M LOOKING FOR?
I RECOMMEND THAT YOU WEAR...
EXACTLY WHAT YOU NORMALLY WOULD.

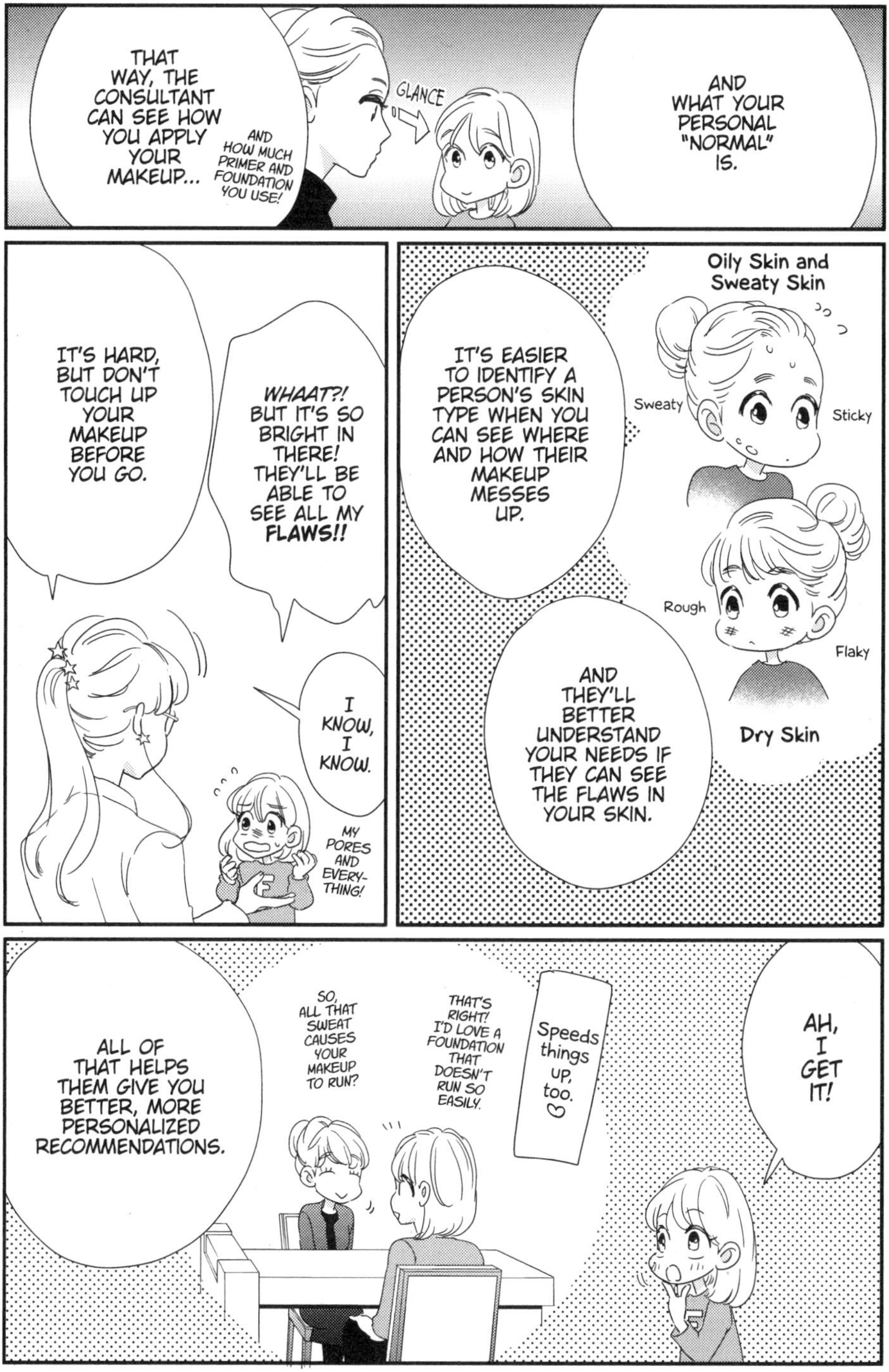
THAT WAY, THE CONSULTANT CAN SEE HOW YOU APPLY YOUR MAKEUP...
AND HOW MUCH PRIMER AND FOUNDATION YOU USE!
GLANCE
AND WHAT YOUR PERSONAL "NORMAL" IS.
IT'S HARD, BUT DON'T TOUCH UP YOUR MAKEUP BEFORE YOU GO.
WHAAT?! BUT IT'S SO BRIGHT IN THERE! THEY'LL BE ABLE TO SEE ALL MY **FLAWS!!**
I KNOW, I KNOW.
MY PORES AND EVERYTHING!
IT'S EASIER TO IDENTIFY A PERSON'S SKIN TYPE WHEN YOU CAN SEE WHERE AND HOW THEIR MAKEUP MESSES UP.
Oily Skin and Sweaty Skin
Sweaty
Sticky
Rough
Flaky
Dry Skin
AND THEY'LL BETTER UNDERSTAND YOUR NEEDS IF THEY CAN SEE THE FLAWS IN YOUR SKIN.
ALL OF THAT HELPS THEM GIVE YOU BETTER, MORE PERSONALIZED RECOMMENDATIONS.
SO, ALL THAT SWEAT CAUSES YOUR MAKEUP TO RUN?
THAT'S RIGHT! I'D LOVE A FOUNDATION THAT DOESN'T RUN SO EASILY.
Speeds things up, too.
AH, I GET IT!

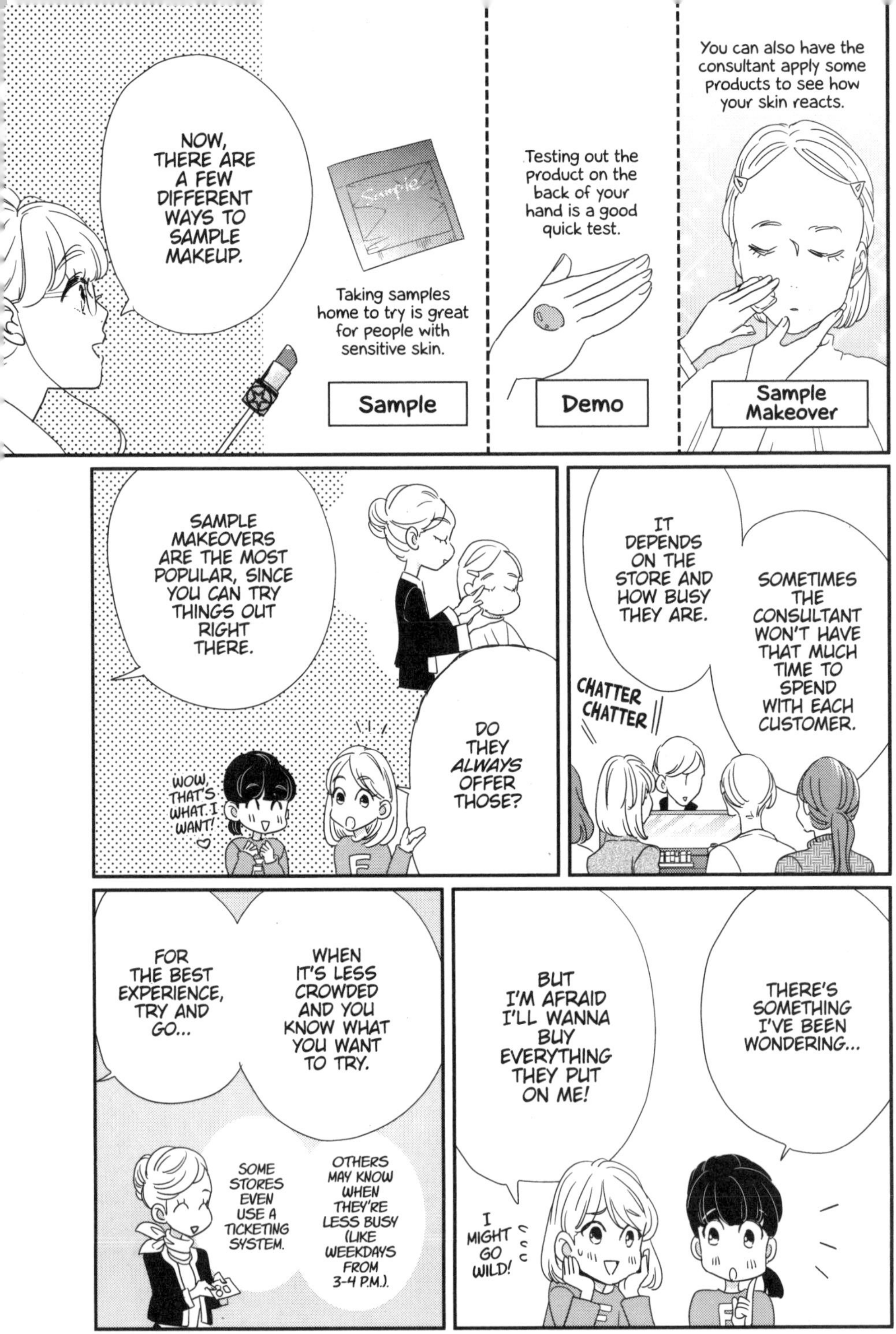
NOW, THERE ARE A FEW DIFFERENT WAYS TO SAMPLE MAKEUP.
Sample
Taking samples home to try is great for people with sensitive skin.
Sample
Testing out the product on the back of your hand is a good quick test.
Demo
You can also have the consultant apply some products to see how your skin reacts.
Sample Makeover
SAMPLE MAKEOVERS ARE THE MOST POPULAR, SINCE YOU CAN TRY THINGS OUT RIGHT THERE.
WOW, THAT'S WHAT I WANT!
DO THEY ALWAYS OFFER THOSE?
IT DEPENDS ON THE STORE AND HOW BUSY THEY ARE.
SOMETIMES THE CONSULTANT WON'T HAVE THAT MUCH TIME TO SPEND WITH EACH CUSTOMER.
CHATTER CHATTER
FOR THE BEST EXPERIENCE, TRY AND GO...
WHEN IT'S LESS CROWDED AND YOU KNOW WHAT YOU WANT TO TRY.
SOME STORES EVEN USE A TICKETING SYSTEM.
OTHERS MAY KNOW WHEN THEY'RE LESS BUSY (LIKE WEEKDAYS FROM 3-4 P.M.).
BUT I'M AFRAID I'LL WANNA BUY EVERYTHING THEY PUT ON ME!
I MIGHT GO WILD!
THERE'S SOMETHING I'VE BEEN WONDERING...

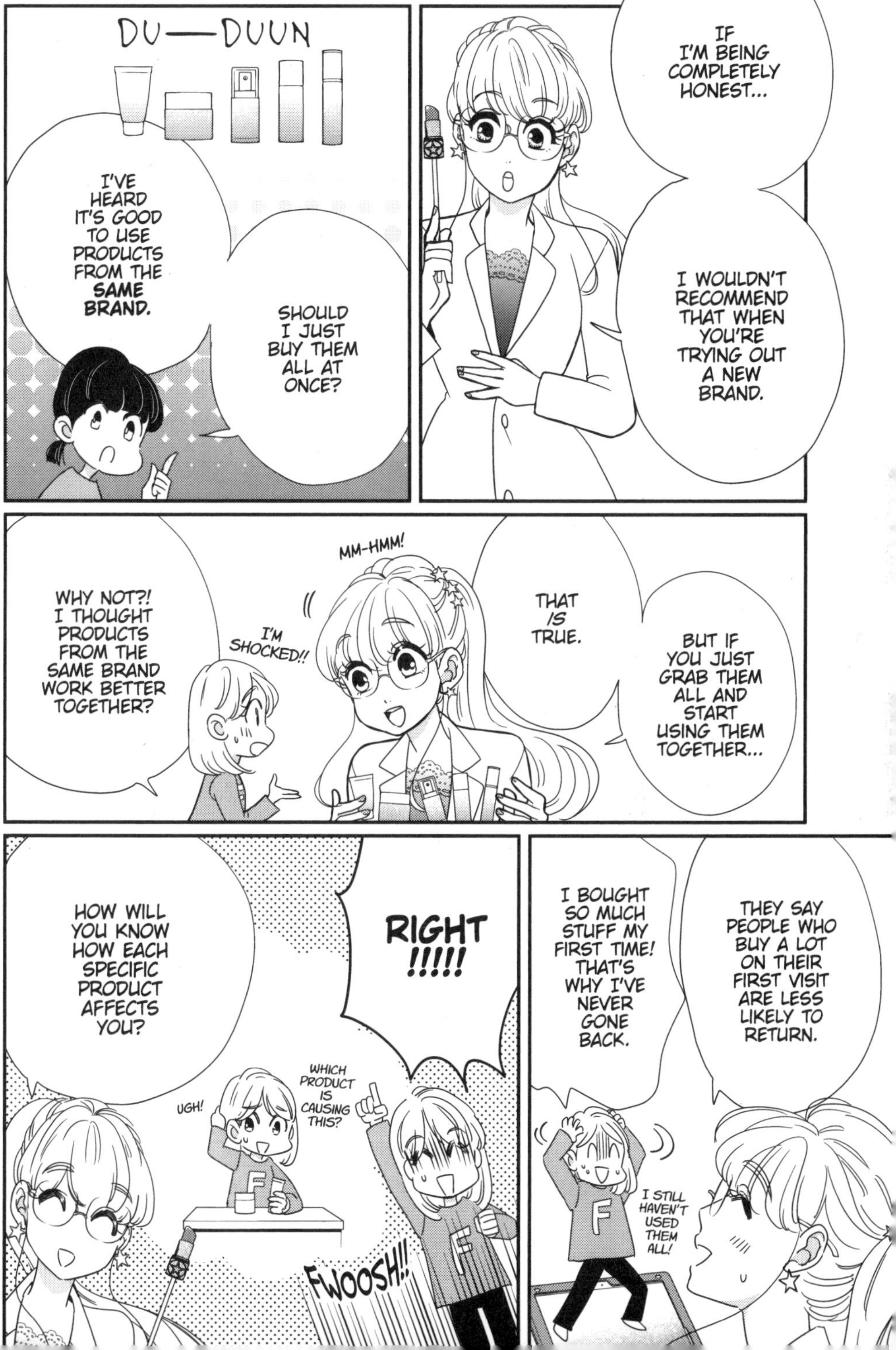
DU—DUUN
I'VE HEARD IT'S GOOD TO USE PRODUCTS FROM THE SAME BRAND.
SHOULD I JUST BUY THEM ALL AT ONCE?
IF I'M BEING COMPLETELY HONEST...
I WOULDN'T RECOMMEND THAT WHEN YOU'RE TRYING OUT A NEW BRAND.
WHY NOT?! I THOUGHT PRODUCTS FROM THE SAME BRAND WORK BETTER TOGETHER?
I'M SHOCKED!!
MM-HMM!
THAT IS TRUE.
BUT IF YOU JUST GRAB THEM ALL AND START USING THEM TOGETHER...
HOW WILL YOU KNOW HOW EACH SPECIFIC PRODUCT AFFECTS YOU?
RIGHT !!!!!
UGH!
WHICH PRODUCT IS CAUSING THIS?
FWOOSH!!
I BOUGHT SO MUCH STUFF MY FIRST TIME! THAT'S WHY I'VE NEVER GONE BACK.
THEY SAY PEOPLE WHO BUY A LOT ON THEIR FIRST VISIT ARE LESS LIKELY TO RETURN.
I STILL HAVEN'T USED THEM ALL!

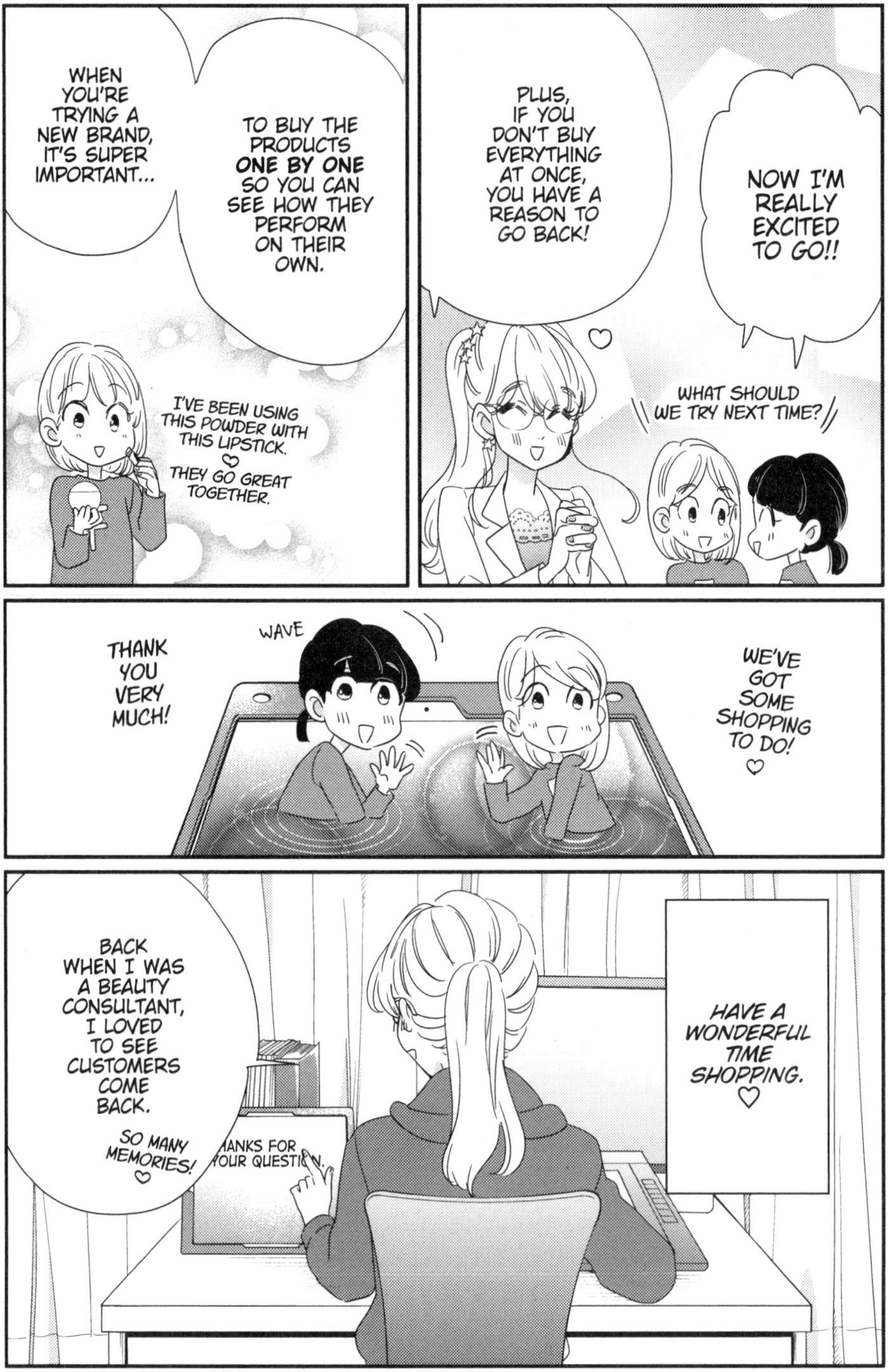

WHEN YOU'RE TRYING A NEW BRAND, IT'S SUPER IMPORTANT...
TO BUY THE PRODUCTS **ONE BY ONE** SO YOU CAN SEE HOW THEY PERFORM ON THEIR OWN.
I'VE BEEN USING THIS POWDER WITH THIS LIPSTICK. ♡ THEY GO GREAT TOGETHER.
PLUS, IF YOU DON'T BUY EVERYTHING AT ONCE, YOU HAVE A REASON TO GO BACK!
NOW I'M REALLY EXCITED TO GO!!
WHAT SHOULD WE TRY NEXT TIME?
THANK YOU VERY MUCH!
WAVE
WE'VE GOT SOME SHOPPING TO DO! ♡
BACK WHEN I WAS A BEAUTY CONSULTANT, I LOVED TO SEE CUSTOMERS COME BACK.
SO MANY MEMORIES! ♡
HANKS FOR YOUR QUESTI N.
HAVE A WONDERFUL TIME SHOPPING. ♡

Let's Ask Rokka-Sensei!

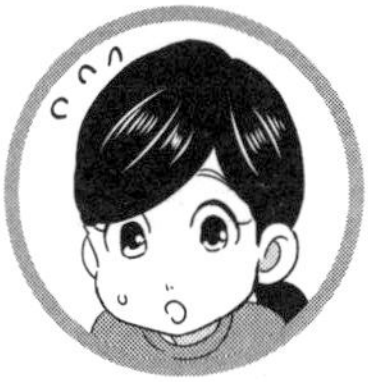

Q. Should I stop using skin care products if my skin gets itchy?

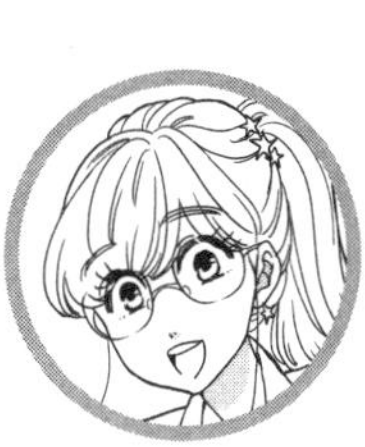

A. Skin care products are meant for healthy skin! If they're causing you problems, you should go ahead and stop. If your symptoms are minor, consider treating them with an over-the-counter ointment. If, however, you're experiencing redness accompanied by itching, burning, or a rash, please see your dermatologist for an evaluation.

Let's Ask Rokka-Sensei!

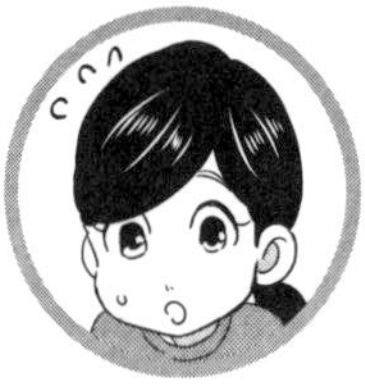

Q. Maybe it's because I normally wear glasses, but my eye makeup isn't very noticeable. Is there another point I should focus more on instead?

A. If you're going more for an intellectual look, focus on your eyebrows. For a cutesy look, intensify your blush or lip color, or add some drama to your lashes.

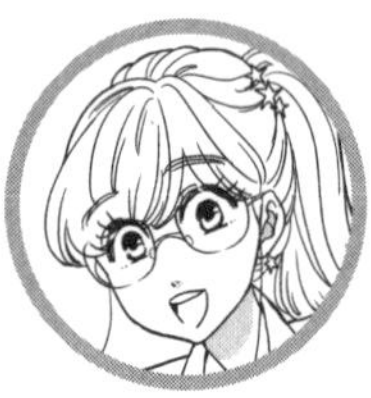

Lesson 4: The Four-Point Makeup Method (Eyebrows)

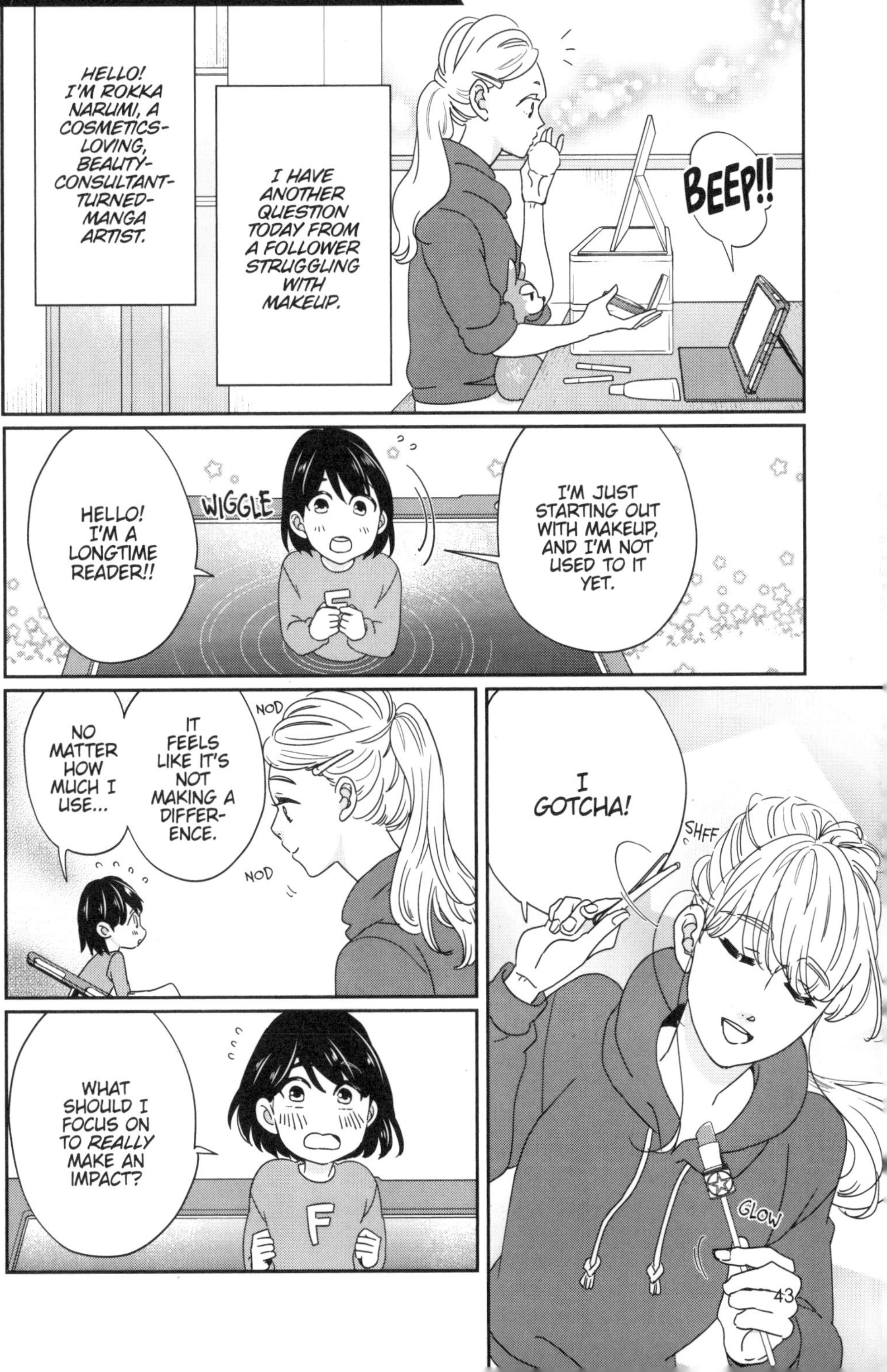
HELLO! I'M ROKKA NARUMI, A COSMETICS-LOVING, BEAUTY-CONSULTANT-TURNED-MANGA ARTIST.
I HAVE ANOTHER QUESTION TODAY FROM A FOLLOWER STRUGGLING WITH MAKEUP.
BEEP!!
HELLO! I'M A LONGTIME READER!!
WIGGLE
I'M JUST STARTING OUT WITH MAKEUP, AND I'M NOT USED TO IT YET.
NO MATTER HOW MUCH I USE...
IT FEELS LIKE IT'S NOT MAKING A DIFFERENCE.
NOD
NOD
WHAT SHOULD I FOCUS ON TO REALLY MAKE AN IMPACT?
I GOTCHA!
SHFF
GLOW

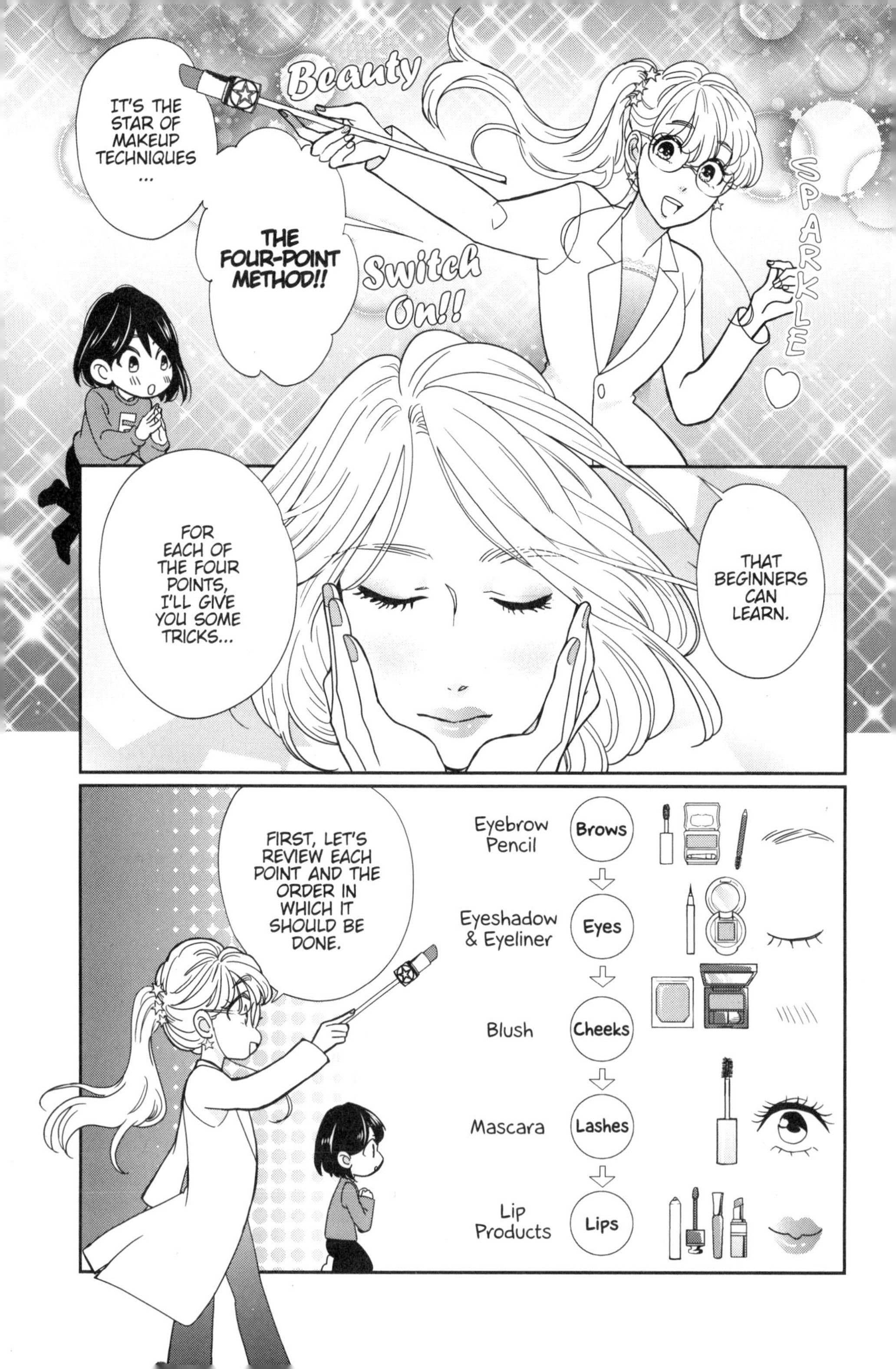
IT'S THE STAR OF MAKEUP TECHNIQUES ...
Beauty
THE FOUR-POINT METHOD!!
Switch On!!
SPARKLE
FOR EACH OF THE FOUR POINTS, I'LL GIVE YOU SOME TRICKS...
THAT BEGINNERS CAN LEARN.
FIRST, LET'S REVIEW EACH POINT AND THE ORDER IN WHICH IT SHOULD BE DONE.
Eyebrow Pencil
Brows
Eyeshadow & Eyeliner
Eyes
Blush
Cheeks
Mascara
Lashes
Lip Products
Lips

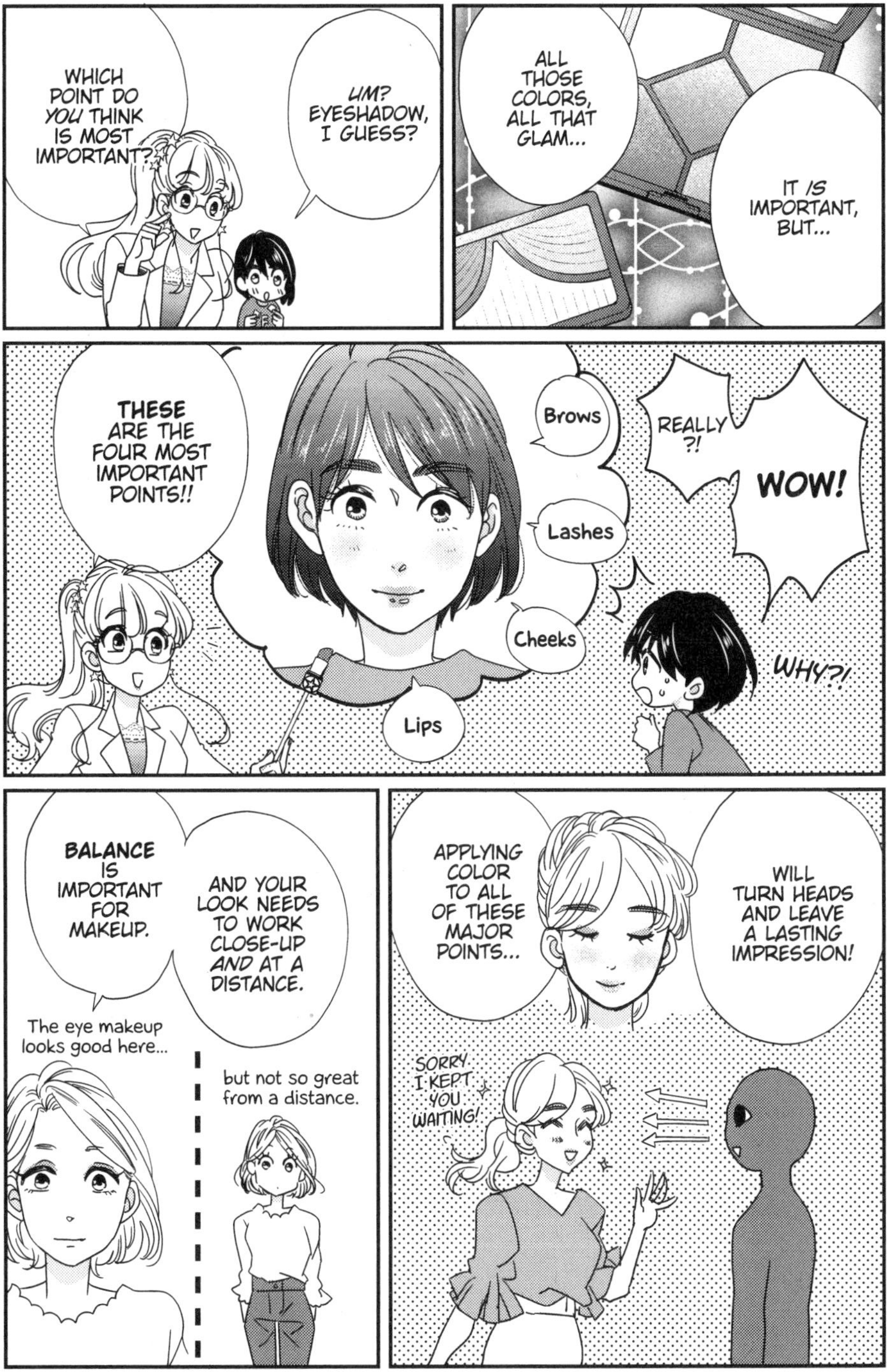

WHICH POINT DO YOU THINK IS MOST IMPORTANT?
UM? EYESHADOW, I GUESS?
ALL THOSE COLORS, ALL THAT GLAM...
IT IS IMPORTANT, BUT...
THESE ARE THE FOUR MOST IMPORTANT POINTS!!
Brows
Lashes
Cheeks
Lips
REALLY?!
WOW!
WHY?!
BALANCE IS IMPORTANT FOR MAKEUP.
AND YOUR LOOK NEEDS TO WORK CLOSE-UP AND AT A DISTANCE.
The eye makeup looks good here...
but not so great from a distance.
APPLYING COLOR TO ALL OF THESE MAJOR POINTS...
WILL TURN HEADS AND LEAVE A LASTING IMPRESSION!
SORRY I KEPT YOU WAITING!

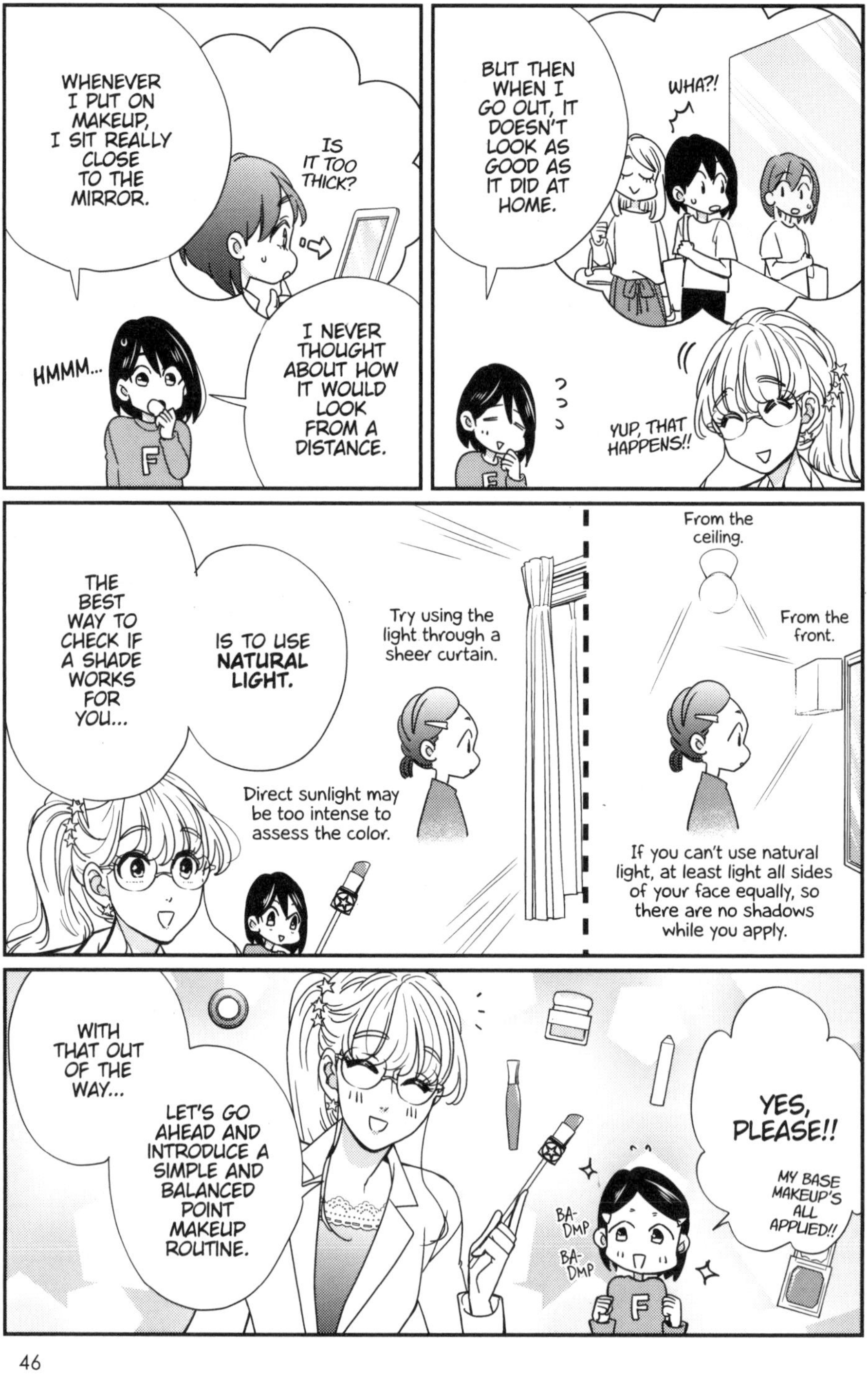
WHENEVER I PUT ON MAKEUP, I SIT REALLY CLOSE TO THE MIRROR.
IS IT TOO THICK?
I NEVER THOUGHT ABOUT HOW IT WOULD LOOK FROM A DISTANCE.
HMMM...
BUT THEN WHEN I GO OUT, IT DOESN'T LOOK AS GOOD AS IT DID AT HOME.
WHA?!
YUP, THAT HAPPENS!!
THE BEST WAY TO CHECK IF A SHADE WORKS FOR YOU...
IS TO USE NATURAL LIGHT.
Try using the light through a sheer curtain.
Direct sunlight may be too intense to assess the color.
From the ceiling.
From the front.
If you can't use natural light, at least light all sides of your face equally, so there are no shadows while you apply.
WITH THAT OUT OF THE WAY...
LET'S GO AHEAD AND INTRODUCE A SIMPLE AND BALANCED POINT MAKEUP ROUTINE.
YES, PLEASE!!
MY BASE MAKEUP'S ALL APPLIED!!
BA-DMP
BA-DMP

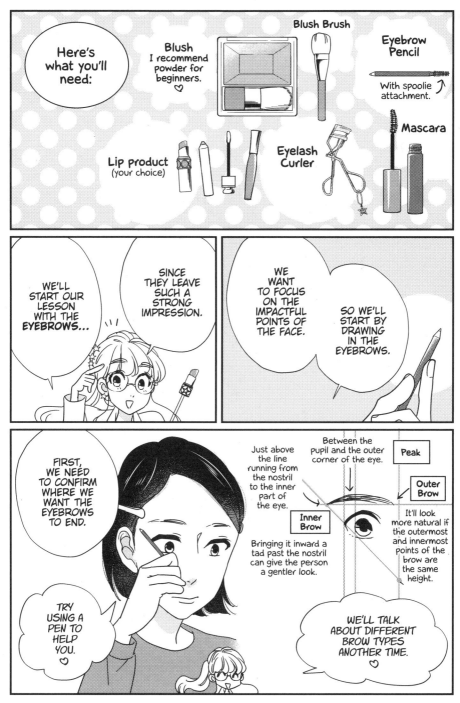

Here's what you'll need:

Blush
I recommend powder for beginners. ♡

Blush Brush

Eyebrow Pencil
With spoolie attachment. ↗

Mascara

Lip product
(your choice)

Eyelash Curler

WE'LL START OUR LESSON WITH THE EYEBROWS...

SINCE THEY LEAVE SUCH A STRONG IMPRESSION.

WE WANT TO FOCUS ON THE IMPACTFUL POINTS OF THE FACE.

SO WE'LL START BY DRAWING IN THE EYEBROWS.

FIRST, WE NEED TO CONFIRM WHERE WE WANT THE EYEBROWS TO END.

TRY USING A PEN TO HELP YOU. ♡

Just above the line running from the nostril to the inner part of the eye.

Between the pupil and the outer corner of the eye.

Peak

Outer Brow

Inner Brow

Bringing it inward a tad past the nostril can give the person a gentler look.

It'll look more natural if the outermost and innermost points of the brow are the same height.

WE'LL TALK ABOUT DIFFERENT BROW TYPES ANOTHER TIME. ♡

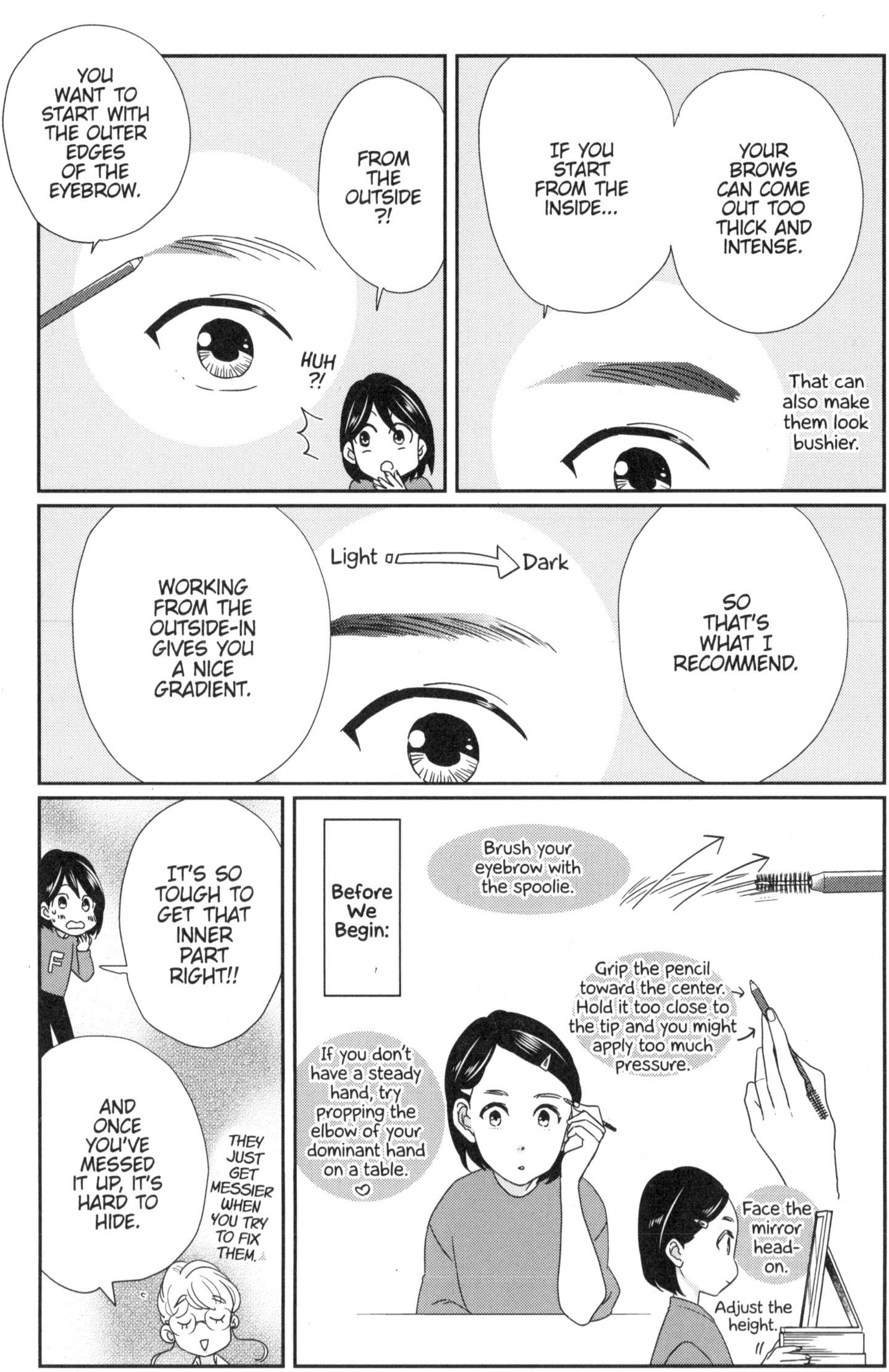
YOU WANT TO START WITH THE OUTER EDGES OF THE EYEBROW.
FROM THE OUTSIDE ?!
HUH ?!
IF YOU START FROM THE INSIDE...
YOUR BROWS CAN COME OUT TOO THICK AND INTENSE.
That can also make them look bushier.
WORKING FROM THE OUTSIDE-IN GIVES YOU A NICE GRADIENT.
Light
Dark
SO THAT'S WHAT I RECOMMEND.
IT'S SO TOUGH TO GET THAT INNER PART RIGHT!!
AND ONCE YOU'VE MESSED IT UP, IT'S HARD TO HIDE.
THEY JUST GET MESSIER WHEN YOU TRY TO FIX THEM.
Before We Begin:
Brush your eyebrow with the spoolie.
Grip the pencil toward the center. Hold it too close to the tip and you might apply too much pressure.
If you don't have a steady hand, try propping the elbow of your dominant hand on a table. ♡
Face the mirror head-on.
Adjust the height.

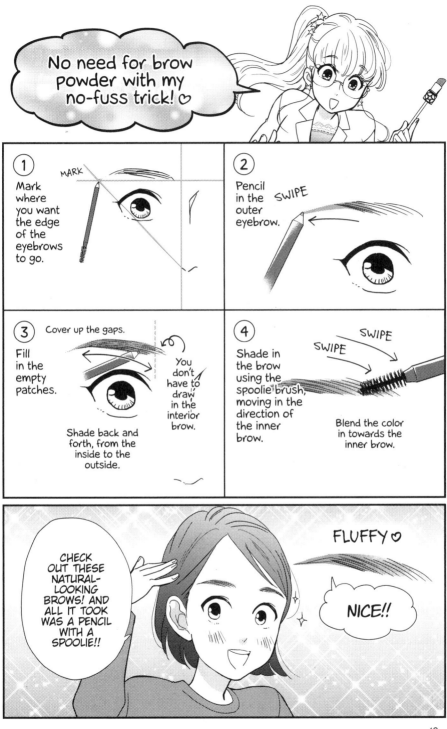

No need for brow powder with my no-fuss trick! ♡

1 Mark where you want the edge of the eyebrows to go.

MARK

2 Pencil in the outer eyebrow.

SWIPE

3 Fill in the empty patches.

Cover up the gaps.

You don't have to draw in the interior brow.

Shade back and forth, from the inside to the outside.

4 Shade in the brow using the spoolie brush, moving in the direction of the inner brow.

SWIPE

SWIPE

Blend the color in towards the inner brow.

CHECK OUT THESE NATURAL-LOOKING BROWS! AND ALL IT TOOK WAS A PENCIL WITH A SPOOLIE!!

FLUFFY ♡

NICE!!

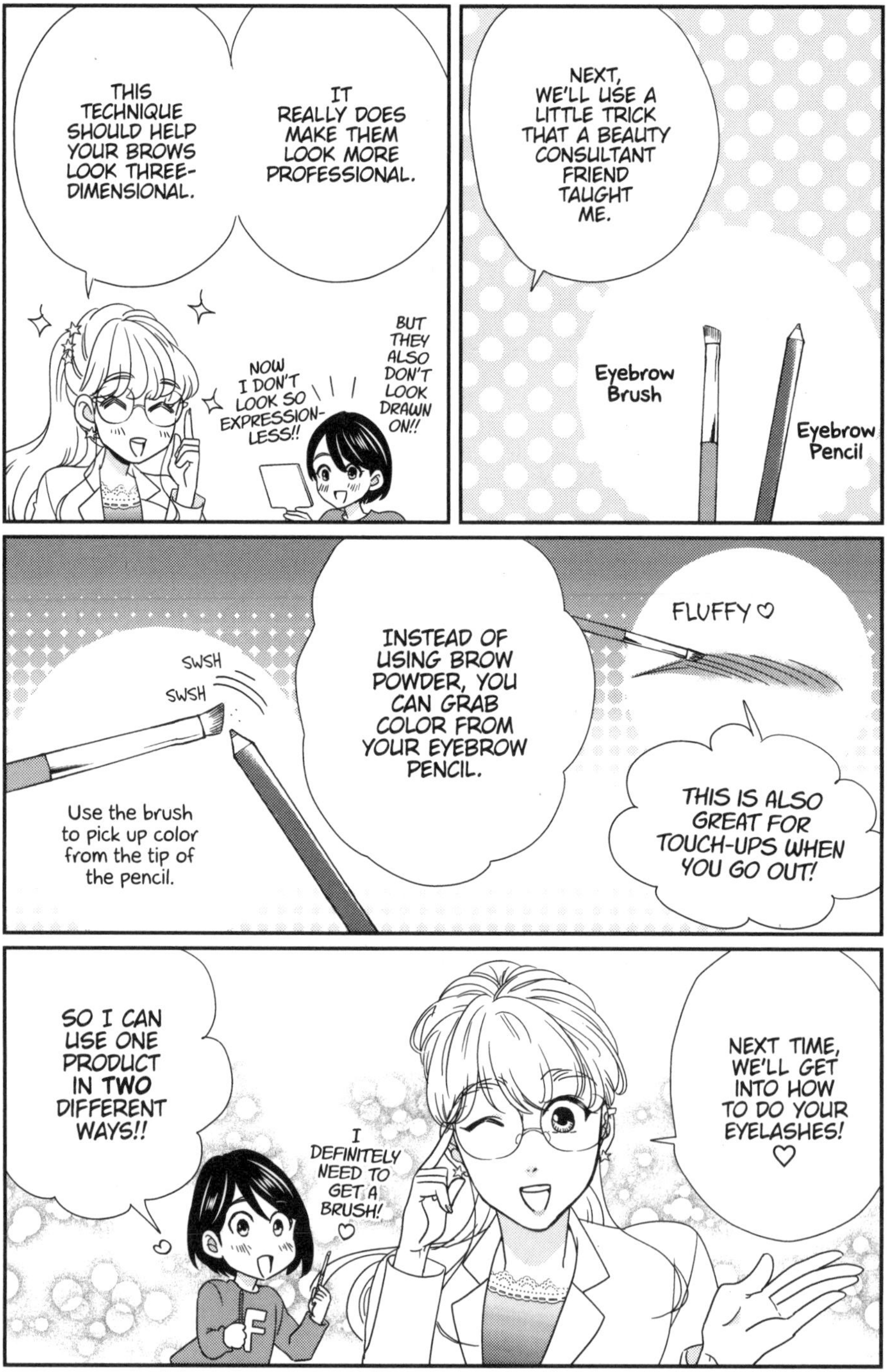
THIS TECHNIQUE SHOULD HELP YOUR BROWS LOOK THREE-DIMENSIONAL.
IT REALLY DOES MAKE THEM LOOK MORE PROFESSIONAL.
NOW I DON'T LOOK SO EXPRESSION-LESS!!
BUT THEY ALSO DON'T LOOK DRAWN ON!!
NEXT, WE'LL USE A LITTLE TRICK THAT A BEAUTY CONSULTANT FRIEND TAUGHT ME.
Eyebrow Brush
Eyebrow Pencil
SWSH
SWSH
Use the brush to pick up color from the tip of the pencil.
INSTEAD OF USING BROW POWDER, YOU CAN GRAB COLOR FROM YOUR EYEBROW PENCIL.
FLUFFY ♡
THIS IS ALSO GREAT FOR TOUCH-UPS WHEN YOU GO OUT!
NEXT TIME, WE'LL GET INTO HOW TO DO YOUR EYELASHES! ♡
I DEFINITELY NEED TO GET A BRUSH! ♡
SO I CAN USE ONE PRODUCT IN TWO DIFFERENT WAYS!! ♡

Lesson 5: The Four-Point Makeup Method (Mascara & Blush)

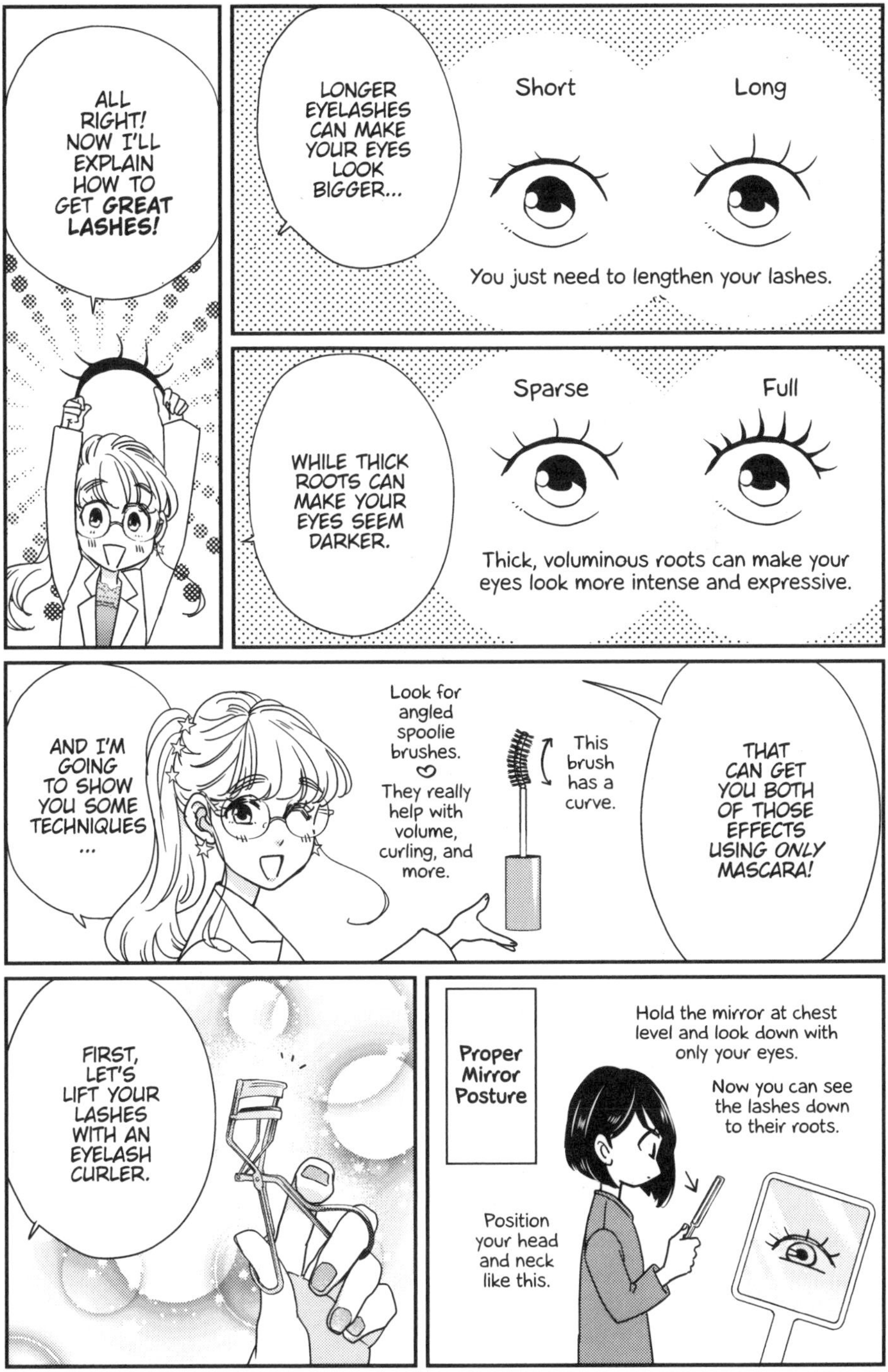

ALL RIGHT! NOW I'LL EXPLAIN HOW TO GET GREAT LASHES!
LONGER EYELASHES CAN MAKE YOUR EYES LOOK BIGGER...
Short
Long
You just need to lengthen your lashes.
WHILE THICK ROOTS CAN MAKE YOUR EYES SEEM DARKER.
Sparse
Full
Thick, voluminous roots can make your eyes look more intense and expressive.
AND I'M GOING TO SHOW YOU SOME TECHNIQUES ...
Look for angled spoolie brushes. ♡ They really help with volume, curling, and more.
This brush has a curve.
THAT CAN GET YOU BOTH OF THOSE EFFECTS USING ONLY MASCARA!
FIRST, LET'S LIFT YOUR LASHES WITH AN EYELASH CURLER.
Proper Mirror Posture
Hold the mirror at chest level and look down with only your eyes.
Now you can see the lashes down to their roots.
Position your head and neck like this.

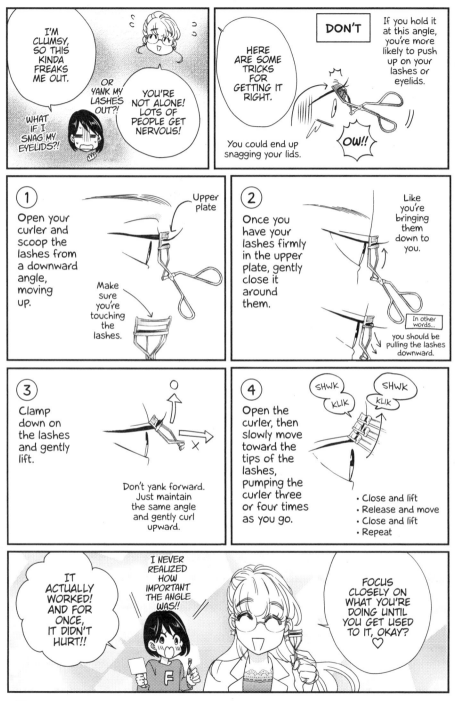

I'M CLUMSY, SO THIS KINDA FREAKS ME OUT.

WHAT IF I SNAG MY EYELIDS?!

OR YANK MY LASHES OUT?!

YOU'RE NOT ALONE! LOTS OF PEOPLE GET NERVOUS!

HERE ARE SOME TRICKS FOR GETTING IT RIGHT.

You could end up snagging your lids.

DON'T

If you hold it at this angle, you're more likely to push up on your lashes or eyelids.

OW!!

1 Open your curler and scoop the lashes from a downward angle, moving up.

Upper plate

Make sure you're touching the lashes.

2 Once you have your lashes firmly in the upper plate, gently close it around them.

Like you're bringing them down to you.

In other words...

you should be pulling the lashes downward.

3 Clamp down on the lashes and gently lift.

Don't yank forward. Just maintain the same angle and gently curl upward.

4 Open the curler, then slowly move toward the tips of the lashes, pumping the curler three or four times as you go.

SHWK KLIK

SHWK KLIK

• Close and lift
• Release and move
• Close and lift
• Repeat

IT ACTUALLY WORKED! AND FOR ONCE, IT DIDN'T HURT!!

I NEVER REALIZED HOW IMPORTANT THE ANGLE WAS!!

FOCUS CLOSELY ON WHAT YOU'RE DOING UNTIL YOU GET USED TO IT, OKAY? ♡

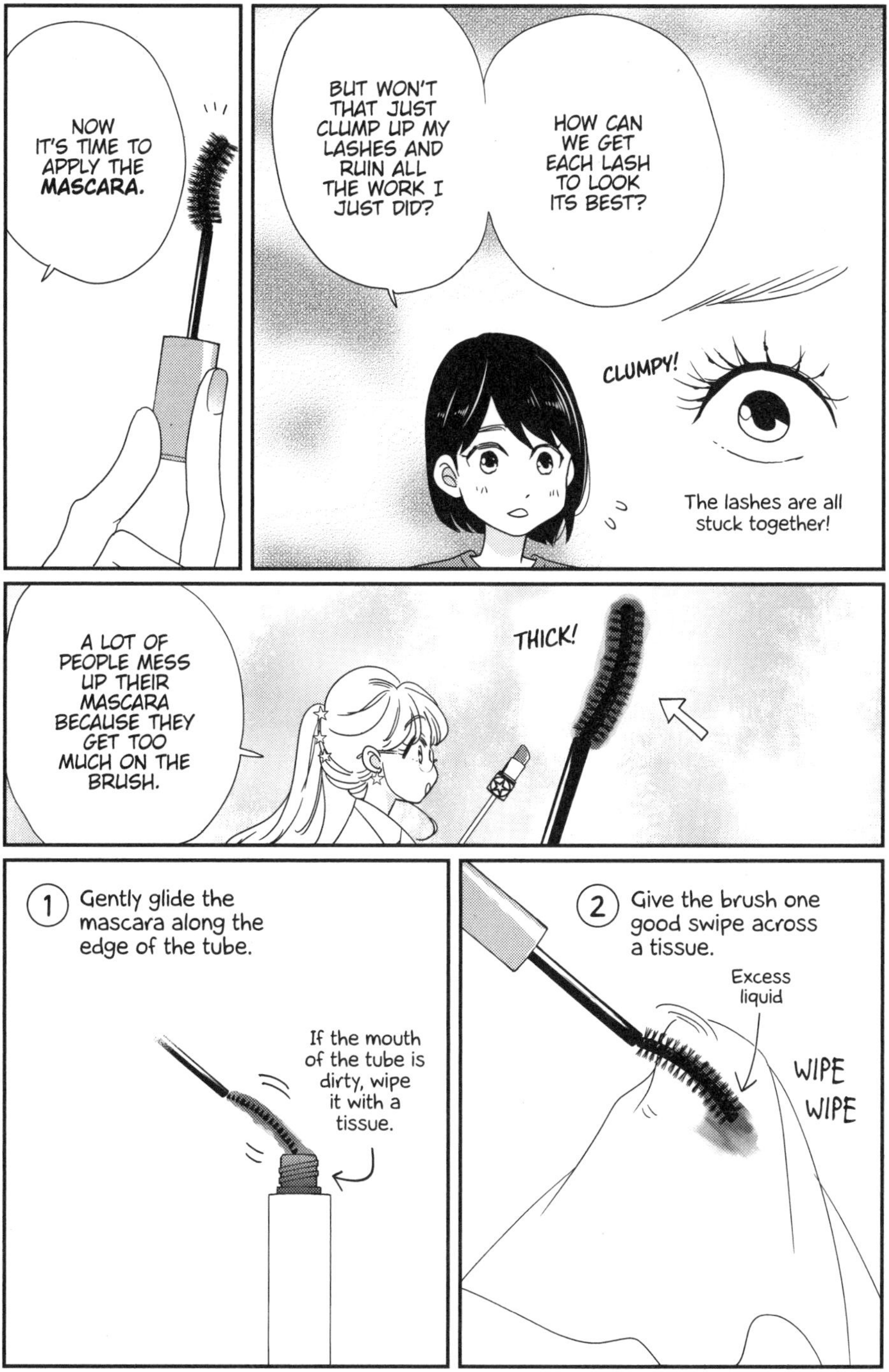
NOW IT'S TIME TO APPLY THE **MASCARA.**
BUT WON'T THAT JUST CLUMP UP MY LASHES AND RUIN ALL THE WORK I JUST DID?
HOW CAN WE GET EACH LASH TO LOOK ITS BEST?
CLUMPY!
The lashes are all stuck together!
A LOT OF PEOPLE MESS UP THEIR MASCARA BECAUSE THEY GET TOO MUCH ON THE BRUSH.
THICK!
1 Gently glide the mascara along the edge of the tube.
If the mouth of the tube is dirty, wipe it with a tissue.
2 Give the brush one good swipe across a tissue.
Excess liquid
WIPE WIPE

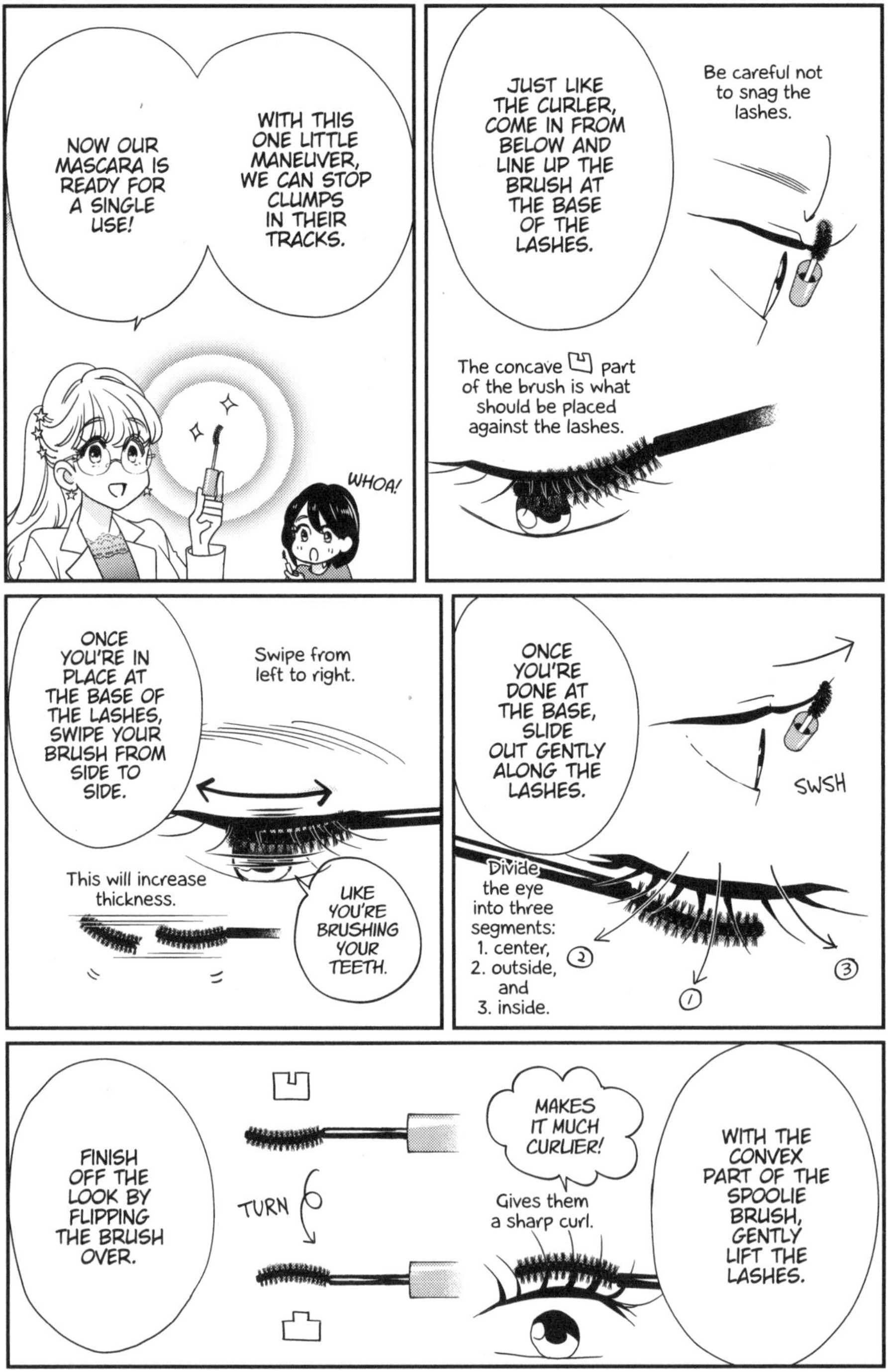
NOW OUR MASCARA IS READY FOR A SINGLE USE!
WITH THIS ONE LITTLE MANEUVER, WE CAN STOP CLUMPS IN THEIR TRACKS.
WHOA!
JUST LIKE THE CURLER, COME IN FROM BELOW AND LINE UP THE BRUSH AT THE BASE OF THE LASHES.
Be careful not to snag the lashes.
The concave part of the brush is what should be placed against the lashes.
ONCE YOU'RE IN PLACE AT THE BASE OF THE LASHES, SWIPE YOUR BRUSH FROM SIDE TO SIDE.
Swipe from left to right.
This will increase thickness.
LIKE YOU'RE BRUSHING YOUR TEETH.
ONCE YOU'RE DONE AT THE BASE, SLIDE OUT GENTLY ALONG THE LASHES.
SWSH
Divide the eye into three segments: 1. center, 2. outside, and 3. inside.
2
1
3
FINISH OFF THE LOOK BY FLIPPING THE BRUSH OVER.
TURN
MAKES IT MUCH CURLIER!
Gives them a sharp curl.
WITH THE CONVEX PART OF THE SPOOLIE BRUSH, GENTLY LIFT THE LASHES.

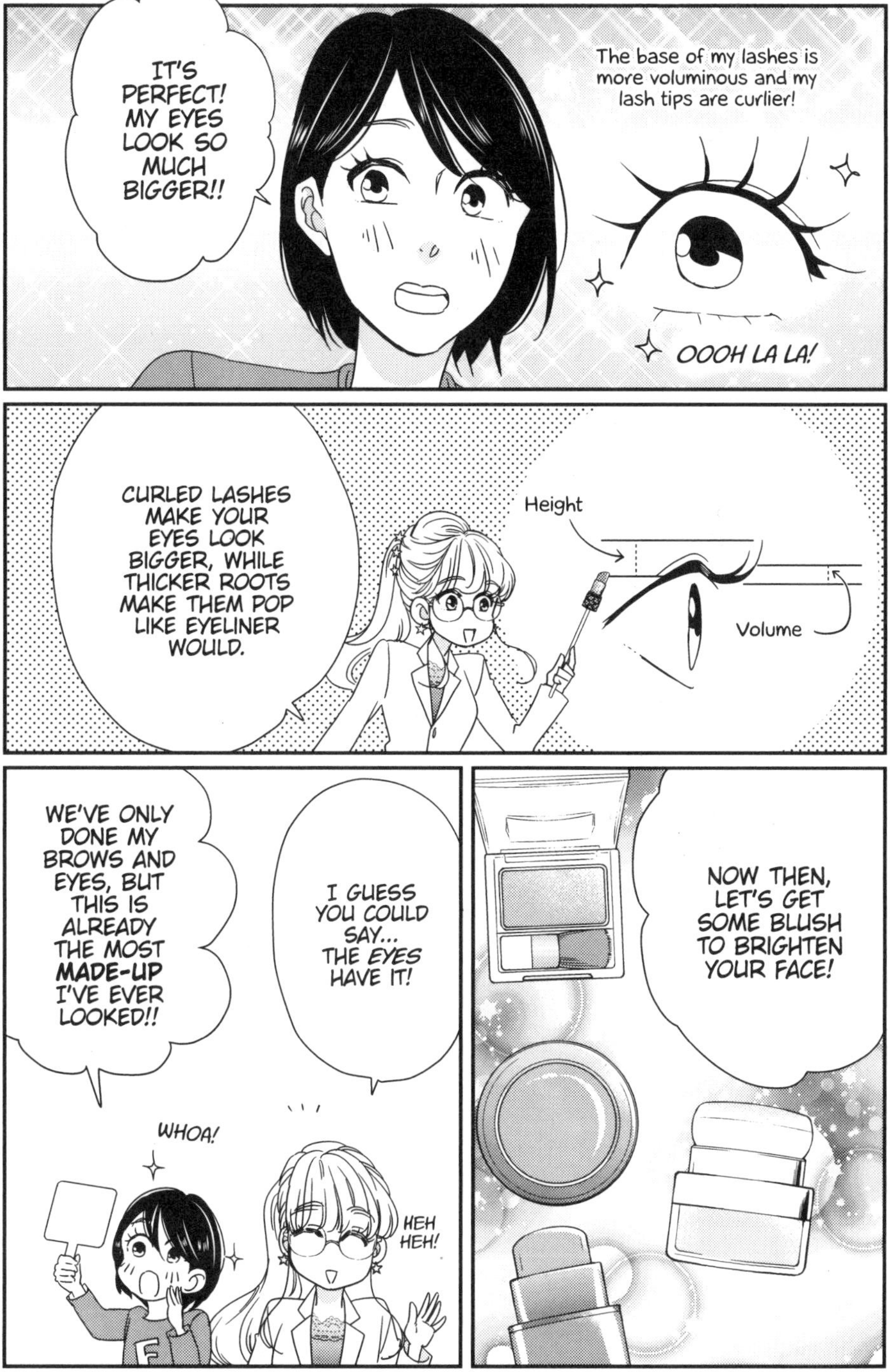
IT'S PERFECT! MY EYES LOOK SO MUCH BIGGER!!
The base of my lashes is more voluminous and my lash tips are curlier!
OOOH LA LA!
CURLED LASHES MAKE YOUR EYES LOOK BIGGER, WHILE THICKER ROOTS MAKE THEM POP LIKE EYELINER WOULD.
Height
Volume
WE'VE ONLY DONE MY BROWS AND EYES, BUT THIS IS ALREADY THE MOST **MADE-UP** I'VE EVER LOOKED!!
I GUESS YOU COULD SAY... THE *EYES* HAVE IT!
WHOA!
HEH HEH!
NOW THEN, LET'S GET SOME BLUSH TO BRIGHTEN YOUR FACE!

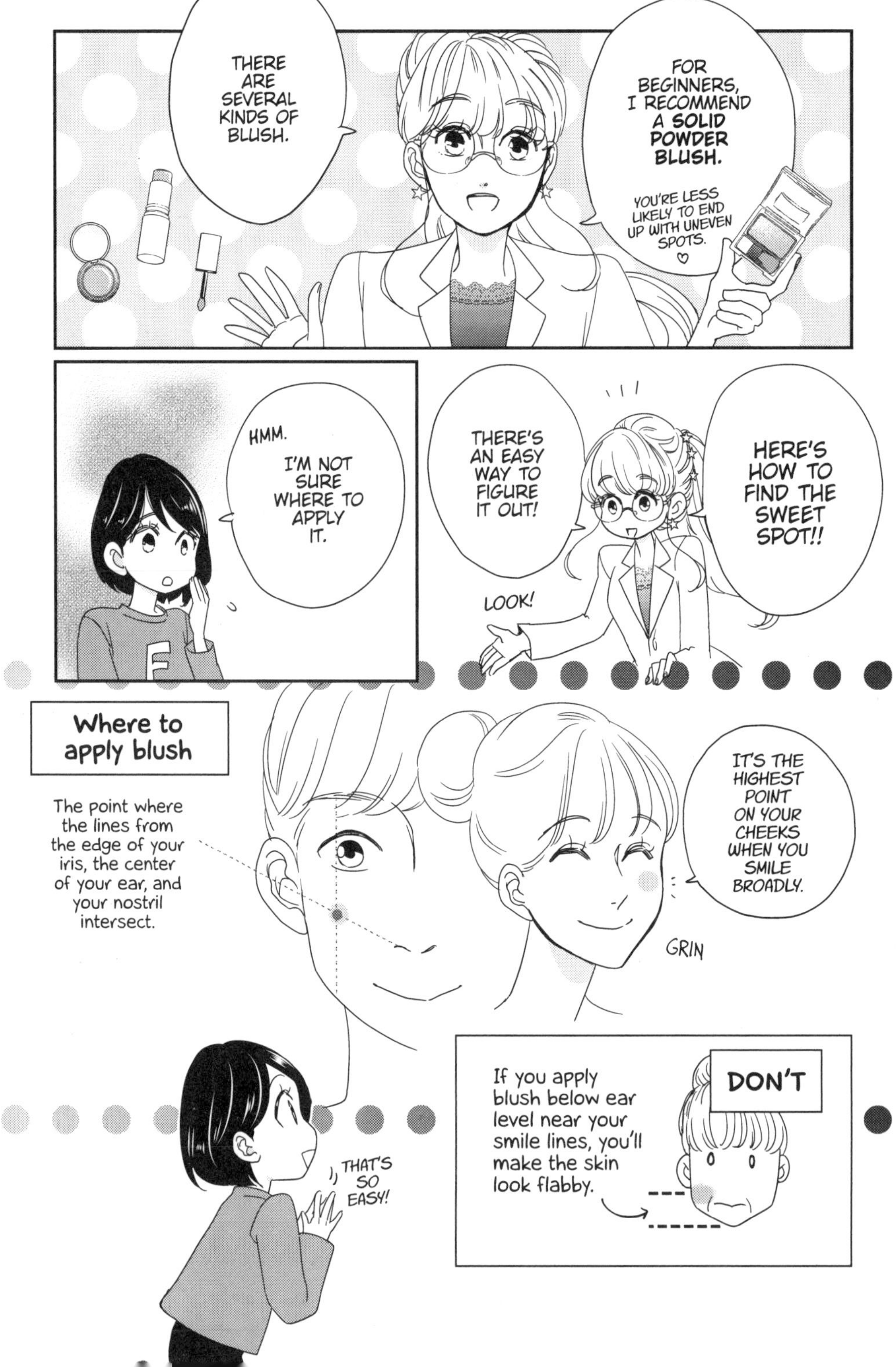

THERE ARE SEVERAL KINDS OF BLUSH.
FOR BEGINNERS, I RECOMMEND A **SOLID POWDER BLUSH.**
YOU'RE LESS LIKELY TO END UP WITH UNEVEN SPOTS. ♡
HMM.
I'M NOT SURE WHERE TO APPLY IT.
THERE'S AN EASY WAY TO FIGURE IT OUT!
HERE'S HOW TO FIND THE SWEET SPOT!!
LOOK!
Where to apply blush
The point where the lines from the edge of your iris, the center of your ear, and your nostril intersect.
IT'S THE HIGHEST POINT ON YOUR CHEEKS WHEN YOU SMILE BROADLY.
GRIN
THAT'S SO EASY!
DON'T
If you apply blush below ear level near your smile lines, you'll make the skin look flabby.

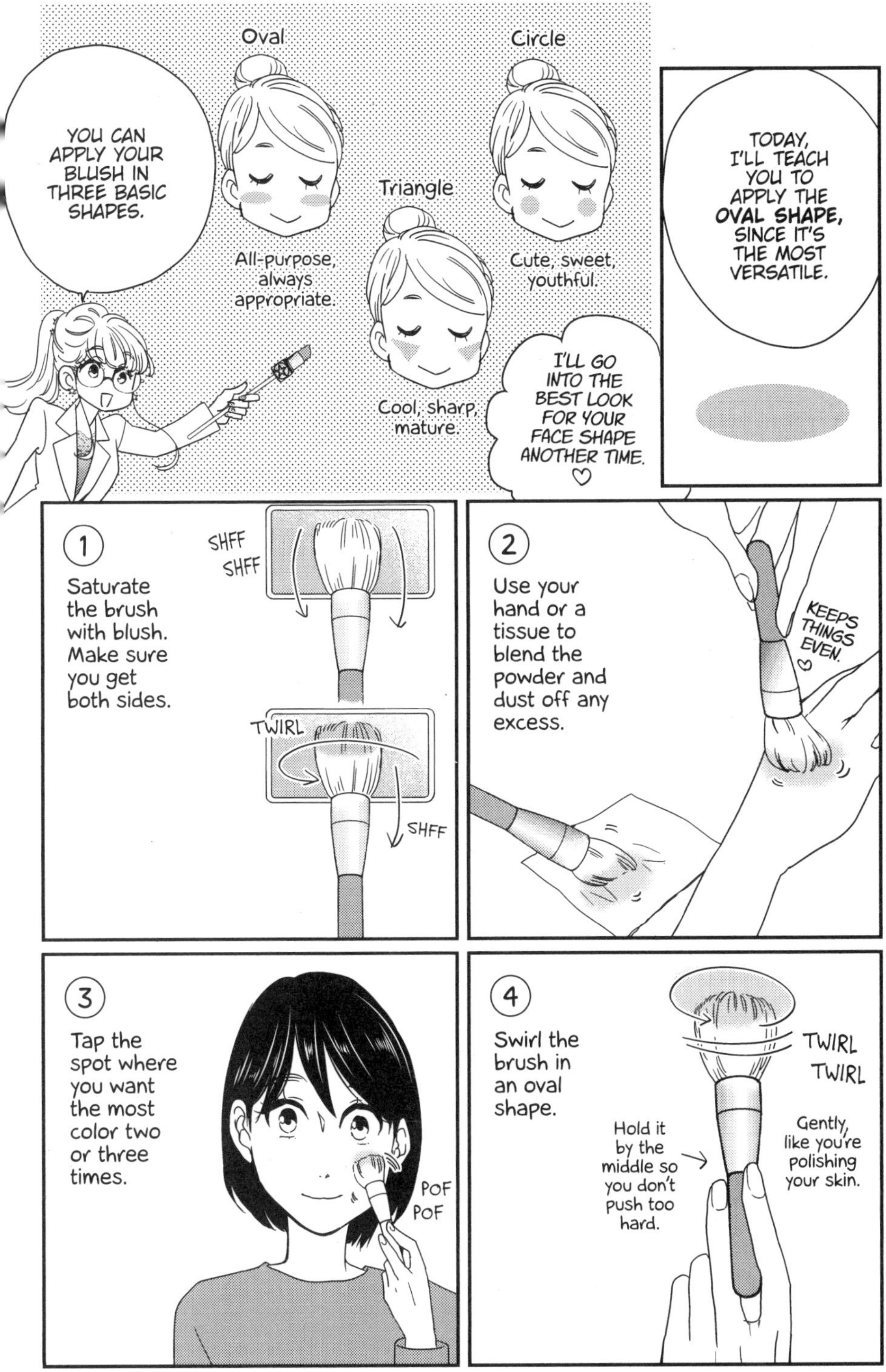
YOU CAN APPLY YOUR BLUSH IN THREE BASIC SHAPES.
Oval
All-purpose, always appropriate.
Triangle
Cool, sharp, mature.
Circle
Cute, sweet, youthful.
I'LL GO INTO THE BEST LOOK FOR YOUR FACE SHAPE ANOTHER TIME. ♡
TODAY, I'LL TEACH YOU TO APPLY THE **OVAL SHAPE,** SINCE IT'S THE MOST VERSATILE.
1
Saturate the brush with blush. Make sure you get both sides.
SHFF
SHFF
TWIRL
SHFF
2
Use your hand or a tissue to blend the powder and dust off any excess.
KEEPS THINGS EVEN. ♡
3
Tap the spot where you want the most color two or three times.
POF
POF
4
Swirl the brush in an oval shape.
TWIRL
TWIRL
Hold it by the middle so you don't push too hard.
Gently, like you're polishing your skin.

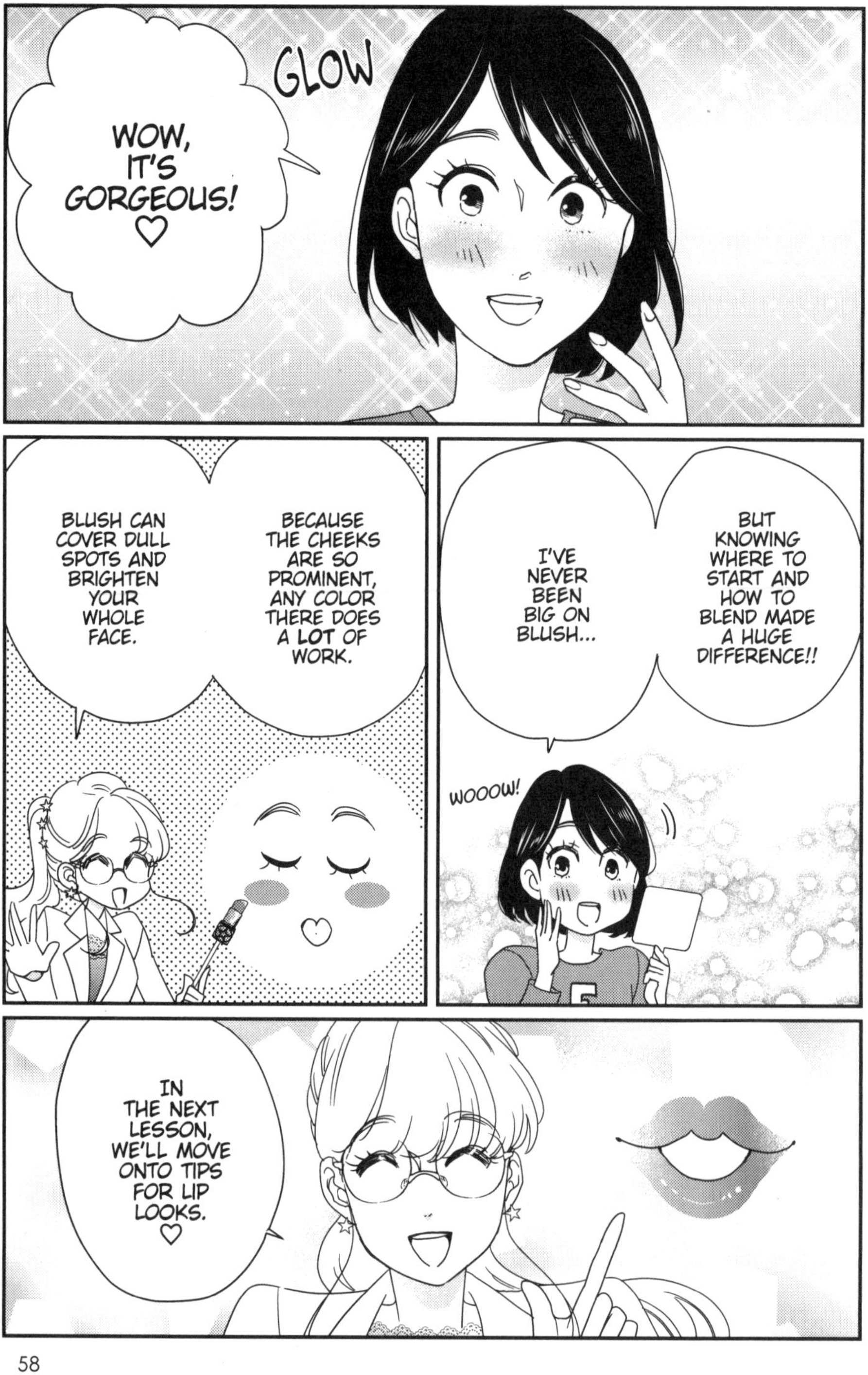
GLOW
WOW, IT'S GORGEOUS! ♡
BLUSH CAN COVER DULL SPOTS AND BRIGHTEN YOUR WHOLE FACE.
BECAUSE THE CHEEKS ARE SO PROMINENT, ANY COLOR THERE DOES A **LOT** OF WORK.
I'VE NEVER BEEN BIG ON BLUSH...
BUT KNOWING WHERE TO START AND HOW TO BLEND MADE A HUGE DIFFERENCE!!
WOOOW!
IN THE NEXT LESSON, WE'LL MOVE ONTO TIPS FOR LIP LOOKS. ♡

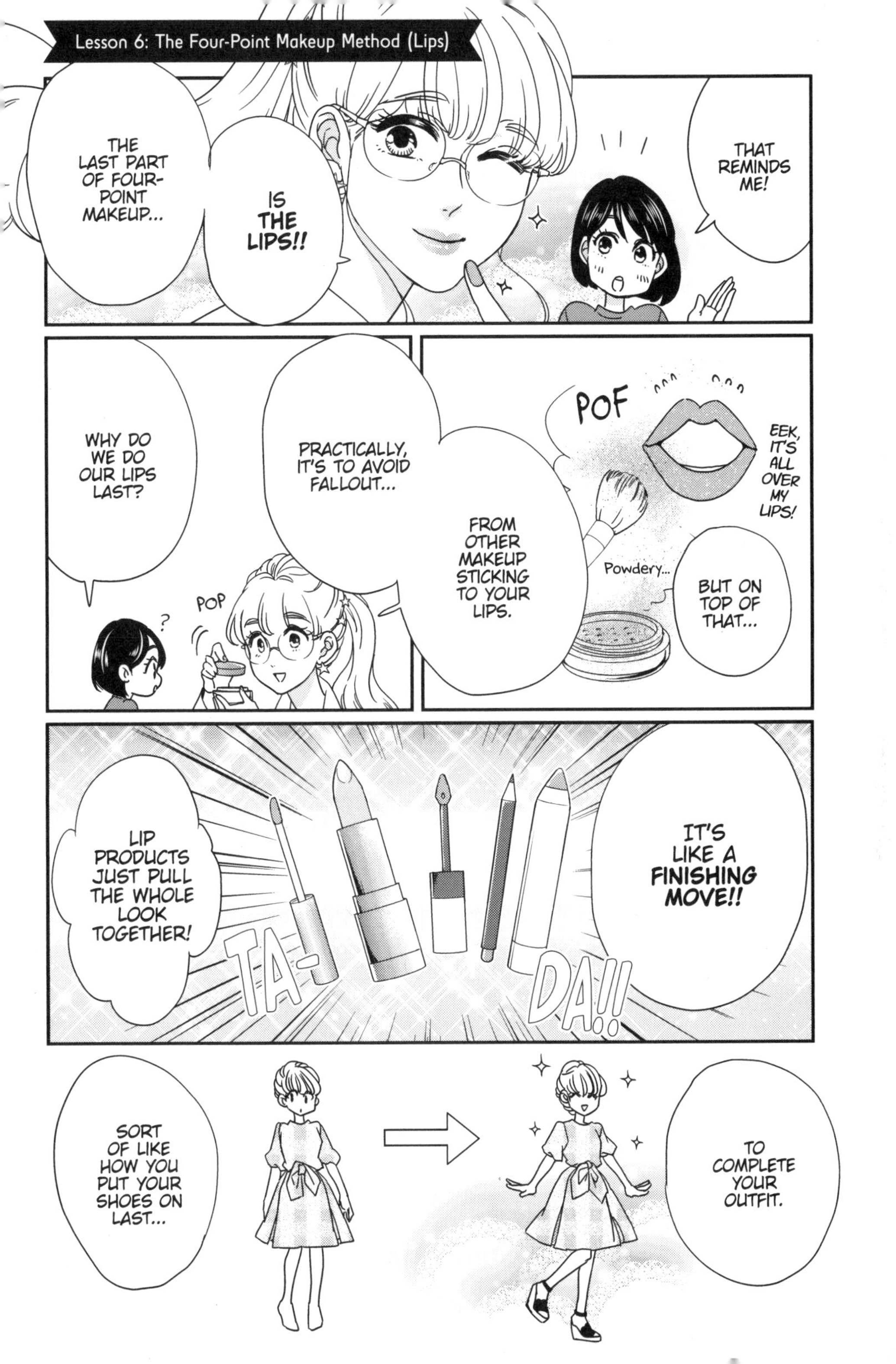
Lesson 6: The Four-Point Makeup Method (Lips)
THE LAST PART OF FOUR-POINT MAKEUP...
IS THE LIPS!!
THAT REMINDS ME!
WHY DO WE DO OUR LIPS LAST?
POP
PRACTICALLY, IT'S TO AVOID FALLOUT...
FROM OTHER MAKEUP STICKING TO YOUR LIPS.
POF
EEK, IT'S ALL OVER MY LIPS!
Powdery...
BUT ON TOP OF THAT...
LIP PRODUCTS JUST PULL THE WHOLE LOOK TOGETHER!
TA-DA!!
IT'S LIKE A FINISHING MOVE!!
SORT OF LIKE HOW YOU PUT YOUR SHOES ON LAST...
TO COMPLETE YOUR OUTFIT.

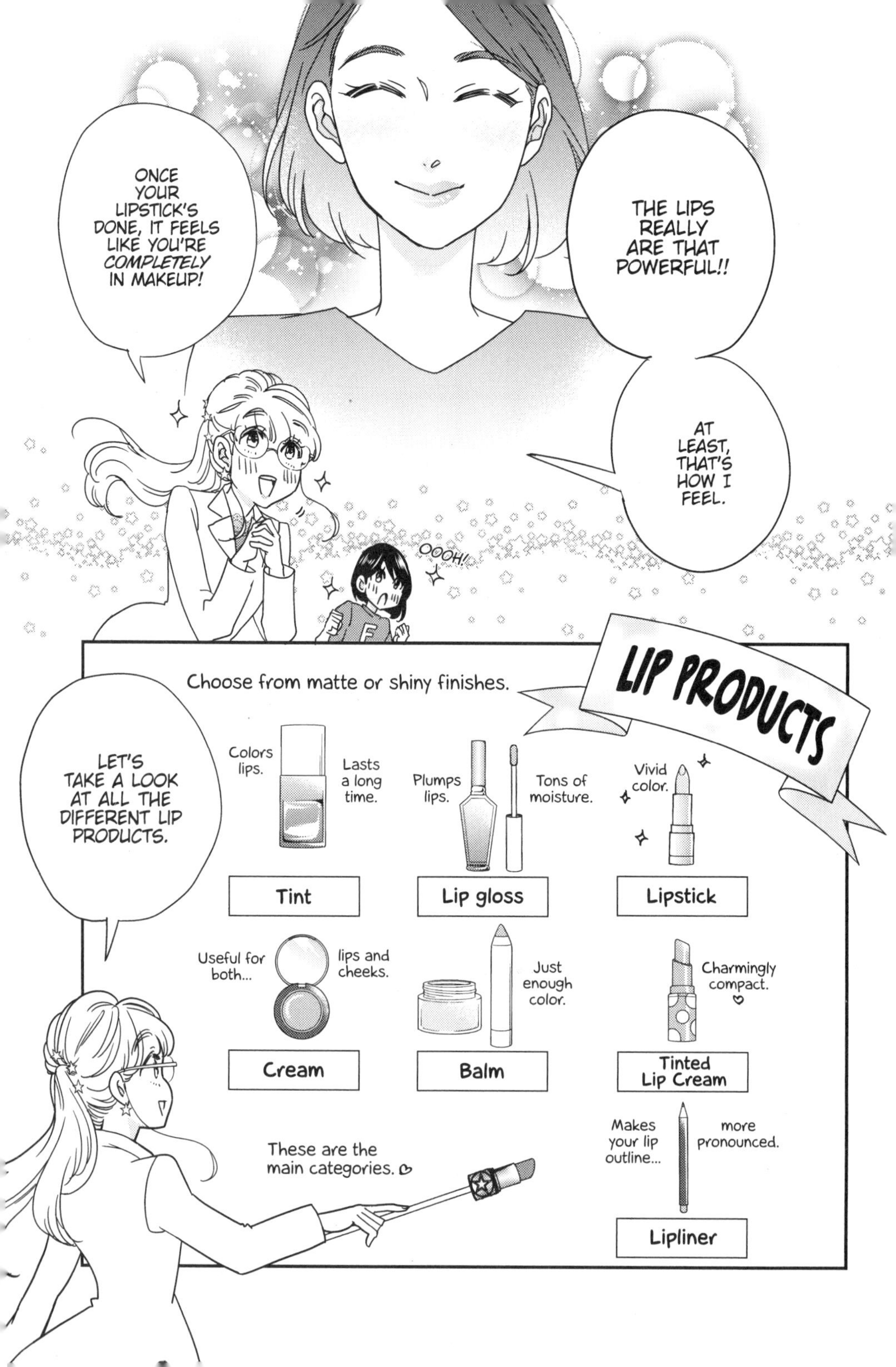
THE LIPS REALLY ARE THAT POWERFUL!!
ONCE YOUR LIPSTICK'S DONE, IT FEELS LIKE YOU'RE COMPLETELY IN MAKEUP!
AT LEAST, THAT'S HOW I FEEL.
OOOH!
LIP PRODUCTS
Choose from matte or shiny finishes.
LET'S TAKE A LOOK AT ALL THE DIFFERENT LIP PRODUCTS.
Colors lips.
Lasts a long time.
Tint
Plumps lips.
Tons of moisture.
Lip gloss
Vivid color.
Lipstick
Useful for both...
lips and cheeks.
Cream
Just enough color.
Balm
Charmingly compact.
Tinted Lip Cream
Makes your lip outline...
more pronounced.
Lipliner
These are the main categories.

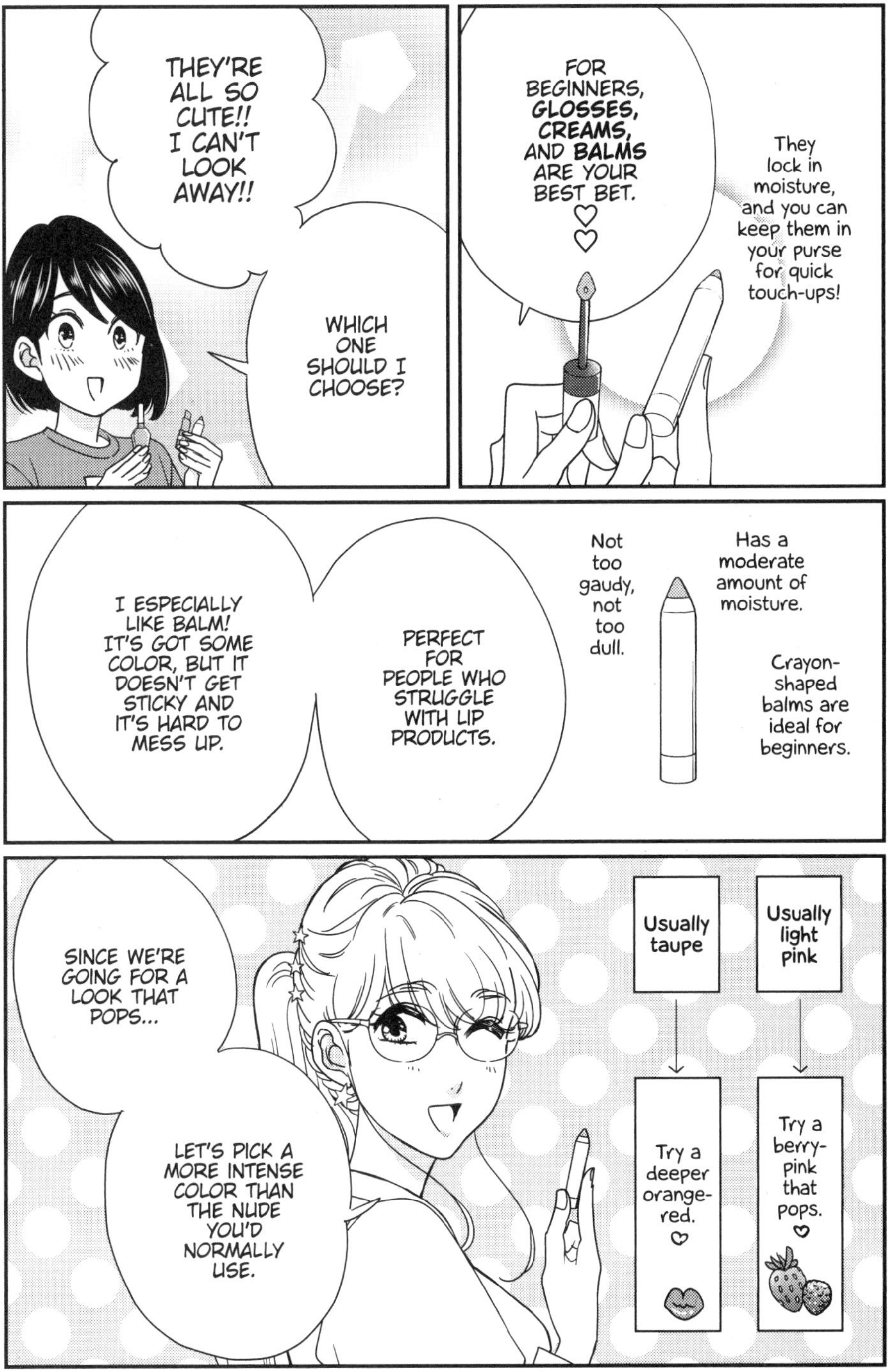
THEY'RE ALL SO CUTE!! I CAN'T LOOK AWAY!!
WHICH ONE SHOULD I CHOOSE?
FOR BEGINNERS, GLOSSES, CREAMS, AND BALMS ARE YOUR BEST BET.
They lock in moisture, and you can keep them in your purse for quick touch-ups!
I ESPECIALLY LIKE BALM! IT'S GOT SOME COLOR, BUT IT DOESN'T GET STICKY AND IT'S HARD TO MESS UP.
PERFECT FOR PEOPLE WHO STRUGGLE WITH LIP PRODUCTS.
Not too gaudy, not too dull.
Has a moderate amount of moisture.
Crayon-shaped balms are ideal for beginners.
SINCE WE'RE GOING FOR A LOOK THAT POPS...
LET'S PICK A MORE INTENSE COLOR THAN THE NUDE YOU'D NORMALLY USE.
Usually taupe
Try a deeper orange-red.
Usually light pink
Try a berry-pink that pops.

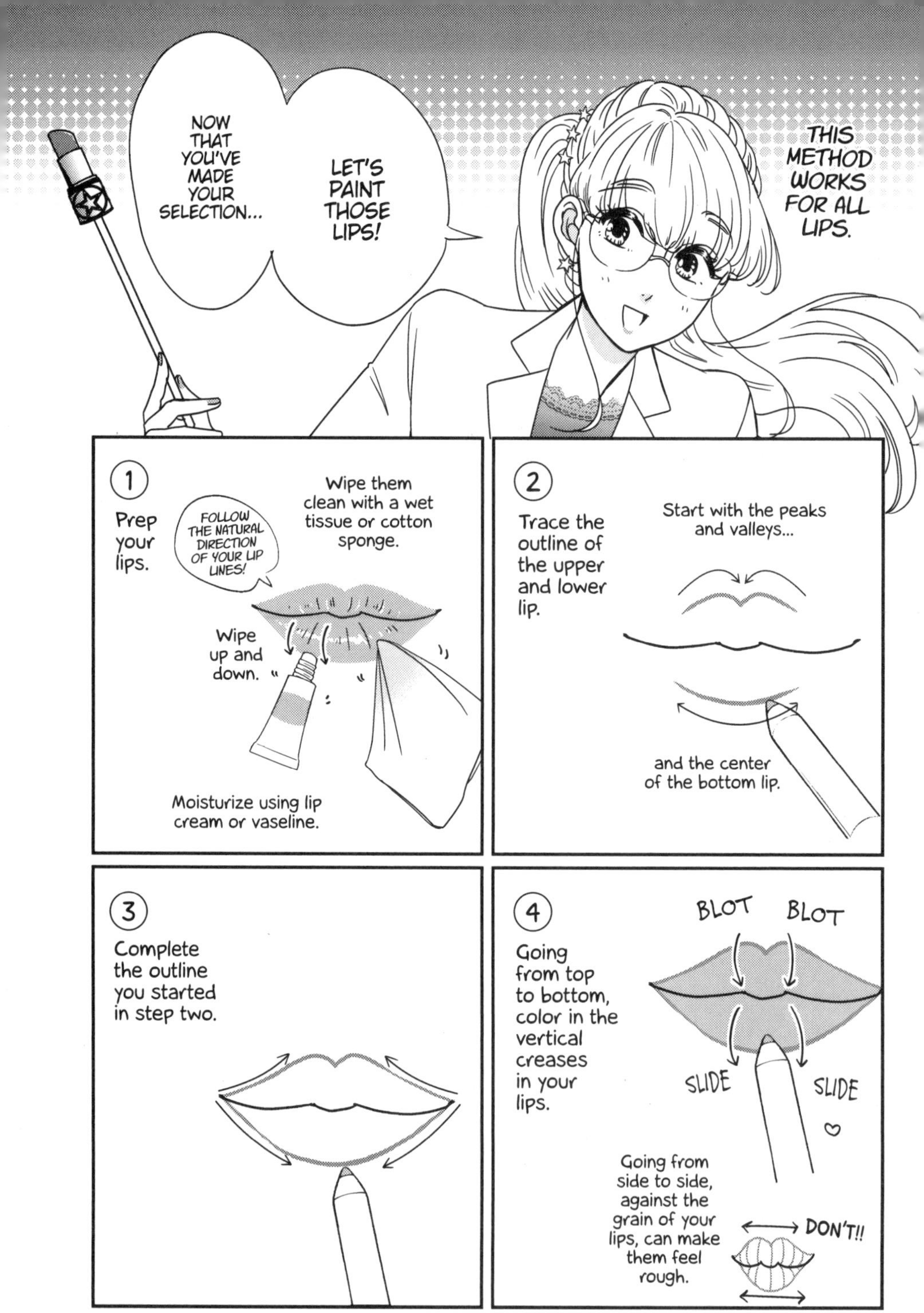
NOW THAT YOU'VE MADE YOUR SELECTION...
LET'S PAINT THOSE LIPS!
THIS METHOD WORKS FOR ALL LIPS.
1
Prep your lips.
FOLLOW THE NATURAL DIRECTION OF YOUR LIP LINES!
Wipe them clean with a wet tissue or cotton sponge.
Wipe up and down.
Moisturize using lip cream or vaseline.
2
Trace the outline of the upper and lower lip.
Start with the peaks and valleys...
and the center of the bottom lip.
3
Complete the outline you started in step two.
4
Going from top to bottom, color in the vertical creases in your lips.
BLOT
BLOT
SLIDE
SLIDE
Going from side to side, against the grain of your lips, can make them feel rough.
DON'T!!

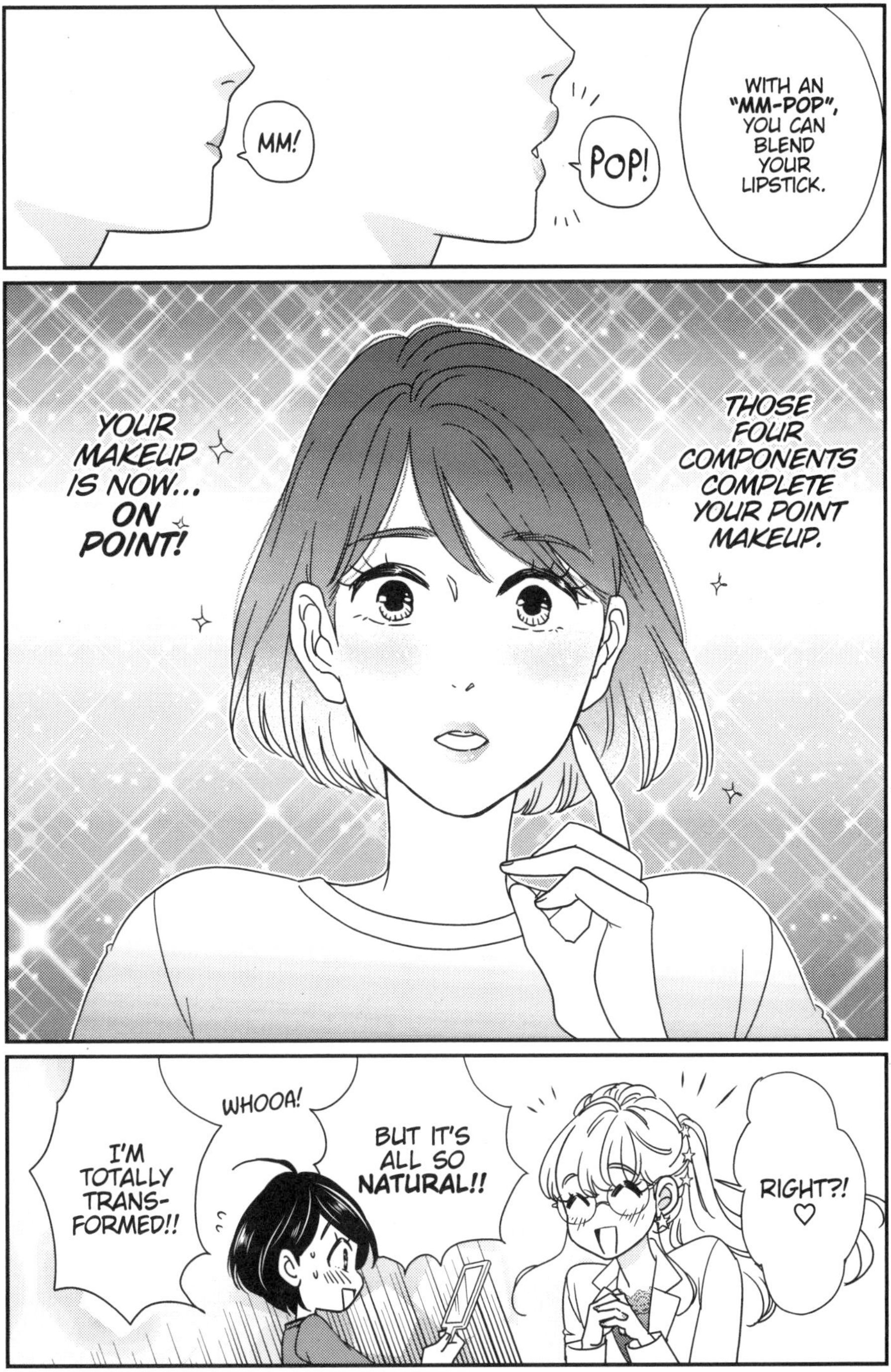
WITH AN "MM-POP", YOU CAN BLEND YOUR LIPSTICK.
MM!
POP!
THOSE FOUR COMPONENTS COMPLETE YOUR POINT MAKEUP.
YOUR MAKEUP IS NOW... ON POINT!
I'M TOTALLY TRANS-FORMED!!
WHOOA!
BUT IT'S ALL SO NATURAL!!
RIGHT?! ♡

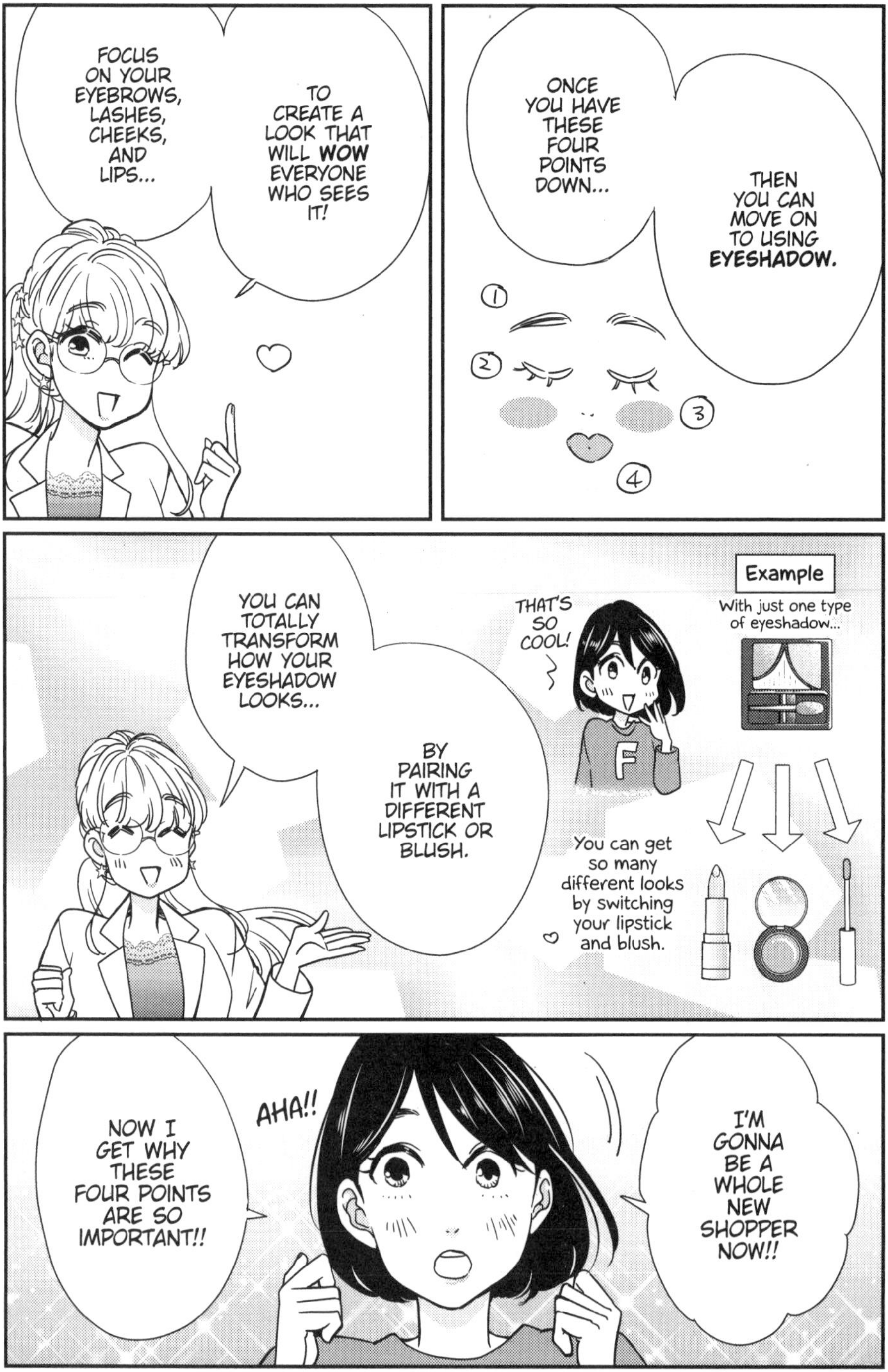
FOCUS ON YOUR EYEBROWS, LASHES, CHEEKS, AND LIPS...
TO CREATE A LOOK THAT WILL **WOW** EVERYONE WHO SEES IT!
ONCE YOU HAVE THESE FOUR POINTS DOWN...
THEN YOU CAN MOVE ON TO USING **EYESHADOW.**
1
2
3
4
YOU CAN TOTALLY TRANSFORM HOW YOUR EYESHADOW LOOKS...
BY PAIRING IT WITH A DIFFERENT LIPSTICK OR BLUSH.
THAT'S SO COOL!
Example
With just one type of eyeshadow...
You can get so many different looks by switching your lipstick and blush.
NOW I GET WHY THESE FOUR POINTS ARE SO IMPORTANT!!
AHA!!
I'M GONNA BE A WHOLE NEW SHOPPER NOW!!

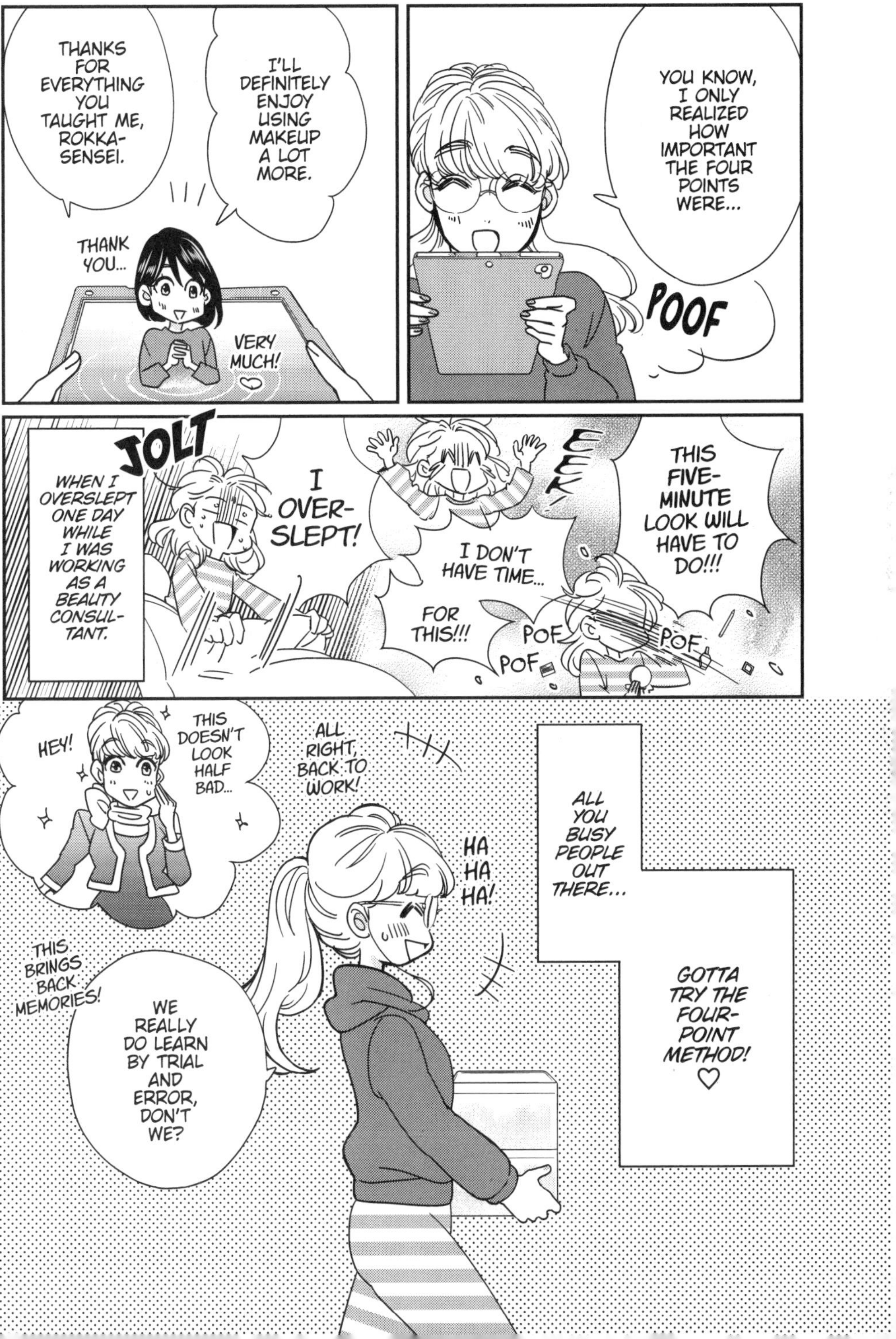
I'LL DEFINITELY ENJOY USING MAKEUP A LOT MORE.
THANKS FOR EVERYTHING YOU TAUGHT ME, ROKKA-SENSEI.
THANK YOU...
VERY MUCH!
YOU KNOW, I ONLY REALIZED HOW IMPORTANT THE FOUR POINTS WERE...
POOF
THIS FIVE-MINUTE LOOK WILL HAVE TO DO!!!
EEK
I DON'T HAVE TIME...
FOR THIS!!!
POF
POF
POF
I OVER-SLEPT!
JOLT
WHEN I OVERSLEPT ONE DAY WHILE I WAS WORKING AS A BEAUTY CONSUL-TANT.
ALL YOU BUSY PEOPLE OUT THERE...
GOTTA TRY THE FOUR-POINT METHOD! ♡
ALL RIGHT, BACK TO WORK!
HA HA HA!
THIS DOESN'T LOOK HALF BAD...
HEY!
THIS BRINGS BACK MEMORIES!
WE REALLY DO LEARN BY TRIAL AND ERROR, DON'T WE?

Let's Ask Rokka-Sensei!

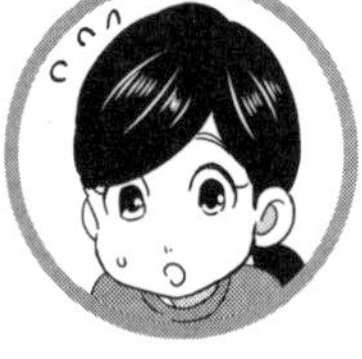

Q. I always wear the same makeup, but it's not doing it for me anymore. If I wanted to change one makeup item, what should it be?

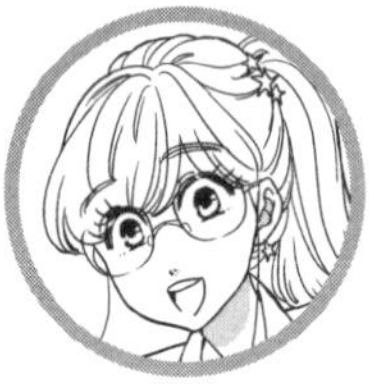

A. I'd try changing your lip look. I touched on this in lesson six, but a brighter lip color can make your whole face more radiant. Pick a new color that's *juuust* enough to look gaudy to you. It'll look great to everyone else!

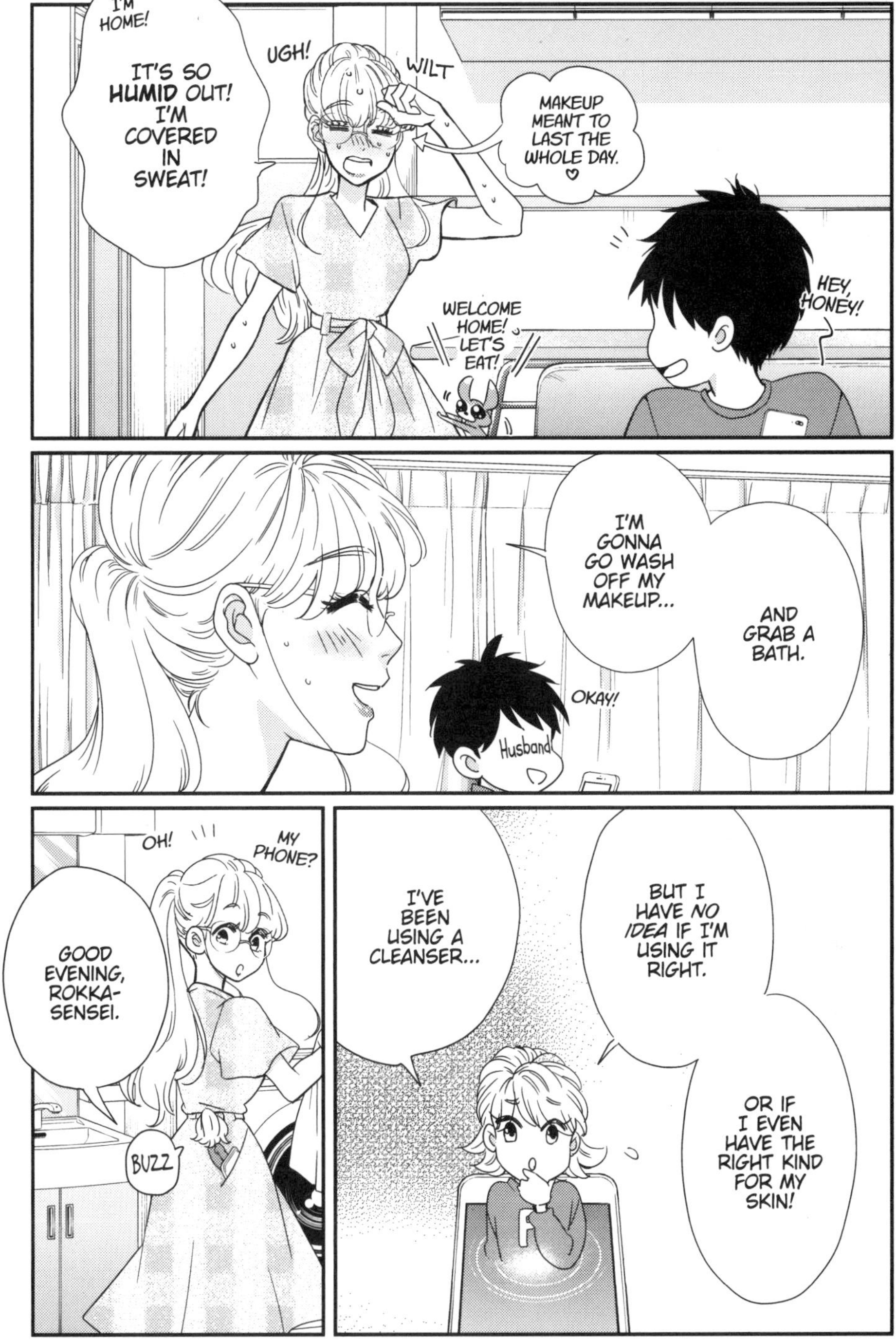
I'M HOME!
IT'S SO HUMID OUT! I'M COVERED IN SWEAT!
UGH!
WILT
MAKEUP MEANT TO LAST THE WHOLE DAY. ♡
HEY, HONEY!
WELCOME HOME! LET'S EAT!
I'M GONNA GO WASH OFF MY MAKEUP...
AND GRAB A BATH.
OKAY!
Husband
OH!
MY PHONE?
GOOD EVENING, ROKKA-SENSEI.
BUZZ
I'VE BEEN USING A CLEANSER...
BUT I HAVE NO IDEA IF I'M USING IT RIGHT.
OR IF I EVEN HAVE THE RIGHT KIND FOR MY SKIN!

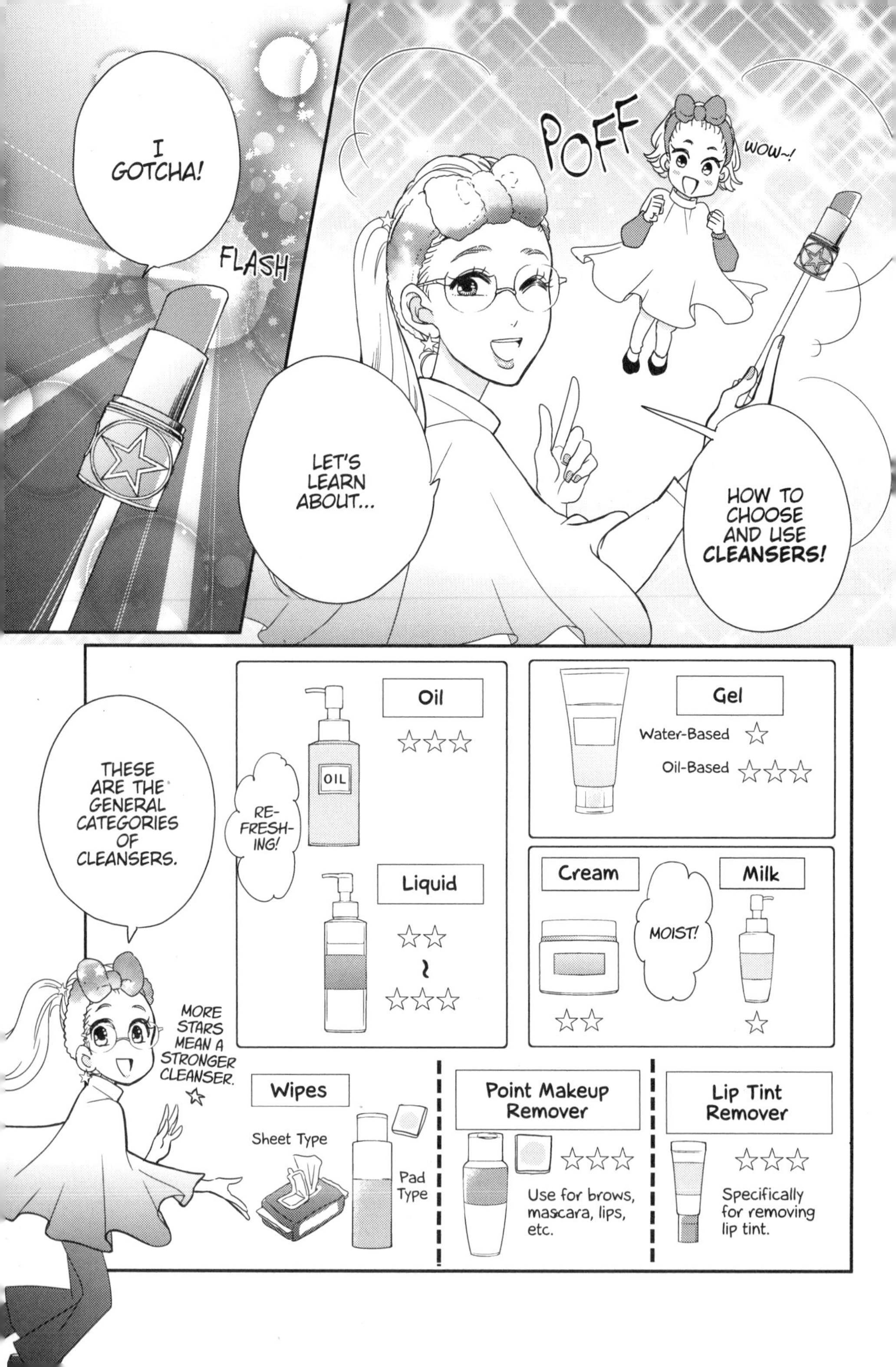

I GOTCHA!
FLASH
POFF
WOW~!
LET'S LEARN ABOUT...
HOW TO CHOOSE AND USE CLEANSERS!
THESE ARE THE GENERAL CATEGORIES OF CLEANSERS.
MORE STARS MEAN A STRONGER CLEANSER.
Oil
☆☆☆
OIL
REFRESHING!
Liquid
☆☆ ~ ☆☆☆
Gel
Water-Based ☆
Oil-Based ☆☆☆
Cream
☆☆
MOIST!
Milk
☆
Wipes
Sheet Type
Pad Type
Point Makeup Remover
☆☆☆
Use for brows, mascara, lips, etc.
Lip Tint Remover
☆☆☆
Specifically for removing lip tint.

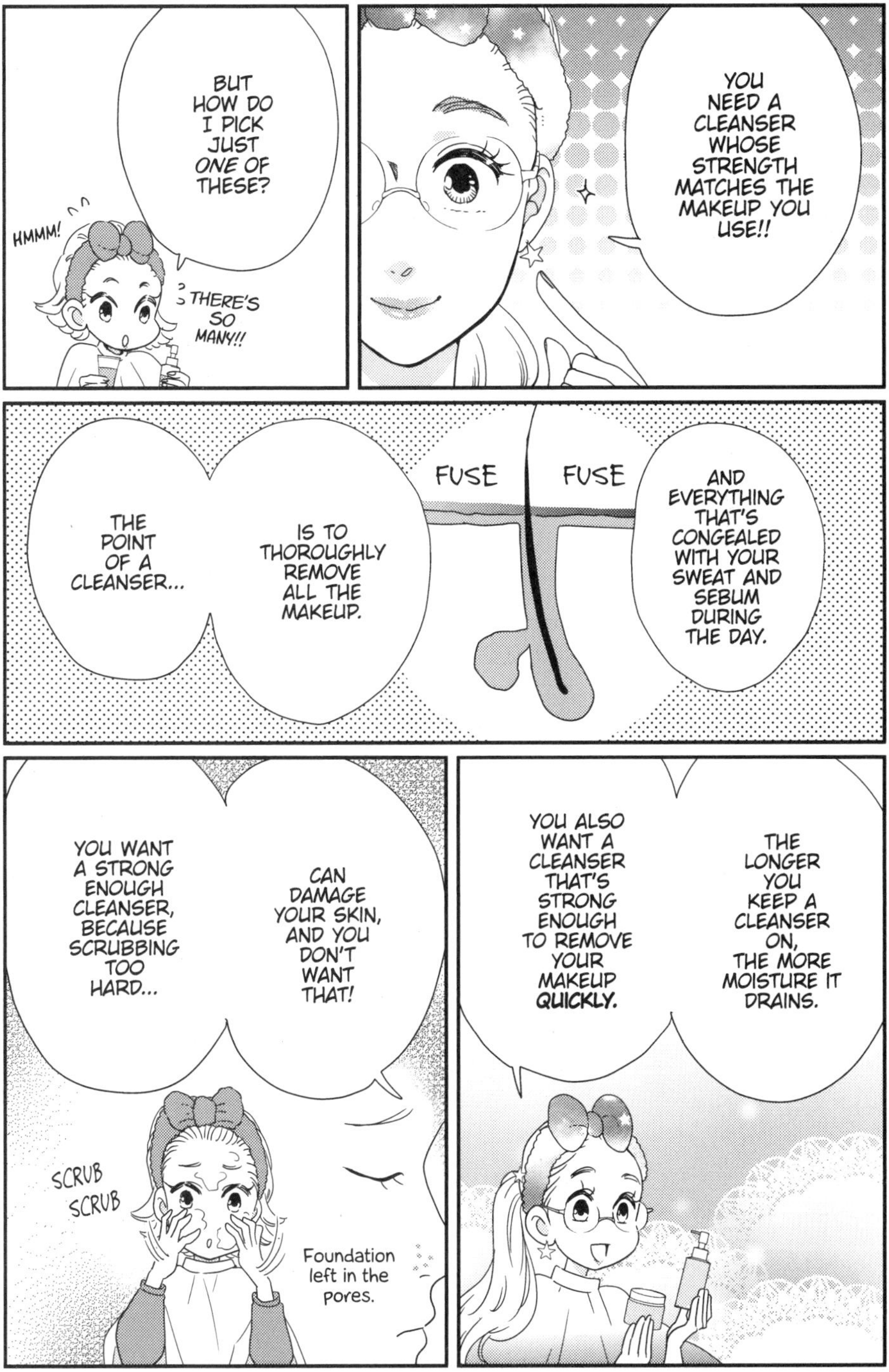
BUT HOW DO I PICK JUST ONE OF THESE?
HMMM!
THERE'S SO MANY!!
YOU NEED A CLEANSER WHOSE STRENGTH MATCHES THE MAKEUP YOU USE!!
THE POINT OF A CLEANSER...
IS TO THOROUGHLY REMOVE ALL THE MAKEUP.
FUSE
FUSE
AND EVERYTHING THAT'S CONGEALED WITH YOUR SWEAT AND SEBUM DURING THE DAY.
YOU WANT A STRONG ENOUGH CLEANSER, BECAUSE SCRUBBING TOO HARD...
CAN DAMAGE YOUR SKIN, AND YOU DON'T WANT THAT!
SCRUB SCRUB
Foundation left in the pores.
YOU ALSO WANT A CLEANSER THAT'S STRONG ENOUGH TO REMOVE YOUR MAKEUP QUICKLY.
THE LONGER YOU KEEP A CLEANSER ON, THE MORE MOISTURE IT DRAINS.

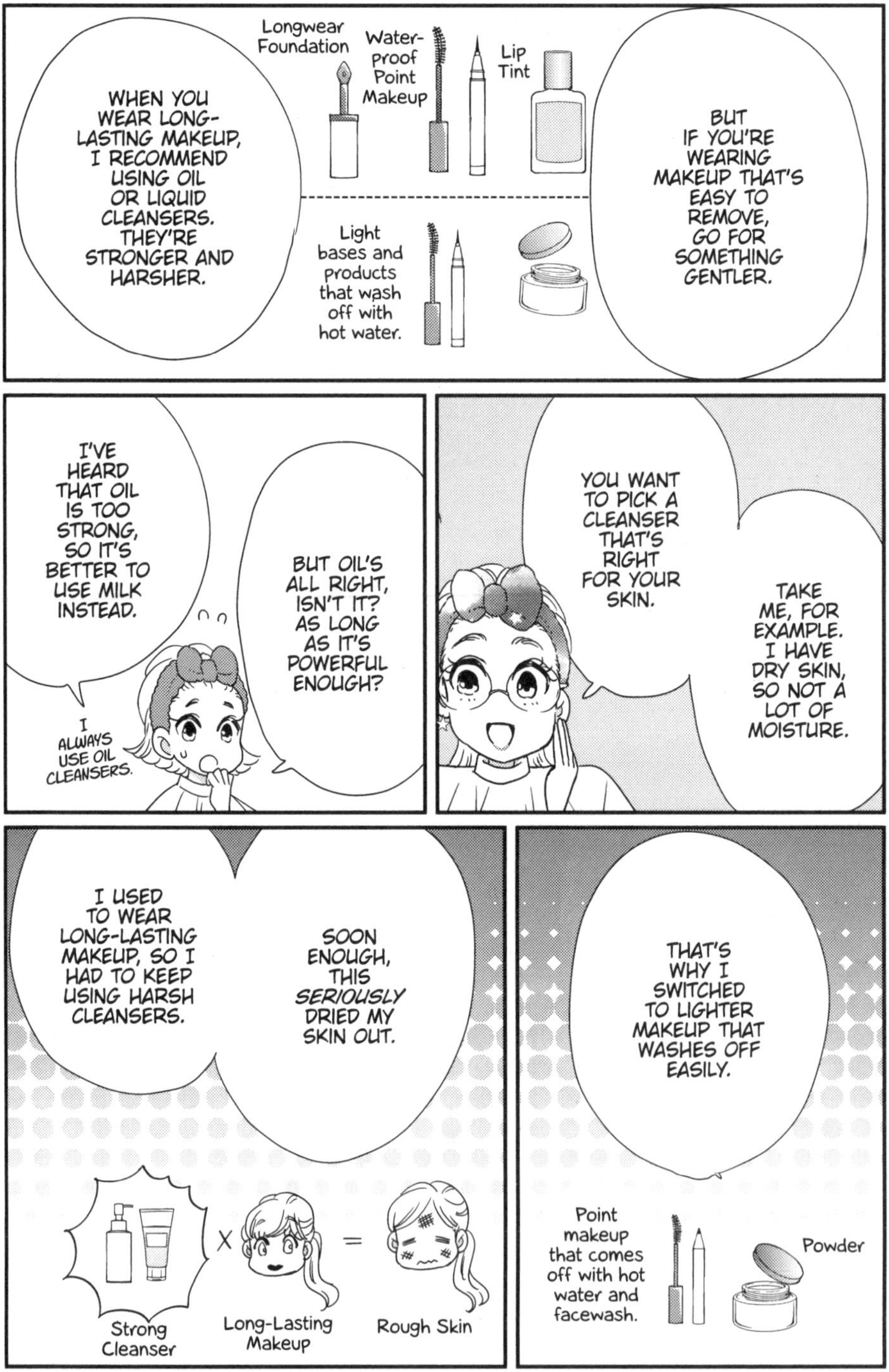

WHEN YOU WEAR LONG-LASTING MAKEUP, I RECOMMEND USING OIL OR LIQUID CLEANSERS. THEY'RE STRONGER AND HARSHER.
Longwear Foundation
Water-proof Point Makeup
Lip Tint
Light bases and products that wash off with hot water.
BUT IF YOU'RE WEARING MAKEUP THAT'S EASY TO REMOVE, GO FOR SOMETHING GENTLER.
I'VE HEARD THAT OIL IS TOO STRONG, SO IT'S BETTER TO USE MILK INSTEAD.
I ALWAYS USE OIL CLEANSERS.
BUT OIL'S ALL RIGHT, ISN'T IT? AS LONG AS IT'S POWERFUL ENOUGH?
YOU WANT TO PICK A CLEANSER THAT'S RIGHT FOR YOUR SKIN.
TAKE ME, FOR EXAMPLE. I HAVE DRY SKIN, SO NOT A LOT OF MOISTURE.
I USED TO WEAR LONG-LASTING MAKEUP, SO I HAD TO KEEP USING HARSH CLEANSERS.
SOON ENOUGH, THIS *SERIOUSLY* DRIED MY SKIN OUT.
Strong Cleanser
X
Long-Lasting Makeup
=
Rough Skin
THAT'S WHY I SWITCHED TO LIGHTER MAKEUP THAT WASHES OFF EASILY.
Point makeup that comes off with hot water and facewash.
Powder

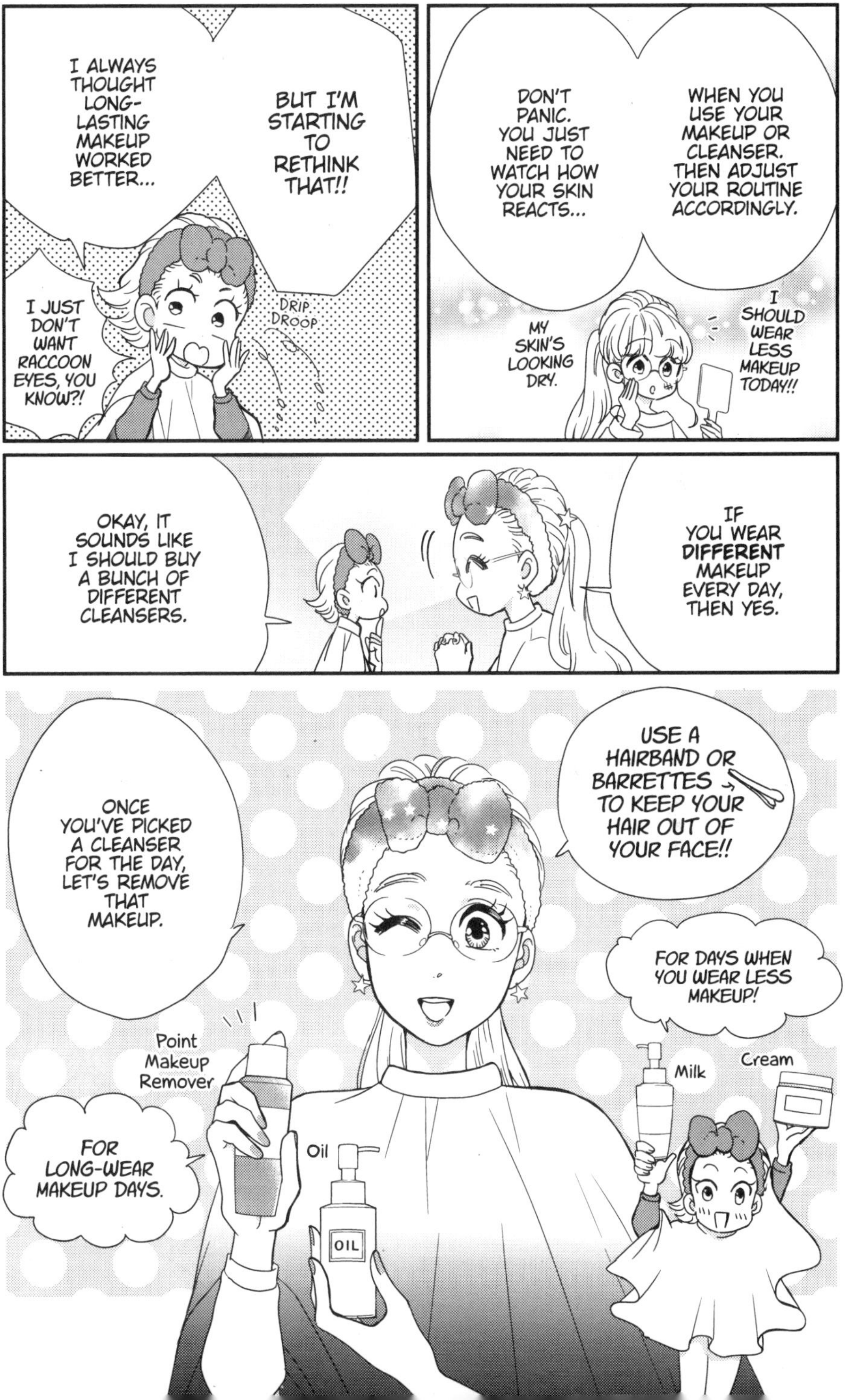
I ALWAYS THOUGHT LONG-LASTING MAKEUP WORKED BETTER...
BUT I'M STARTING TO RETHINK THAT!!
I JUST DON'T WANT RACCOON EYES, YOU KNOW?!
DRIP DROOP
DON'T PANIC. YOU JUST NEED TO WATCH HOW YOUR SKIN REACTS...
WHEN YOU USE YOUR MAKEUP OR CLEANSER. THEN ADJUST YOUR ROUTINE ACCORDINGLY.
MY SKIN'S LOOKING DRY.
I SHOULD WEAR LESS MAKEUP TODAY!!
OKAY, IT SOUNDS LIKE I SHOULD BUY A BUNCH OF DIFFERENT CLEANSERS.
IF YOU WEAR **DIFFERENT** MAKEUP EVERY DAY, THEN YES.
ONCE YOU'VE PICKED A CLEANSER FOR THE DAY, LET'S REMOVE THAT MAKEUP.
USE A HAIRBAND OR BARRETTES → TO KEEP YOUR HAIR OUT OF YOUR FACE!!
FOR DAYS WHEN YOU WEAR LESS MAKEUP!
Milk
Cream
Point Makeup Remover
Oil
OIL
FOR LONG-WEAR MAKEUP DAYS.

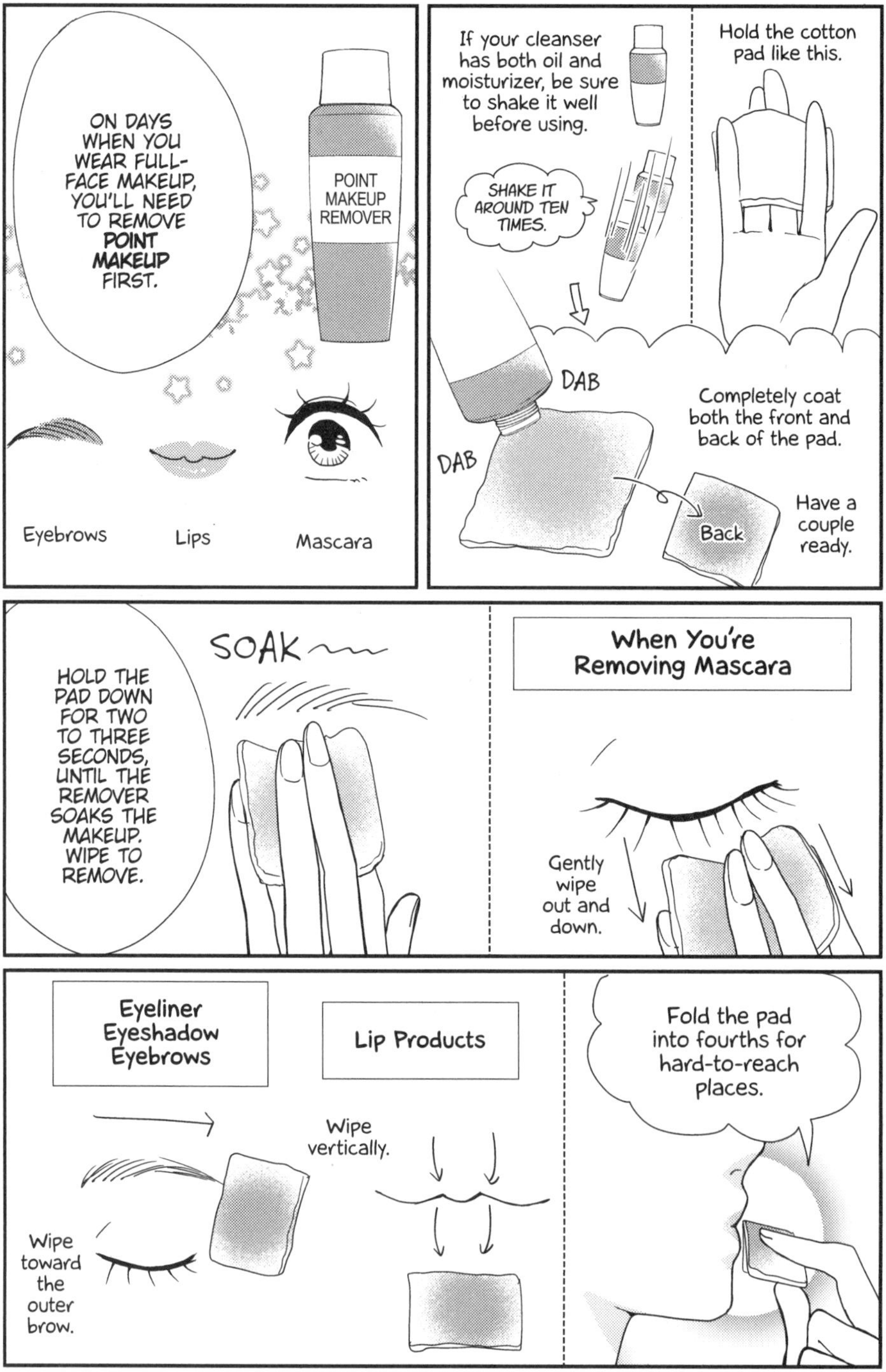
ON DAYS WHEN YOU WEAR FULL-FACE MAKEUP, YOU'LL NEED TO REMOVE **POINT MAKEUP** FIRST.
POINT MAKEUP REMOVER
Eyebrows
Lips
Mascara
If your cleanser has both oil and moisturizer, be sure to shake it well before using.
SHAKE IT AROUND TEN TIMES.
Hold the cotton pad like this.
DAB
DAB
Completely coat both the front and back of the pad.
Back
Have a couple ready.
HOLD THE PAD DOWN FOR TWO TO THREE SECONDS, UNTIL THE REMOVER SOAKS THE MAKEUP. WIPE TO REMOVE.
SOAK
When You're Removing Mascara
Gently wipe out and down.
Eyeliner Eyeshadow Eyebrows
Wipe toward the outer brow.
Lip Products
Wipe vertically.
Fold the pad into fourths for hard-to-reach places.

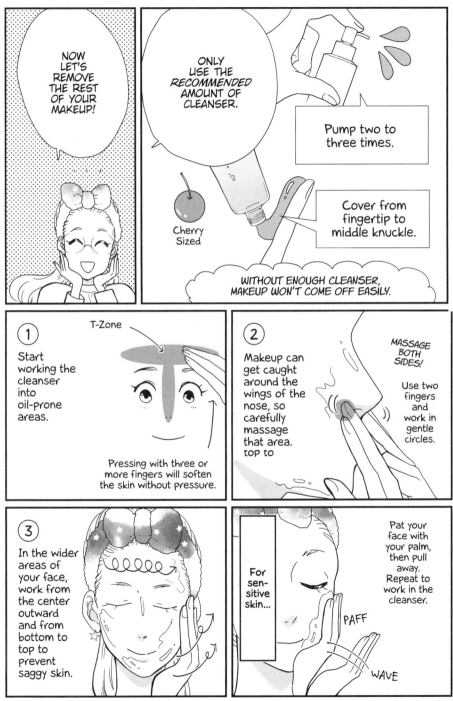

NOW LET'S REMOVE THE REST OF YOUR MAKEUP!

ONLY USE THE *RECOMMENDED* AMOUNT OF CLEANSER.

Pump two to three times.

Cover from fingertip to middle knuckle.

Cherry Sized

WITHOUT ENOUGH CLEANSER, MAKEUP WON'T COME OFF EASILY.

① Start working the cleanser into oil-prone areas.

T-Zone

Pressing with three or more fingers will soften the skin without pressure.

② Makeup can get caught around the wings of the nose, so carefully massage that area. top to

MASSAGE BOTH SIDES!

Use two fingers and work in gentle circles.

③ In the wider areas of your face, work from the center outward and from bottom to top to prevent saggy skin.

For sensitive skin...

Pat your face with your palm, then pull away. Repeat to work in the cleanser.

PAFF

WAVE

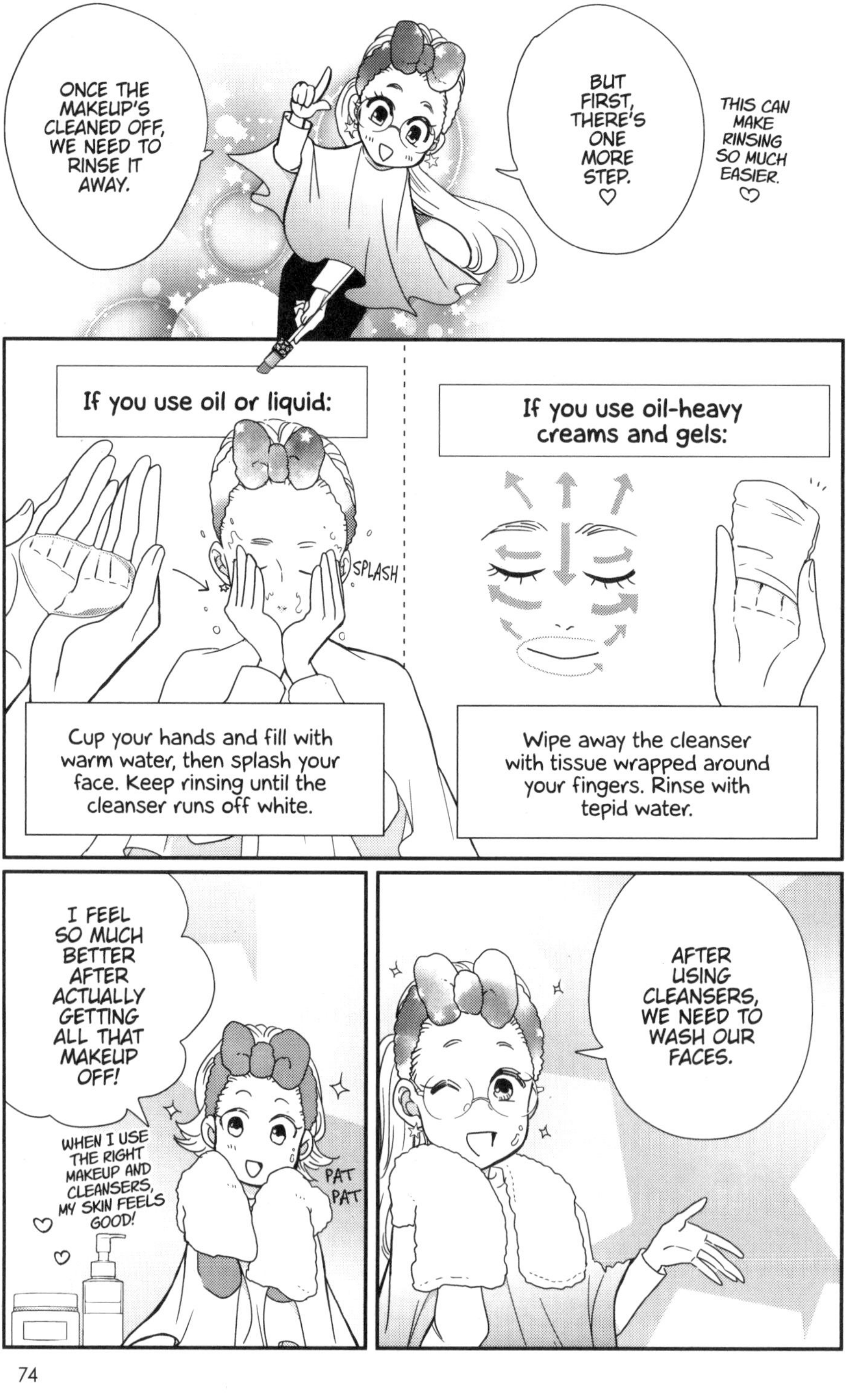
ONCE THE MAKEUP'S CLEANED OFF, WE NEED TO RINSE IT AWAY.
BUT FIRST, THERE'S ONE MORE STEP. ♡
THIS CAN MAKE RINSING SO MUCH EASIER. ♡
If you use oil or liquid:
SPLASH
Cup your hands and fill with warm water, then splash your face. Keep rinsing until the cleanser runs off white.
If you use oil-heavy creams and gels:
Wipe away the cleanser with tissue wrapped around your fingers. Rinse with tepid water.
I FEEL SO MUCH BETTER AFTER ACTUALLY GETTING ALL THAT MAKEUP OFF!
WHEN I USE THE RIGHT MAKEUP AND CLEANSERS, MY SKIN FEELS GOOD!
PAT PAT
AFTER USING CLEANSERS, WE NEED TO WASH OUR FACES.

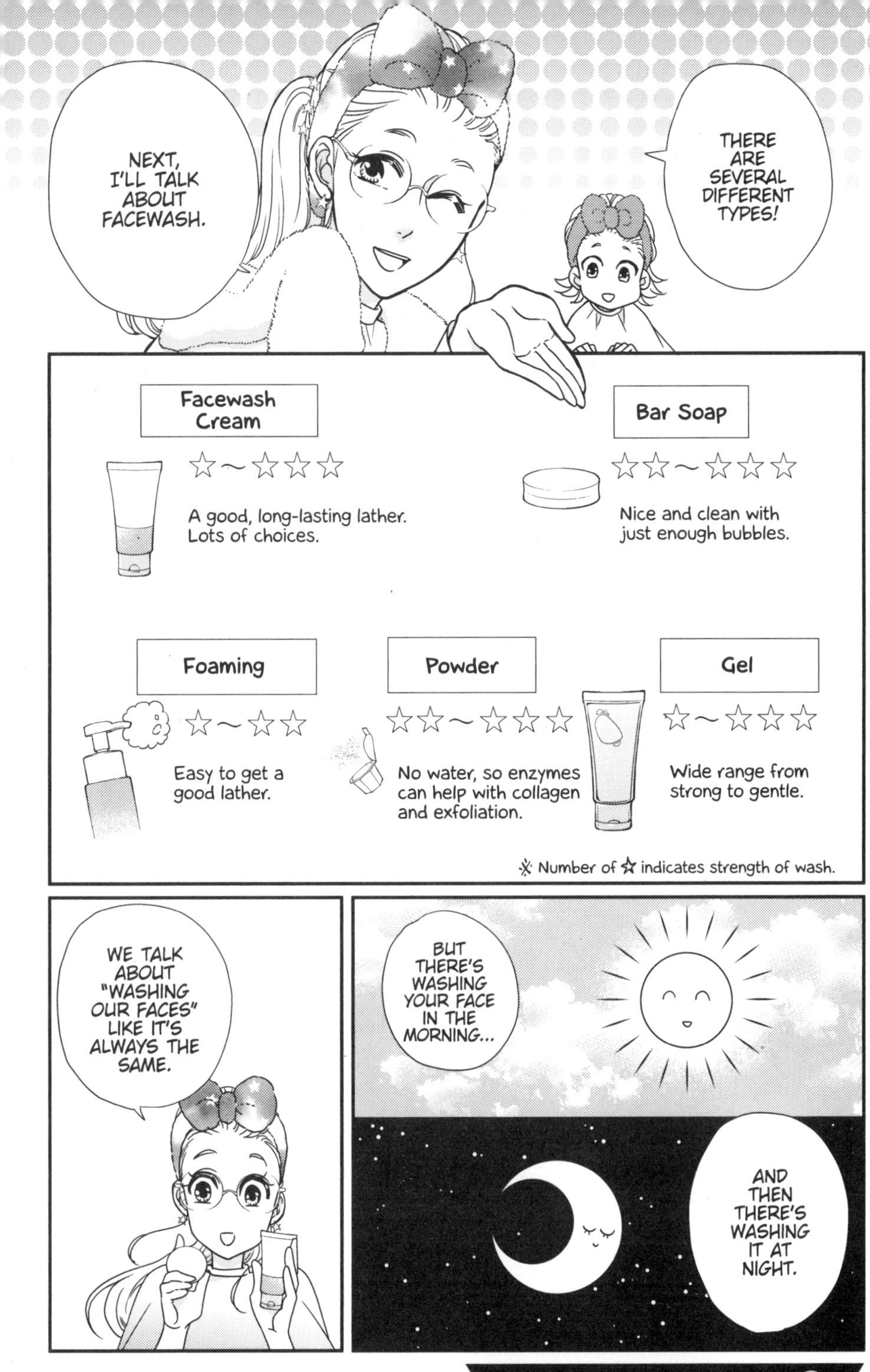
NEXT, I'LL TALK ABOUT FACEWASH.
THERE ARE SEVERAL DIFFERENT TYPES!
Facewash Cream
☆～☆☆☆
A good, long-lasting lather. Lots of choices.
Bar Soap
☆☆～☆☆☆
Nice and clean with just enough bubbles.
Foaming
☆～☆☆
Easy to get a good lather.
Powder
☆☆～☆☆☆
No water, so enzymes can help with collagen and exfoliation.
Gel
☆～☆☆☆
Wide range from strong to gentle.
※ Number of ☆ indicates strength of wash.
WE TALK ABOUT "WASHING OUR FACES" LIKE IT'S ALWAYS THE SAME.
BUT THERE'S WASHING YOUR FACE IN THE MORNING...
AND THEN THERE'S WASHING IT AT NIGHT.

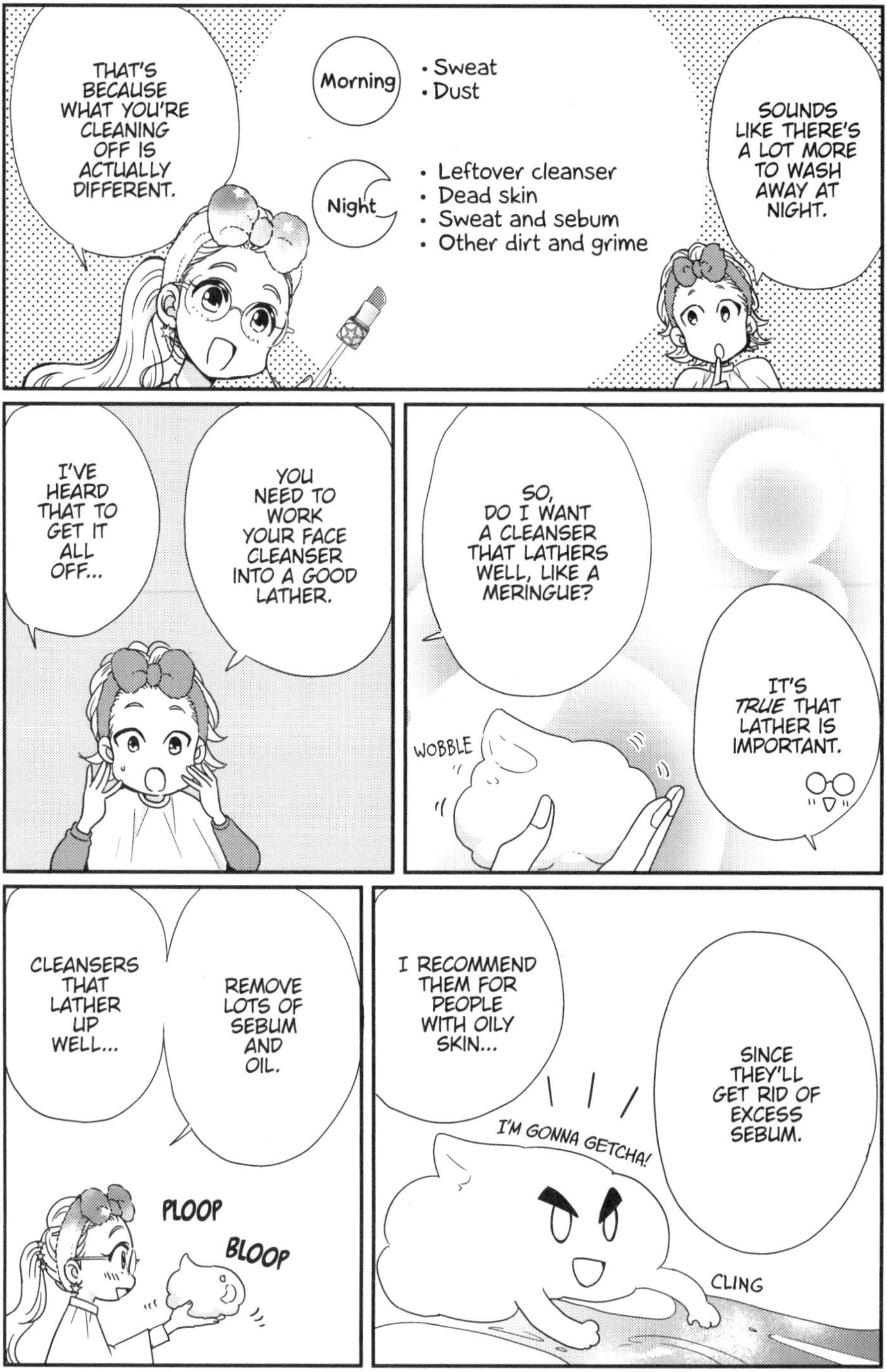
THAT'S BECAUSE WHAT YOU'RE CLEANING OFF IS ACTUALLY DIFFERENT.
Morning
• Sweat
• Dust
Night
• Leftover cleanser
• Dead skin
• Sweat and sebum
• Other dirt and grime
SOUNDS LIKE THERE'S A LOT MORE TO WASH AWAY AT NIGHT.
I'VE HEARD THAT TO GET IT ALL OFF...
YOU NEED TO WORK YOUR FACE CLEANSER INTO A GOOD LATHER.
SO, DO I WANT A CLEANSER THAT LATHERS WELL, LIKE A MERINGUE?
WOBBLE
IT'S *TRUE* THAT LATHER IS IMPORTANT.
CLEANSERS THAT LATHER UP WELL...
REMOVE LOTS OF SEBUM AND OIL.
PLOOP
BLOOP
I RECOMMEND THEM FOR PEOPLE WITH OILY SKIN...
SINCE THEY'LL GET RID OF EXCESS SEBUM.
I'M GONNA GETCHA!
CLING

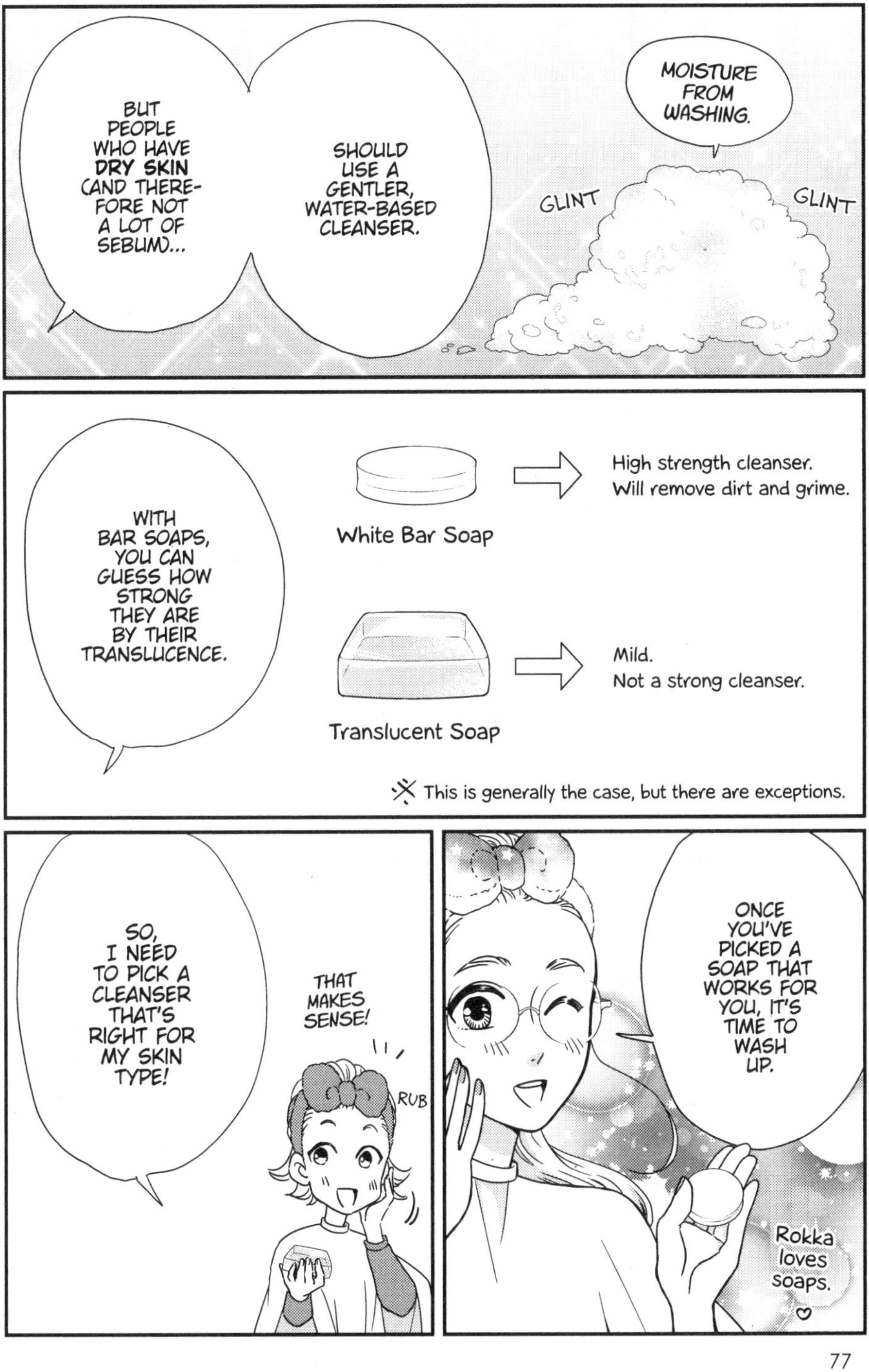
BUT PEOPLE WHO HAVE **DRY SKIN** (AND THEREFORE NOT A LOT OF SEBUM)...
SHOULD USE A GENTLER, WATER-BASED CLEANSER.
MOISTURE FROM WASHING.
GLINT
GLINT
WITH BAR SOAPS, YOU CAN GUESS HOW STRONG THEY ARE BY THEIR TRANSLUCENCE.
White Bar Soap
High strength cleanser.
Will remove dirt and grime.
Translucent Soap
Mild.
Not a strong cleanser.
※ This is generally the case, but there are exceptions.
SO, I NEED TO PICK A CLEANSER THAT'S RIGHT FOR MY SKIN TYPE!
THAT MAKES SENSE!
RUB
ONCE YOU'VE PICKED A SOAP THAT WORKS FOR YOU, IT'S TIME TO WASH UP.
Rokka loves soaps. ♡

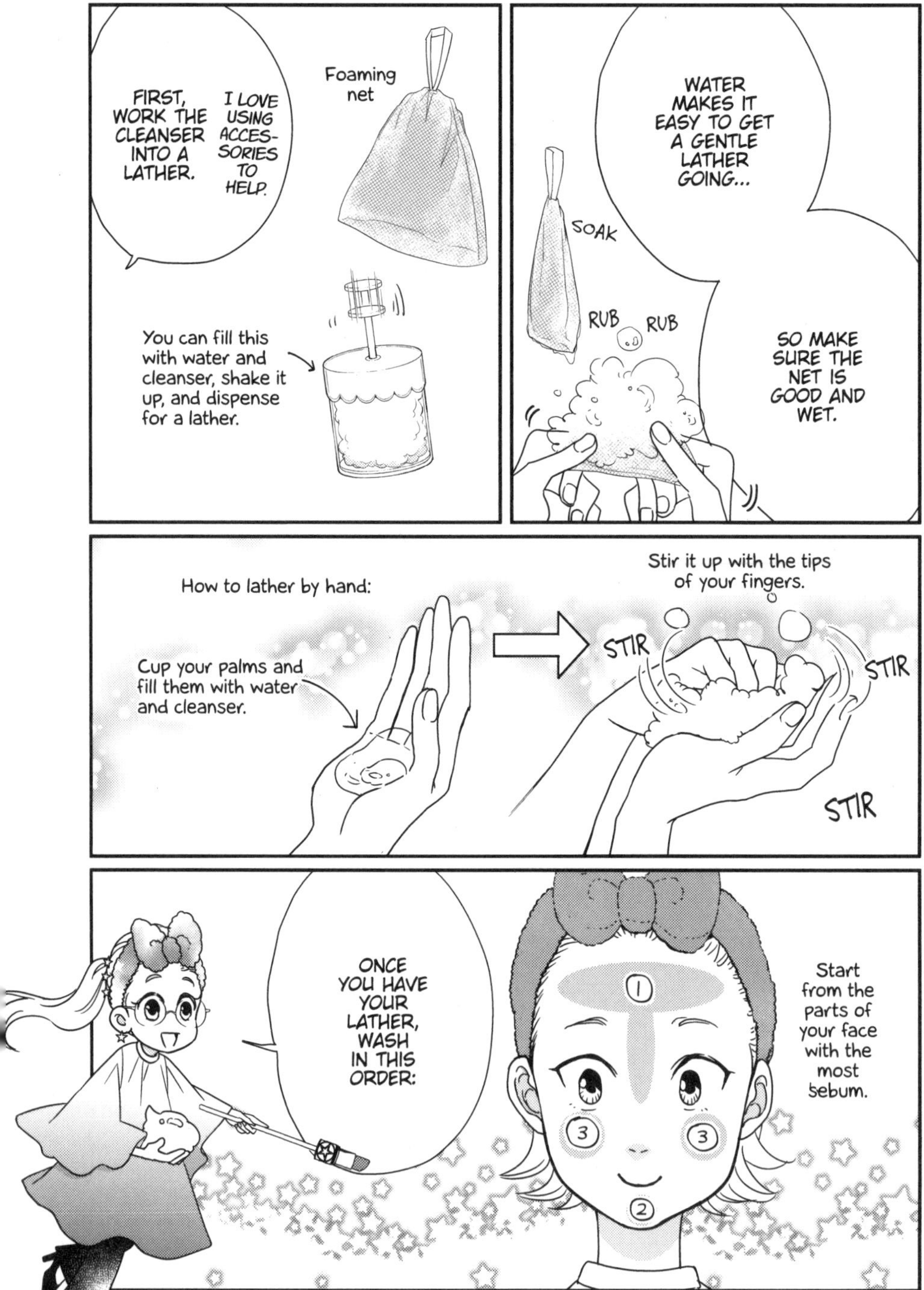
FIRST, WORK THE CLEANSER INTO A LATHER.
I LOVE USING ACCESSORIES TO HELP.
Foaming net
You can fill this with water and cleanser, shake it up, and dispense for a lather.
WATER MAKES IT EASY TO GET A GENTLE LATHER GOING...
SOAK
RUB RUB
SO MAKE SURE THE NET IS GOOD AND WET.
How to lather by hand:
Cup your palms and fill them with water and cleanser.
Stir it up with the tips of your fingers.
STIR
STIR
STIR
ONCE YOU HAVE YOUR LATHER, WASH IN THIS ORDER:
1
2
3
3
Start from the parts of your face with the most sebum.

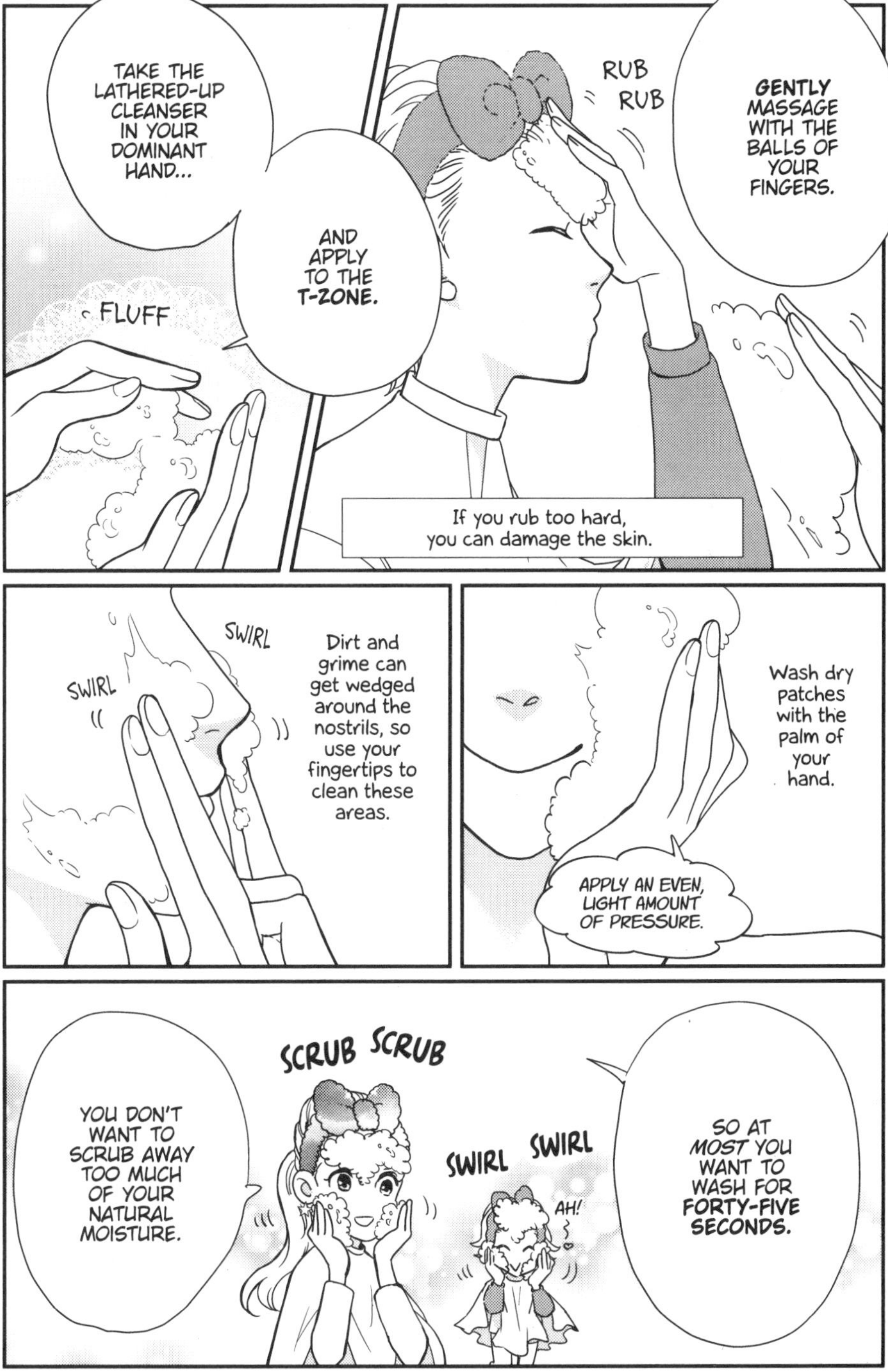

TAKE THE LATHERED-UP CLEANSER IN YOUR DOMINANT HAND...
FLUFF
AND APPLY TO THE **T-ZONE.**
RUB RUB
GENTLY MASSAGE WITH THE BALLS OF YOUR FINGERS.
If you rub too hard, you can damage the skin.
SWIRL
SWIRL
Dirt and grime can get wedged around the nostrils, so use your fingertips to clean these areas.
Wash dry patches with the palm of your hand.
APPLY AN EVEN, LIGHT AMOUNT OF PRESSURE.
SCRUB SCRUB
YOU DON'T WANT TO SCRUB AWAY TOO MUCH OF YOUR NATURAL MOISTURE.
SWIRL SWIRL
AH!
SO AT *MOST* YOU WANT TO WASH FOR **FORTY-FIVE SECONDS.**

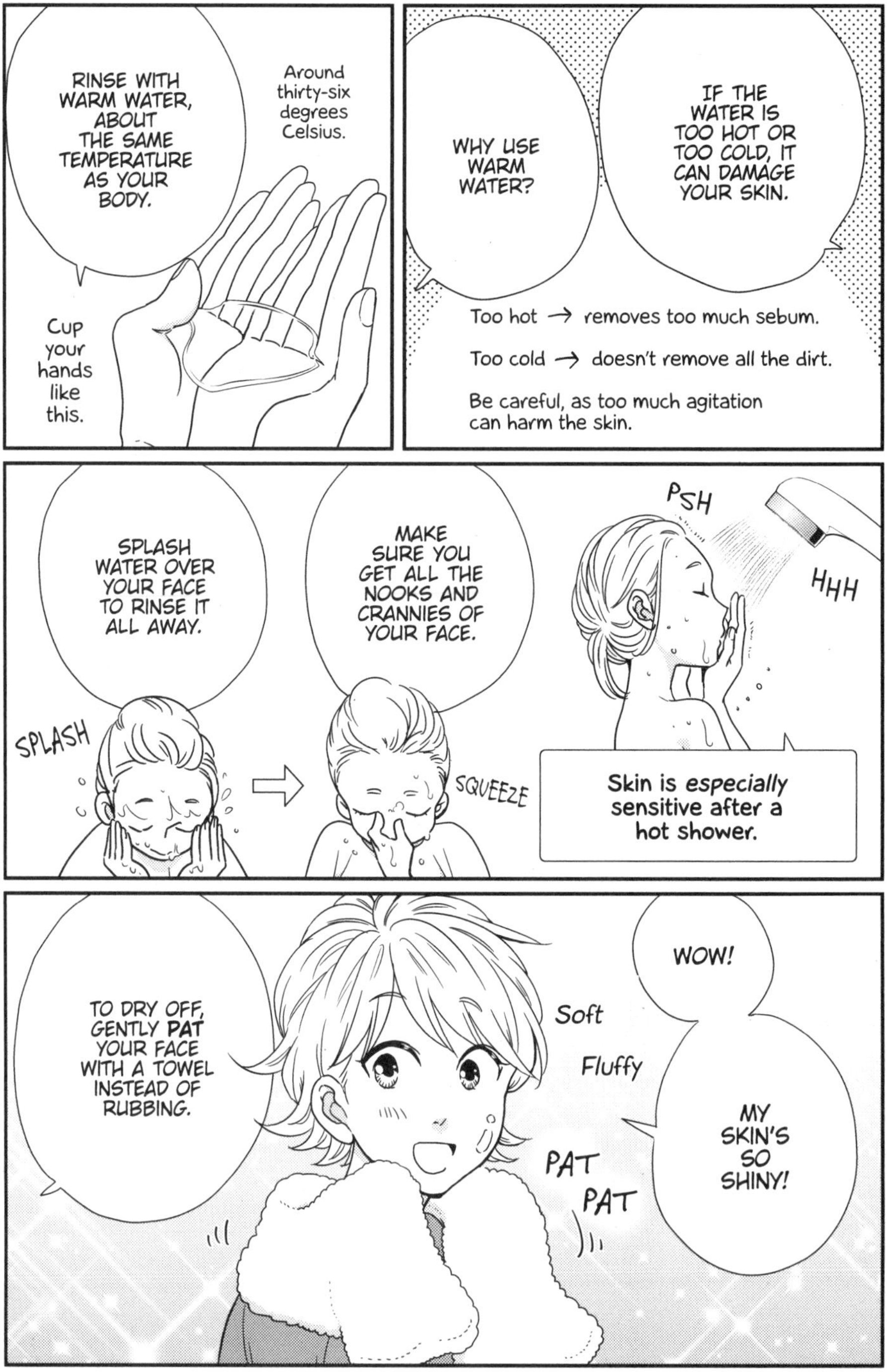
RINSE WITH WARM WATER, ABOUT THE SAME TEMPERATURE AS YOUR BODY.
Around thirty-six degrees Celsius.
Cup your hands like this.
WHY USE WARM WATER?
IF THE WATER IS TOO HOT OR TOO COLD, IT CAN DAMAGE YOUR SKIN.
Too hot → removes too much sebum.
Too cold → doesn't remove all the dirt.
Be careful, as too much agitation can harm the skin.
SPLASH WATER OVER YOUR FACE TO RINSE IT ALL AWAY.
MAKE SURE YOU GET ALL THE NOOKS AND CRANNIES OF YOUR FACE.
PSH
HHH
SPLASH
SQUEEZE
Skin is especially sensitive after a hot shower.
TO DRY OFF, GENTLY PAT YOUR FACE WITH A TOWEL INSTEAD OF RUBBING.
WOW!
Soft
Fluffy
MY SKIN'S SO SHINY!
PAT
PAT

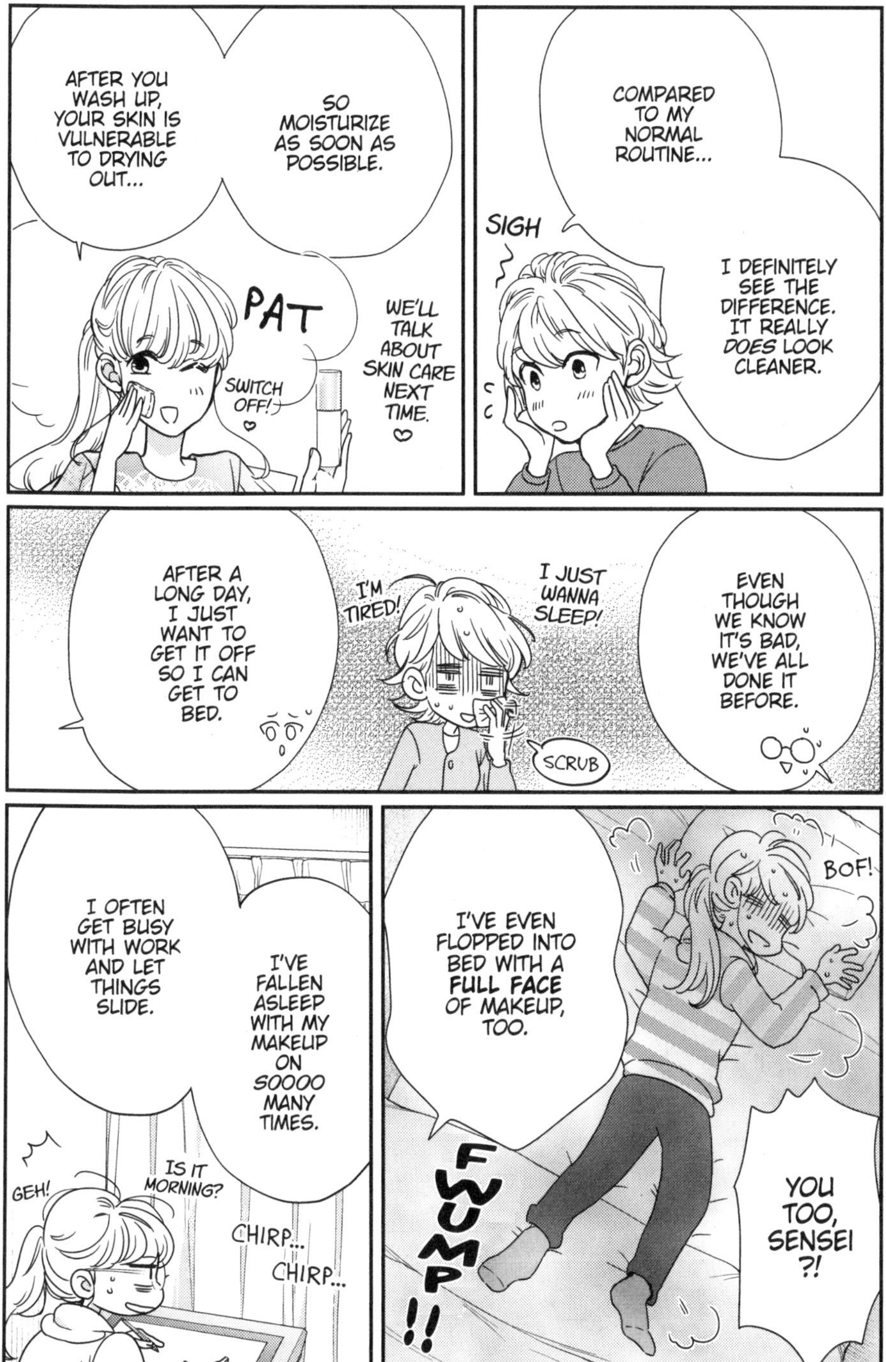
AFTER YOU WASH UP, YOUR SKIN IS VULNERABLE TO DRYING OUT...
SO MOISTURIZE AS SOON AS POSSIBLE.
PAT
SWITCH OFF!
WE'LL TALK ABOUT SKIN CARE NEXT TIME.
COMPARED TO MY NORMAL ROUTINE...
SIGH
I DEFINITELY SEE THE DIFFERENCE. IT REALLY *DOES* LOOK CLEANER.
AFTER A LONG DAY, I JUST WANT TO GET IT OFF SO I CAN GET TO BED.
I'M TIRED!
I JUST WANNA SLEEP!
SCRUB
EVEN THOUGH WE KNOW IT'S BAD, WE'VE ALL DONE IT BEFORE.
I OFTEN GET BUSY WITH WORK AND LET THINGS SLIDE.
I'VE FALLEN ASLEEP WITH MY MAKEUP ON SOOOO MANY TIMES.
GEH!
IS IT MORNING?
CHIRP... CHIRP...
I'VE EVEN FLOPPED INTO BED WITH A **FULL FACE** OF MAKEUP, TOO.
BOF!
FWUMP!!
YOU TOO, SENSEI?!

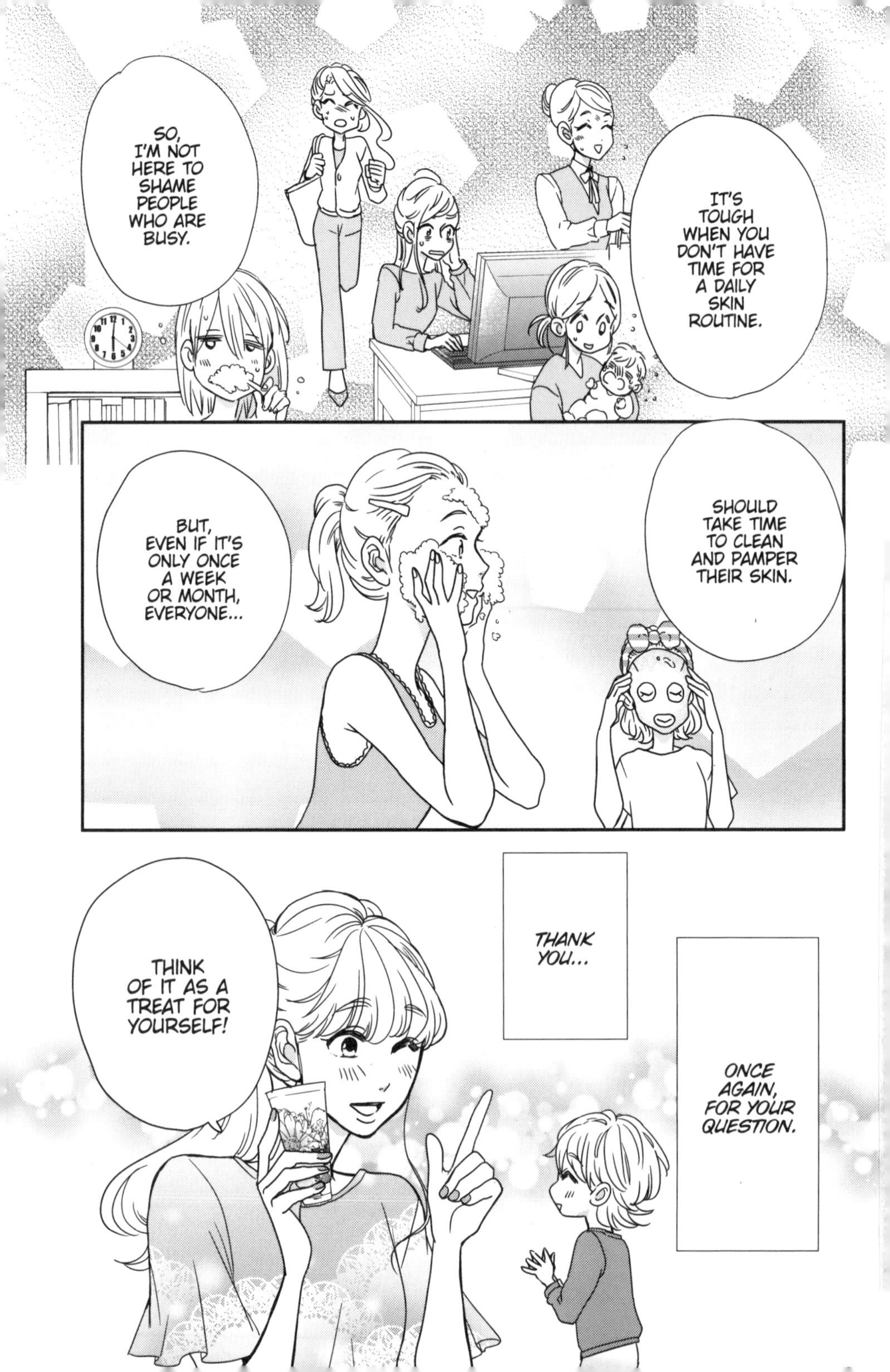

SO, I'M NOT HERE TO SHAME PEOPLE WHO ARE BUSY.
IT'S TOUGH WHEN YOU DON'T HAVE TIME FOR A DAILY SKIN ROUTINE.
BUT, EVEN IF IT'S ONLY ONCE A WEEK OR MONTH, EVERYONE...
SHOULD TAKE TIME TO CLEAN AND PAMPER THEIR SKIN.
THINK OF IT AS A TREAT FOR YOURSELF!
THANK YOU...
ONCE AGAIN, FOR YOUR QUESTION.

Lesson 9: Skin Care for Beginners ①

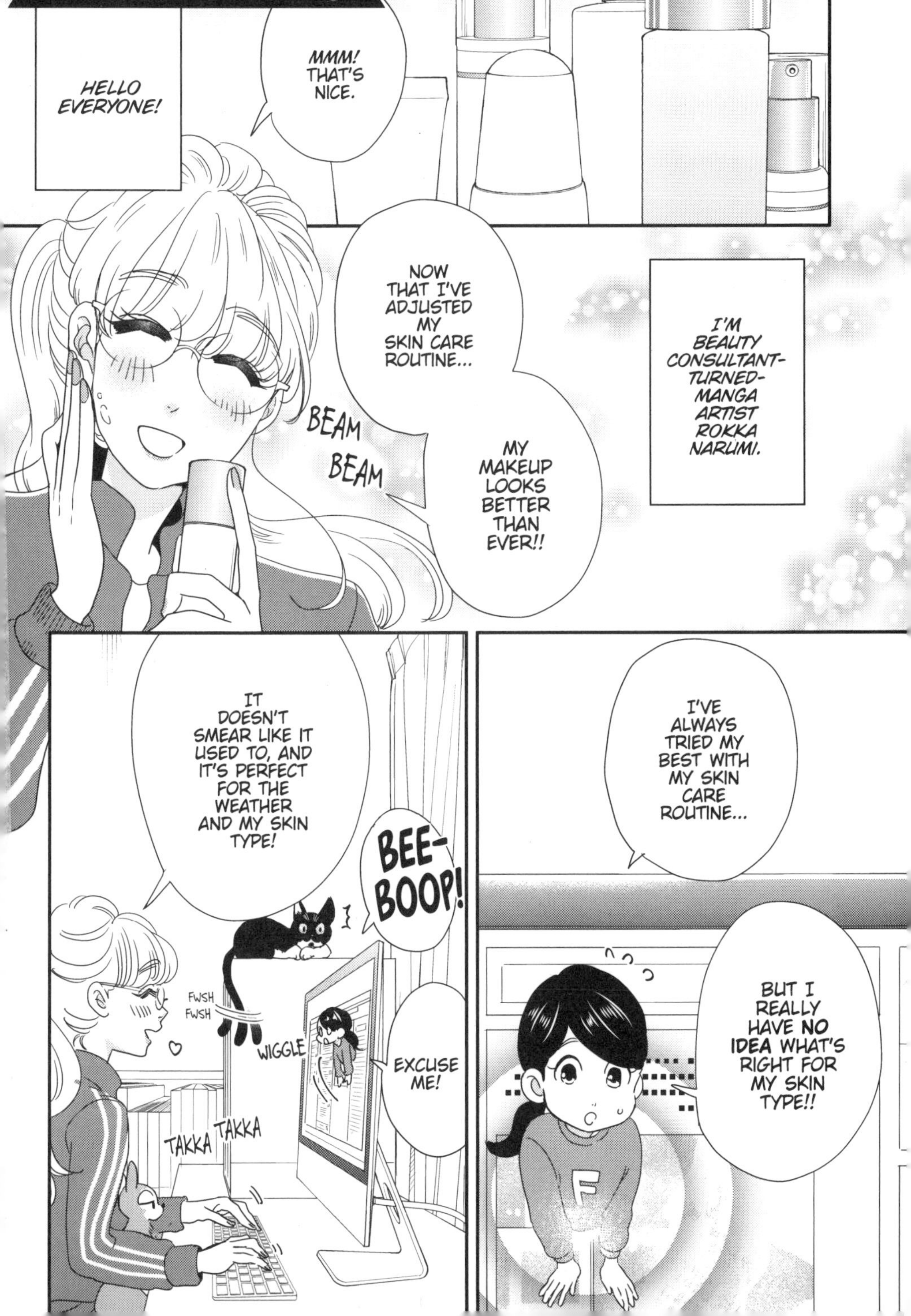
HELLO EVERYONE!
MMM! THAT'S NICE.
I'M BEAUTY CONSULTANT-TURNED-MANGA ARTIST ROKKA NARUMI.
NOW THAT I'VE ADJUSTED MY SKIN CARE ROUTINE...
BEAM BEAM
MY MAKEUP LOOKS BETTER THAN EVER!!
IT DOESN'T SMEAR LIKE IT USED TO, AND IT'S PERFECT FOR THE WEATHER AND MY SKIN TYPE!
BEE-BOOP!
FWSH FWSH
WIGGLE
EXCUSE ME!
TAKKA TAKKA
I'VE ALWAYS TRIED MY BEST WITH MY SKIN CARE ROUTINE...
BUT I REALLY HAVE **NO IDEA** WHAT'S RIGHT FOR MY SKIN TYPE!!

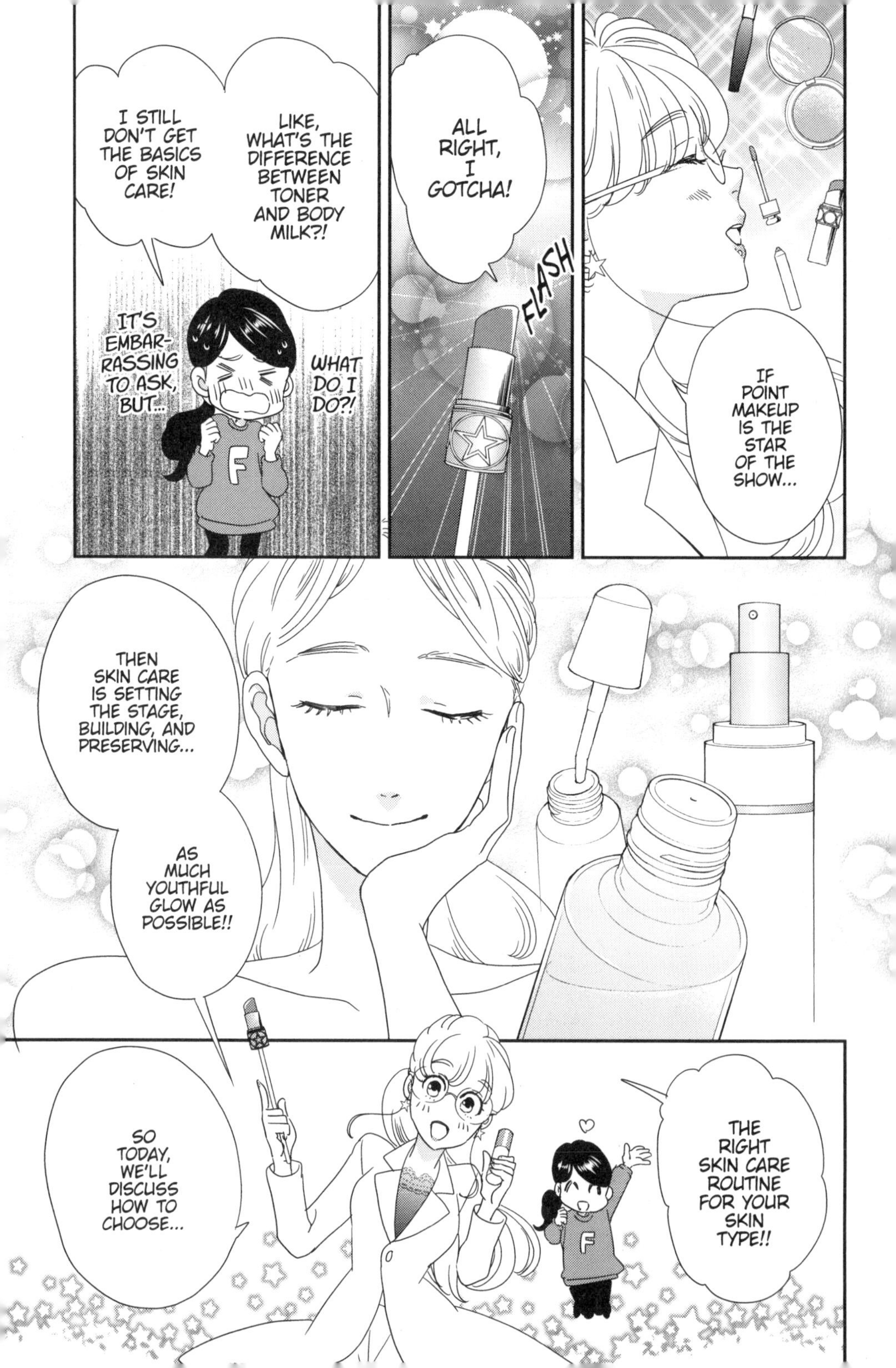
I STILL DON'T GET THE BASICS OF SKIN CARE!
LIKE, WHAT'S THE DIFFERENCE BETWEEN TONER AND BODY MILK?!
IT'S EMBARRASSING TO ASK, BUT...
WHAT DO I DO?!
ALL RIGHT, I GOTCHA!
FLASH
IF POINT MAKEUP IS THE STAR OF THE SHOW...
THEN SKIN CARE IS SETTING THE STAGE, BUILDING, AND PRESERVING...
AS MUCH YOUTHFUL GLOW AS POSSIBLE!!
SO TODAY, WE'LL DISCUSS HOW TO CHOOSE...
THE RIGHT SKIN CARE ROUTINE FOR YOUR SKIN TYPE!!

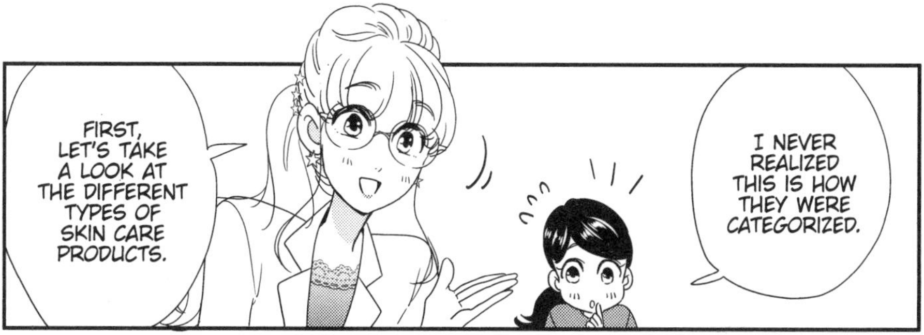
FIRST, LET'S TAKE A LOOK AT THE DIFFERENT TYPES OF SKIN CARE PRODUCTS.
I NEVER REALIZED THIS IS HOW THEY WERE CATEGORIZED.

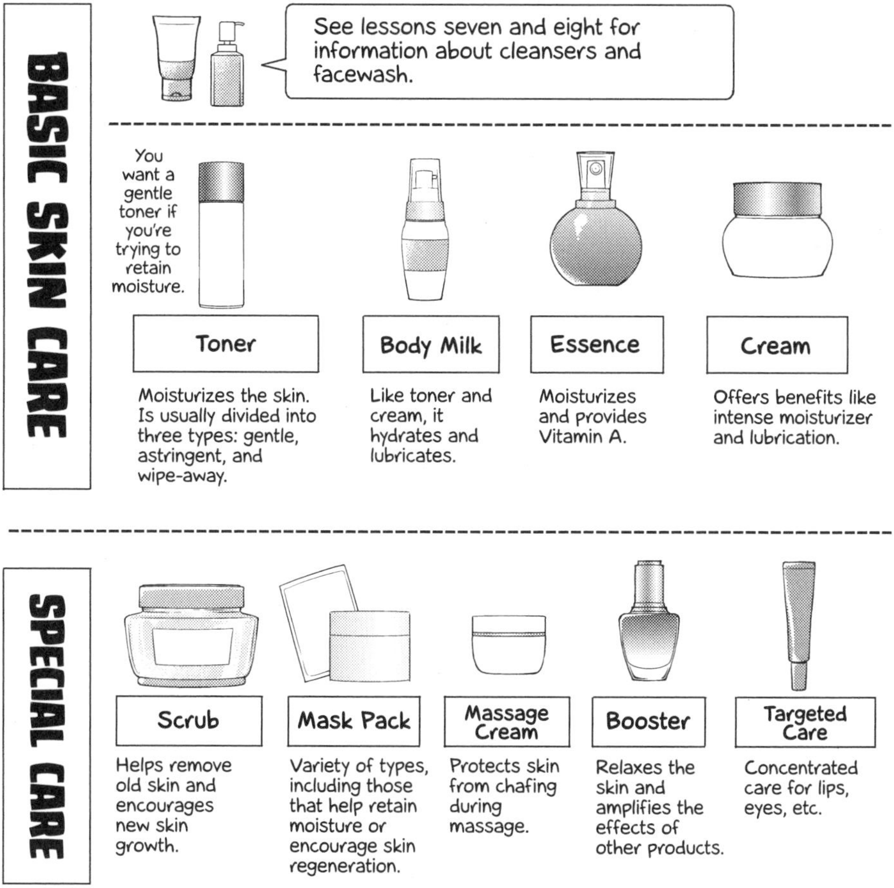
BASIC SKIN CARE
See lessons seven and eight for information about cleansers and facewash.
You want a gentle toner if you're trying to retain moisture.
Toner
Moisturizes the skin. Is usually divided into three types: gentle, astringent, and wipe-away.
Body Milk
Like toner and cream, it hydrates and lubricates.
Essence
Moisturizes and provides Vitamin A.
Cream
Offers benefits like intense moisturizer and lubrication.
SPECIAL CARE
Scrub
Helps remove old skin and encourages new skin growth.
Mask Pack
Variety of types, including those that help retain moisture or encourage skin regeneration.
Massage Cream
Protects skin from chafing during massage.
Booster
Relaxes the skin and amplifies the effects of other products.
Targeted Care
Concentrated care for lips, eyes, etc.

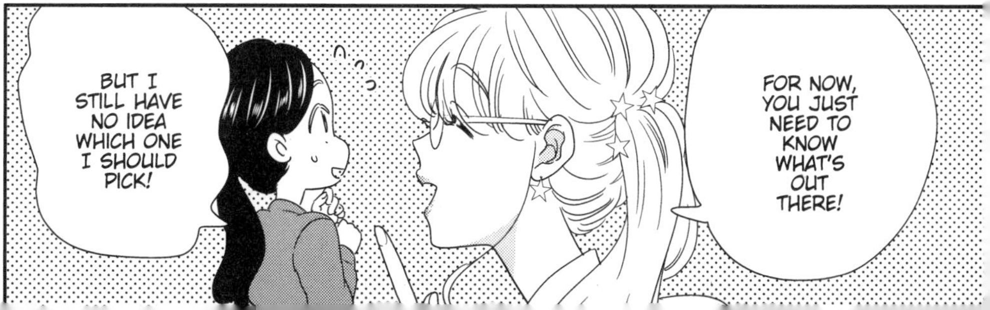
BUT I STILL HAVE NO IDEA WHICH ONE I SHOULD PICK!
FOR NOW, YOU JUST NEED TO KNOW WHAT'S OUT THERE!

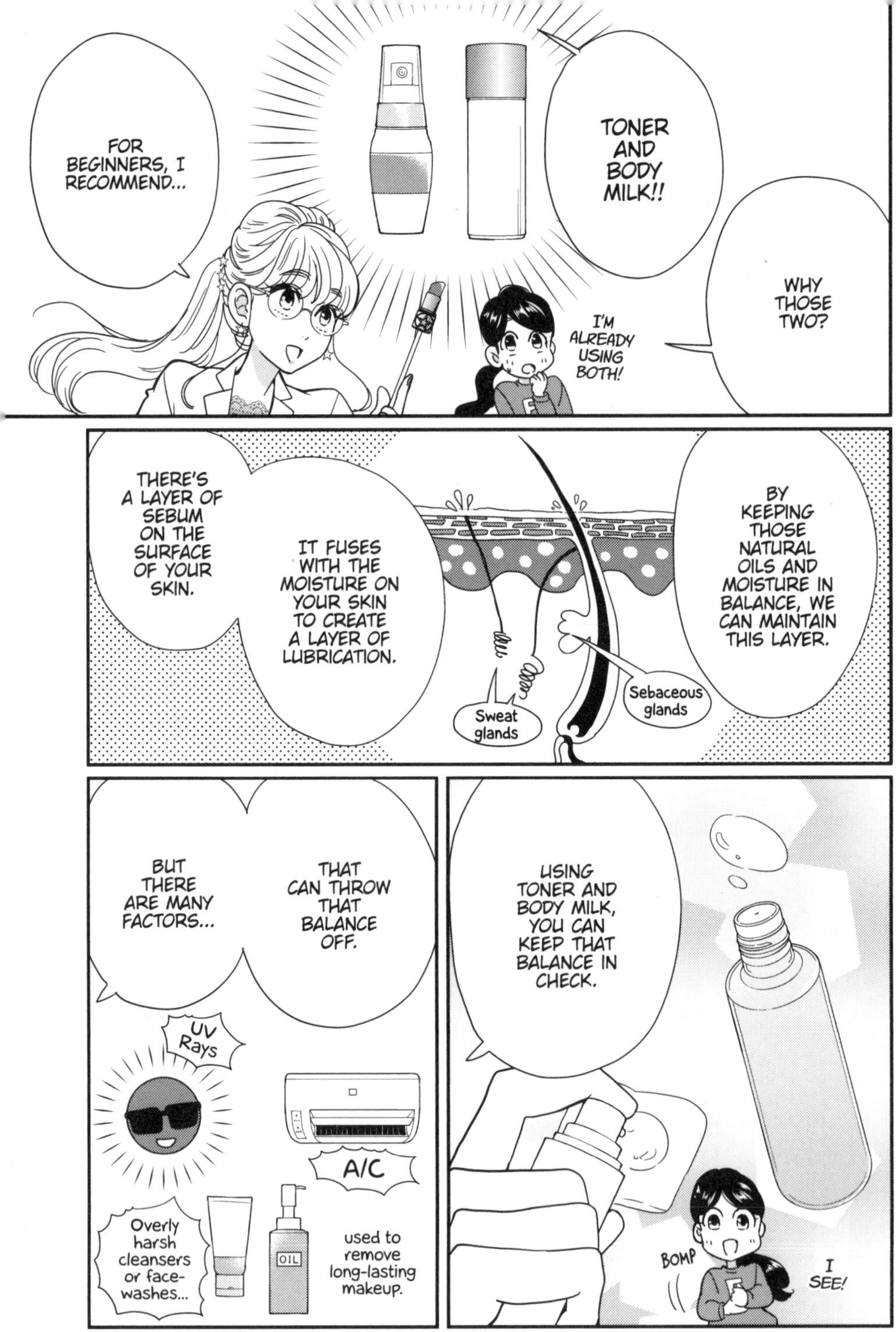
FOR BEGINNERS, I RECOMMEND...
TONER AND BODY MILK!!
I'M ALREADY USING BOTH!
WHY THOSE TWO?
THERE'S A LAYER OF SEBUM ON THE SURFACE OF YOUR SKIN.
IT FUSES WITH THE MOISTURE ON YOUR SKIN TO CREATE A LAYER OF LUBRICATION.
Sweat glands
Sebaceous glands
BY KEEPING THOSE NATURAL OILS AND MOISTURE IN BALANCE, WE CAN MAINTAIN THIS LAYER.
BUT THERE ARE MANY FACTORS...
THAT CAN THROW THAT BALANCE OFF.
UV Rays
A/C
Overly harsh cleansers or face-washes...
OIL
used to remove long-lasting makeup.
USING TONER AND BODY MILK, YOU CAN KEEP THAT BALANCE IN CHECK.
BOMP
I SEE!

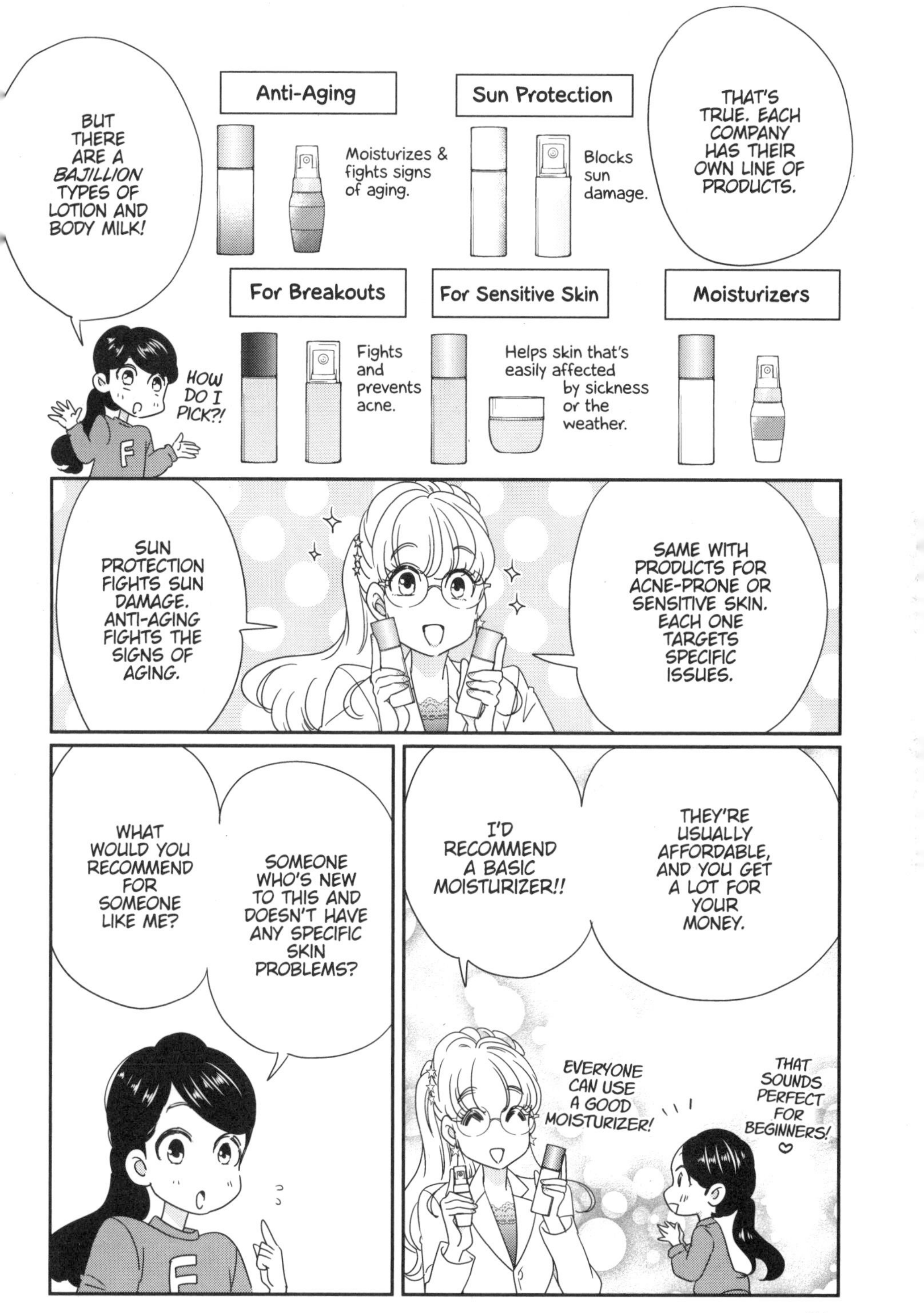
BUT THERE ARE A BAJILLION TYPES OF LOTION AND BODY MILK!
Anti-Aging
Moisturizes & fights signs of aging.
Sun Protection
Blocks sun damage.
THAT'S TRUE. EACH COMPANY HAS THEIR OWN LINE OF PRODUCTS.
HOW DO I PICK?!
For Breakouts
Fights and prevents acne.
For Sensitive Skin
Helps skin that's easily affected by sickness or the weather.
Moisturizers
SAME WITH PRODUCTS FOR ACNE-PRONE OR SENSITIVE SKIN. EACH ONE TARGETS SPECIFIC ISSUES.
SUN PROTECTION FIGHTS SUN DAMAGE. ANTI-AGING FIGHTS THE SIGNS OF AGING.
SOMEONE WHO'S NEW TO THIS AND DOESN'T HAVE ANY SPECIFIC SKIN PROBLEMS?
WHAT WOULD YOU RECOMMEND FOR SOMEONE LIKE ME?
THEY'RE USUALLY AFFORDABLE, AND YOU GET A LOT FOR YOUR MONEY.
I'D RECOMMEND A BASIC MOISTURIZER!!
THAT SOUNDS PERFECT FOR BEGINNERS!
EVERYONE CAN USE A GOOD MOISTURIZER!

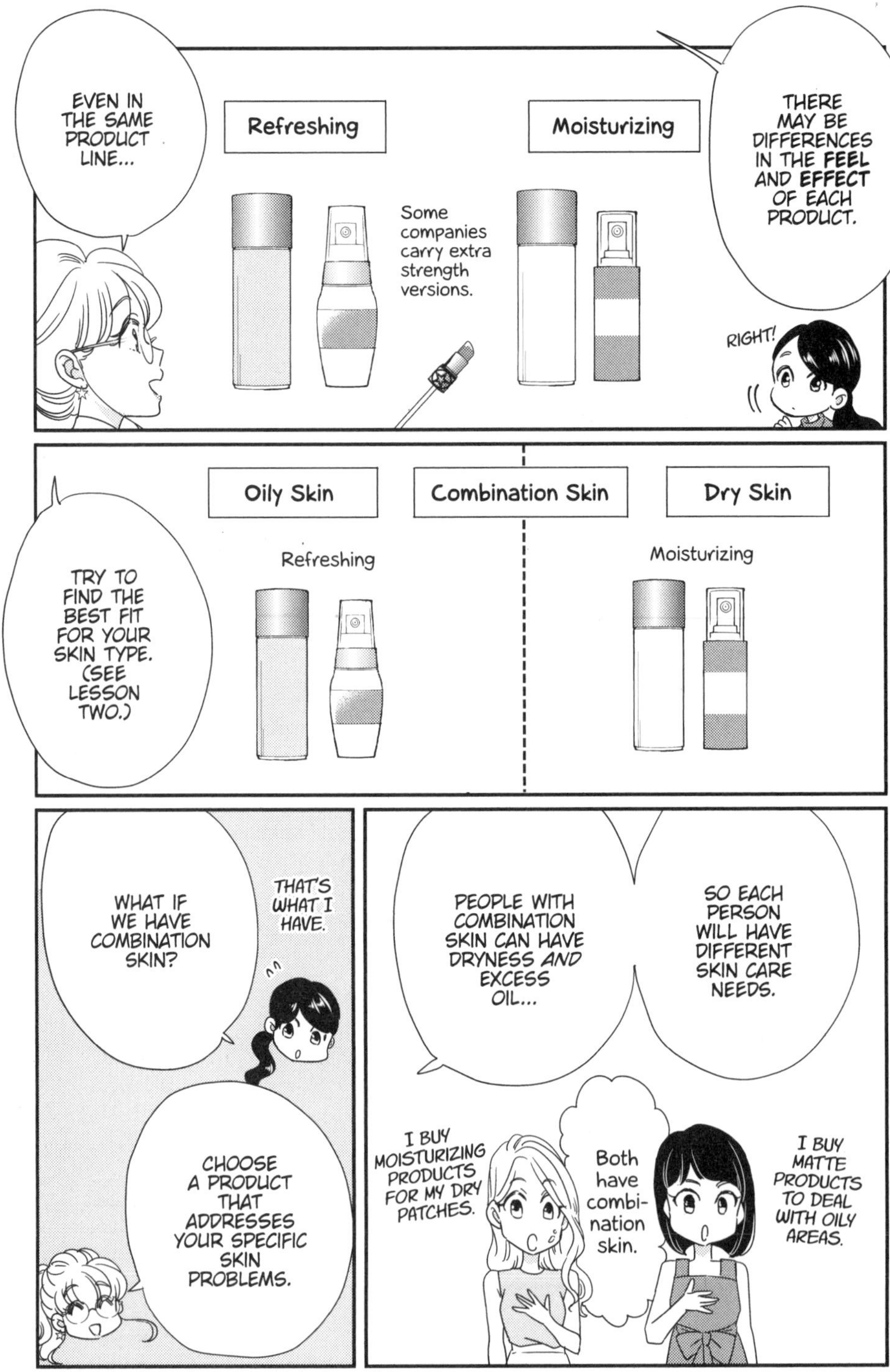
EVEN IN THE SAME PRODUCT LINE...
Refreshing
Moisturizing
Some companies carry extra strength versions.
THERE MAY BE DIFFERENCES IN THE FEEL AND EFFECT OF EACH PRODUCT.
RIGHT!
Oily Skin
Combination Skin
Dry Skin
Refreshing
Moisturizing
TRY TO FIND THE BEST FIT FOR YOUR SKIN TYPE. (SEE LESSON TWO.)
WHAT IF WE HAVE COMBINATION SKIN?
THAT'S WHAT I HAVE.
CHOOSE A PRODUCT THAT ADDRESSES YOUR SPECIFIC SKIN PROBLEMS.
PEOPLE WITH COMBINATION SKIN CAN HAVE DRYNESS AND EXCESS OIL...
SO EACH PERSON WILL HAVE DIFFERENT SKIN CARE NEEDS.
I BUY MOISTURIZING PRODUCTS FOR MY DRY PATCHES.
Both have combi-nation skin.
I BUY MATTE PRODUCTS TO DEAL WITH OILY AREAS.

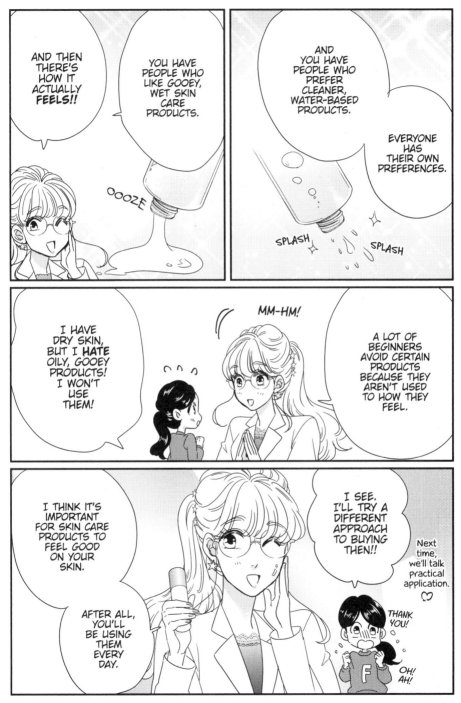

AND THEN THERE'S HOW IT ACTUALLY **FEELS!!**

YOU HAVE PEOPLE WHO LIKE GOOEY, WET SKIN CARE PRODUCTS.

OOOZE

AND YOU HAVE PEOPLE WHO PREFER CLEANER, WATER-BASED PRODUCTS.

EVERYONE HAS THEIR OWN PREFERENCES.

SPLASH   SPLASH

I HAVE DRY SKIN, BUT I **HATE** OILY, GOOEY PRODUCTS! I WON'T USE THEM!

MM-HM!

A LOT OF BEGINNERS AVOID CERTAIN PRODUCTS BECAUSE THEY AREN'T USED TO HOW THEY FEEL.

I THINK IT'S IMPORTANT FOR SKIN CARE PRODUCTS TO FEEL GOOD ON YOUR SKIN.

AFTER ALL, YOU'LL BE USING THEM EVERY DAY.

I SEE. I'LL TRY A DIFFERENT APPROACH TO BUYING THEN!!

Next time, we'll talk practical application. ♡

THANK YOU!

OH! AH!

89

Let's Ask Rokka-Sensei!

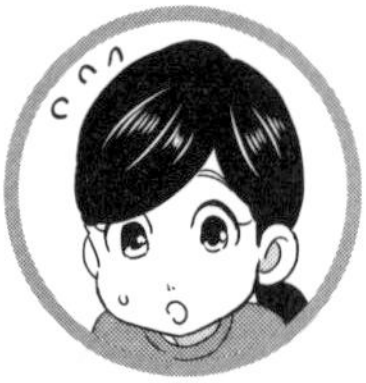

Q. I can't seem to get rich color from my brow pencil. What should I do when that happens?

A. Your eyebrows may not absorb the color because of excess oil, either from your lotions or excess sebum. Try lightly dabbing the area around your eyebrows with a tissue, and then applying a little powder (take care not to overdo it). This should help you see more color from your eyebrow pencil.

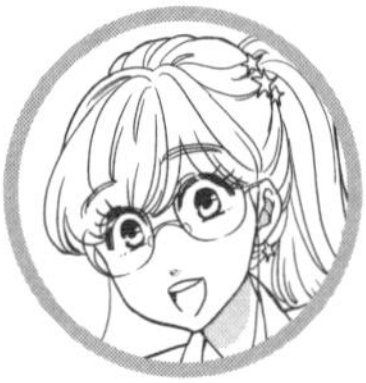

Lesson 10: Skin Care for Beginners ②

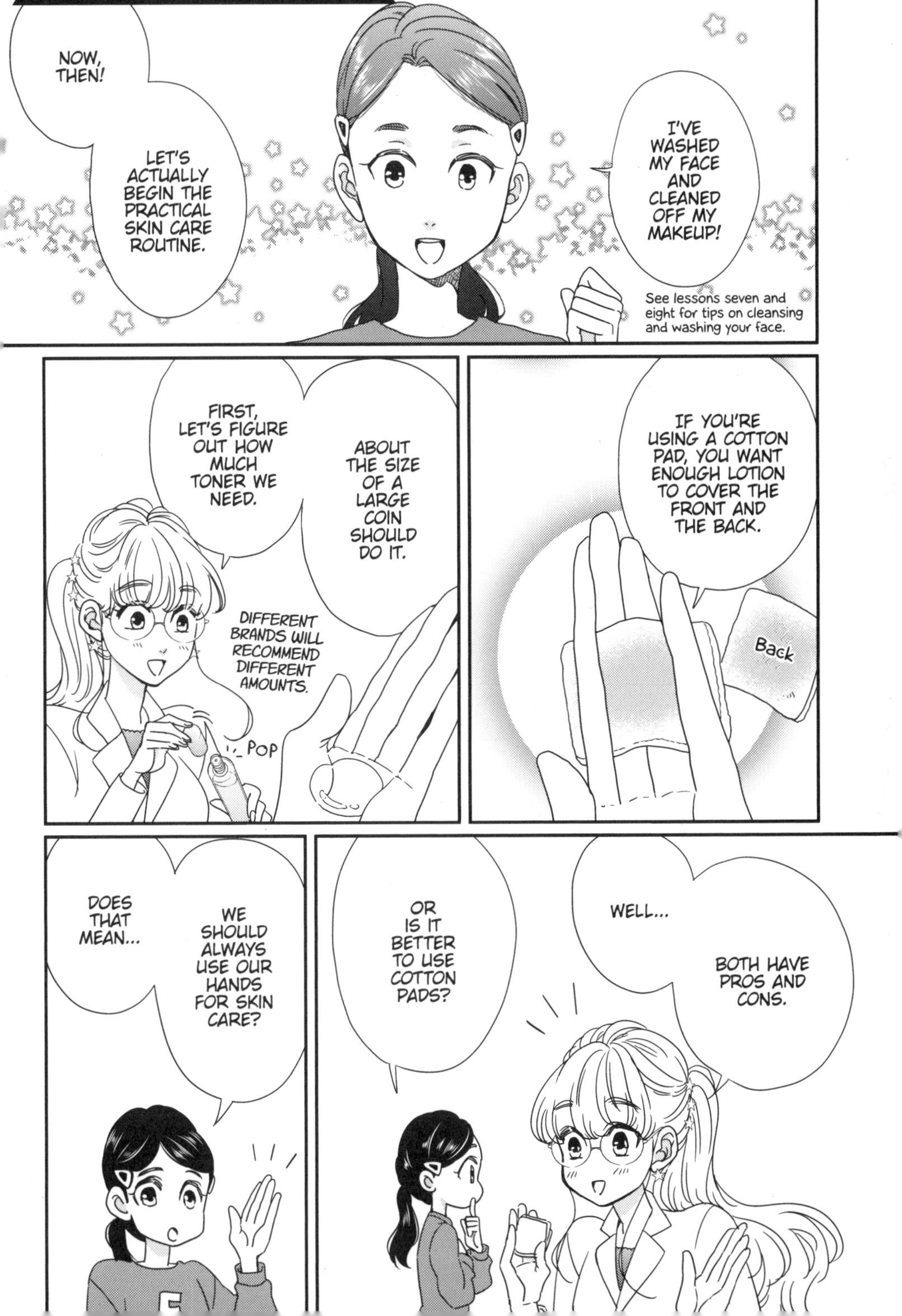

NOW, THEN!
LET'S ACTUALLY BEGIN THE PRACTICAL SKIN CARE ROUTINE.
I'VE WASHED MY FACE AND CLEANED OFF MY MAKEUP!
See lessons seven and eight for tips on cleansing and washing your face.
FIRST, LET'S FIGURE OUT HOW MUCH TONER WE NEED.
ABOUT THE SIZE OF A LARGE COIN SHOULD DO IT.
DIFFERENT BRANDS WILL RECOMMEND DIFFERENT AMOUNTS.
POP
IF YOU'RE USING A COTTON PAD, YOU WANT ENOUGH LOTION TO COVER THE FRONT AND THE BACK.
Back
DOES THAT MEAN...
WE SHOULD ALWAYS USE OUR HANDS FOR SKIN CARE?
OR IS IT BETTER TO USE COTTON PADS?
WELL...
BOTH HAVE PROS AND CONS.

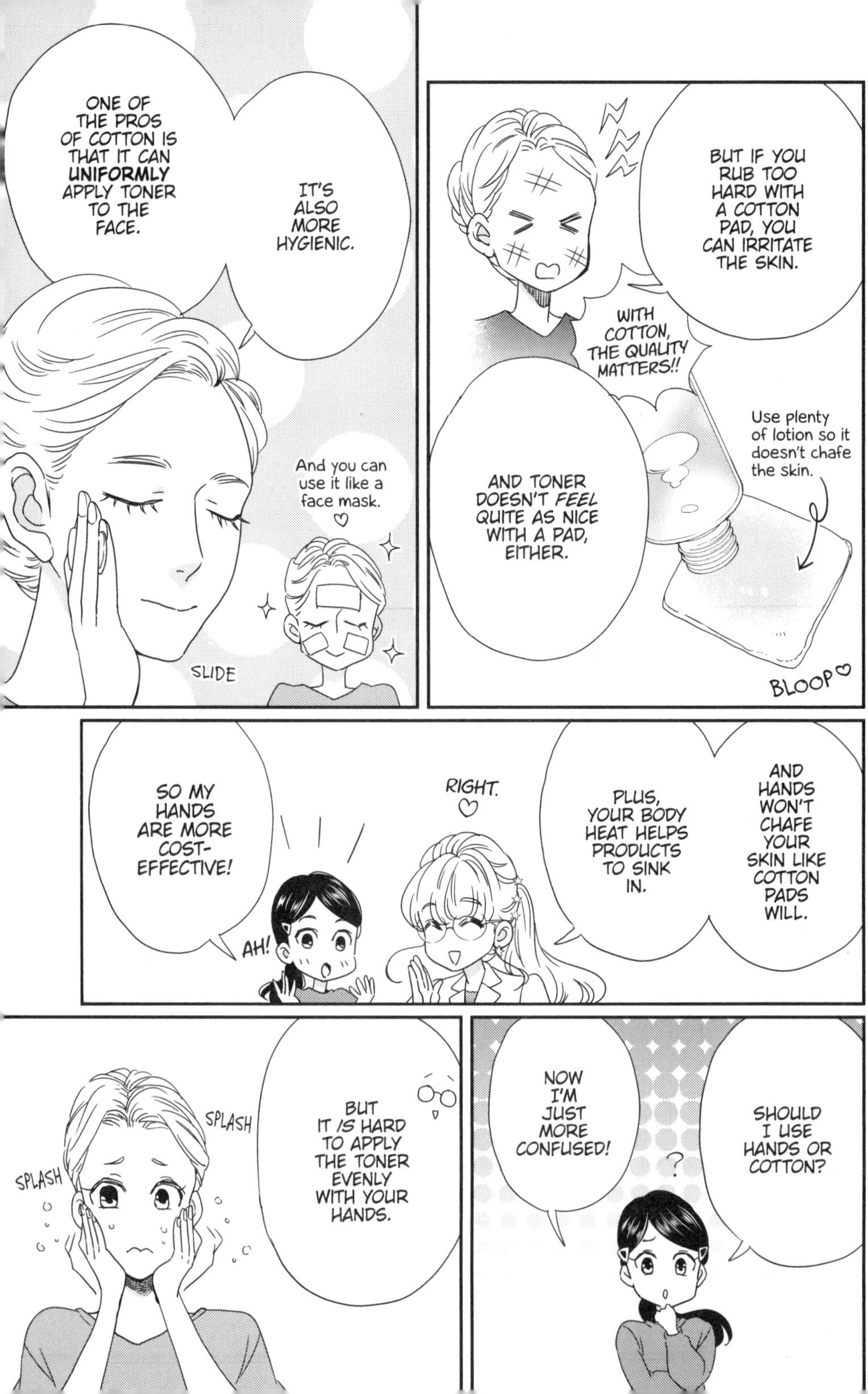
ONE OF THE PROS OF COTTON IS THAT IT CAN **UNIFORMLY** APPLY TONER TO THE FACE.
IT'S ALSO MORE HYGIENIC.
And you can use it like a face mask. ♡
SLIDE
BUT IF YOU RUB TOO HARD WITH A COTTON PAD, YOU CAN IRRITATE THE SKIN.
WITH COTTON, THE QUALITY MATTERS!!
AND TONER DOESN'T *FEEL* QUITE AS NICE WITH A PAD, EITHER.
Use plenty of lotion so it doesn't chafe the skin.
BLOOP♡
SO MY HANDS ARE MORE COST-EFFECTIVE!
AH!
RIGHT. ♡
PLUS, YOUR BODY HEAT HELPS PRODUCTS TO SINK IN.
AND HANDS WON'T CHAFE YOUR SKIN LIKE COTTON PADS WILL.
SPLASH
SPLASH
BUT IT *IS* HARD TO APPLY THE TONER EVENLY WITH YOUR HANDS.
SHOULD I USE HANDS OR COTTON?
NOW I'M JUST MORE CONFUSED!

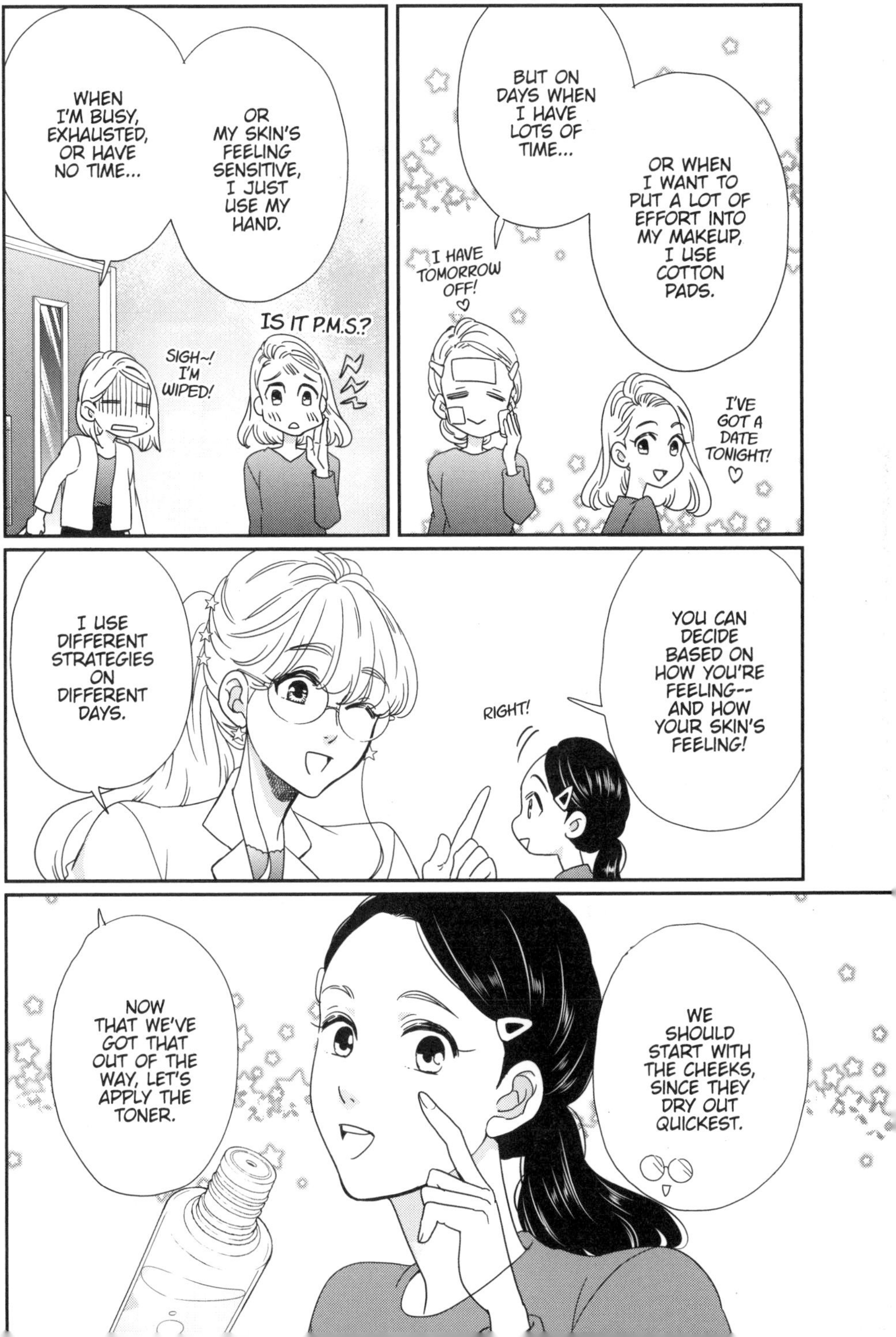
WHEN I'M BUSY, EXHAUSTED, OR HAVE NO TIME...
OR MY SKIN'S FEELING SENSITIVE, I JUST USE MY HAND.
SIGH~! I'M WIPED!
IS IT P.M.S.?
BUT ON DAYS WHEN I HAVE LOTS OF TIME...
I HAVE TOMORROW OFF! ♡
OR WHEN I WANT TO PUT A LOT OF EFFORT INTO MY MAKEUP, I USE COTTON PADS.
I'VE GOT A DATE TONIGHT! ♡
I USE DIFFERENT STRATEGIES ON DIFFERENT DAYS.
RIGHT!
YOU CAN DECIDE BASED ON HOW YOU'RE FEELING-- AND HOW YOUR SKIN'S FEELING!
NOW THAT WE'VE GOT THAT OUT OF THE WAY, LET'S APPLY THE TONER.
WE SHOULD START WITH THE CHEEKS, SINCE THEY DRY OUT QUICKEST.

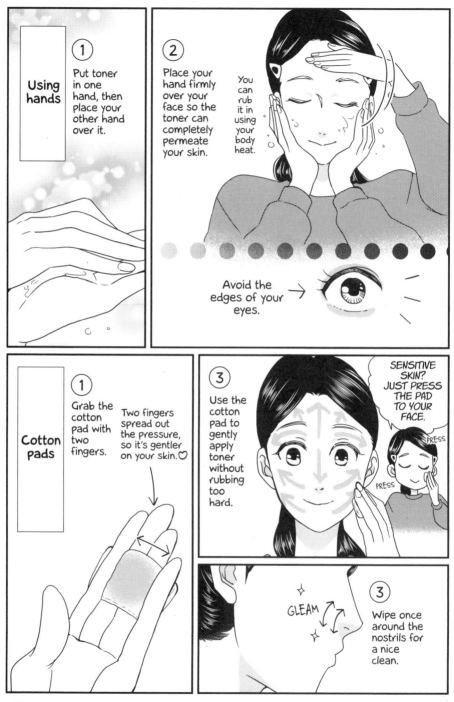

Using hands

① Put toner in one hand, then place your other hand over it.

② Place your hand firmly over your face so the toner can completely permeate your skin.

You can rub it in using your body heat.

Avoid the edges of your eyes. →

Cotton pads

① Grab the cotton pad with two fingers.

Two fingers spread out the pressure, so it's gentler on your skin.♡

③ Use the cotton pad to gently apply toner without rubbing too hard.

SENSITIVE SKIN? JUST PRESS THE PAD TO YOUR FACE.

PRESS

PRESS

GLEAM

③ Wipe once around the nostrils for a nice clean.

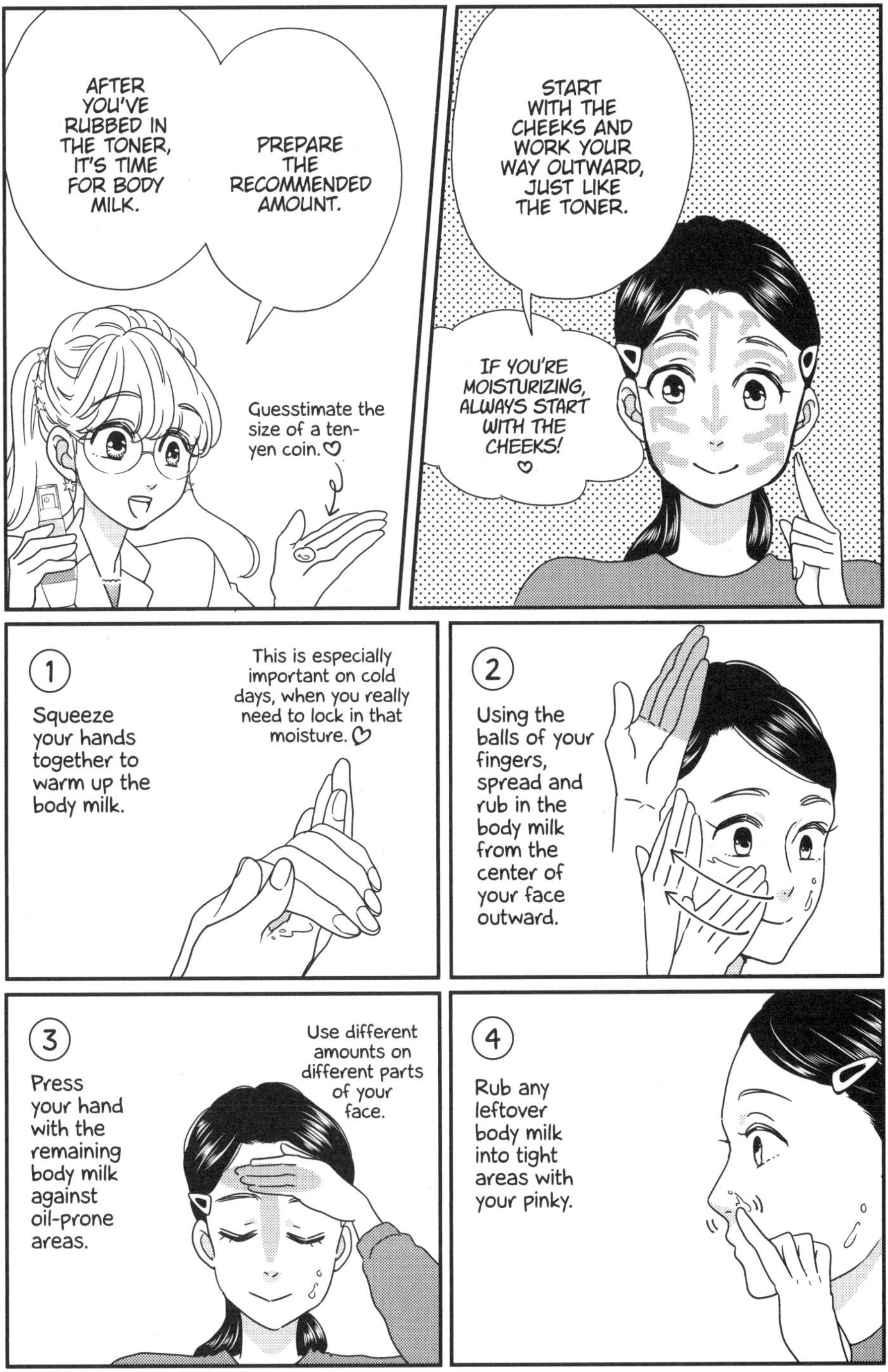

AFTER YOU'VE RUBBED IN THE TONER, IT'S TIME FOR BODY MILK.
PREPARE THE RECOMMENDED AMOUNT.
Guesstimate the size of a ten-yen coin. ♡
START WITH THE CHEEKS AND WORK YOUR WAY OUTWARD, JUST LIKE THE TONER.
IF YOU'RE MOISTURIZING, ALWAYS START WITH THE CHEEKS! ♡
1
Squeeze your hands together to warm up the body milk.
This is especially important on cold days, when you really need to lock in that moisture. ♡
2
Using the balls of your fingers, spread and rub in the body milk from the center of your face outward.
3
Press your hand with the remaining body milk against oil-prone areas.
Use different amounts on different parts of your face.
4
Rub any leftover body milk into tight areas with your pinky.

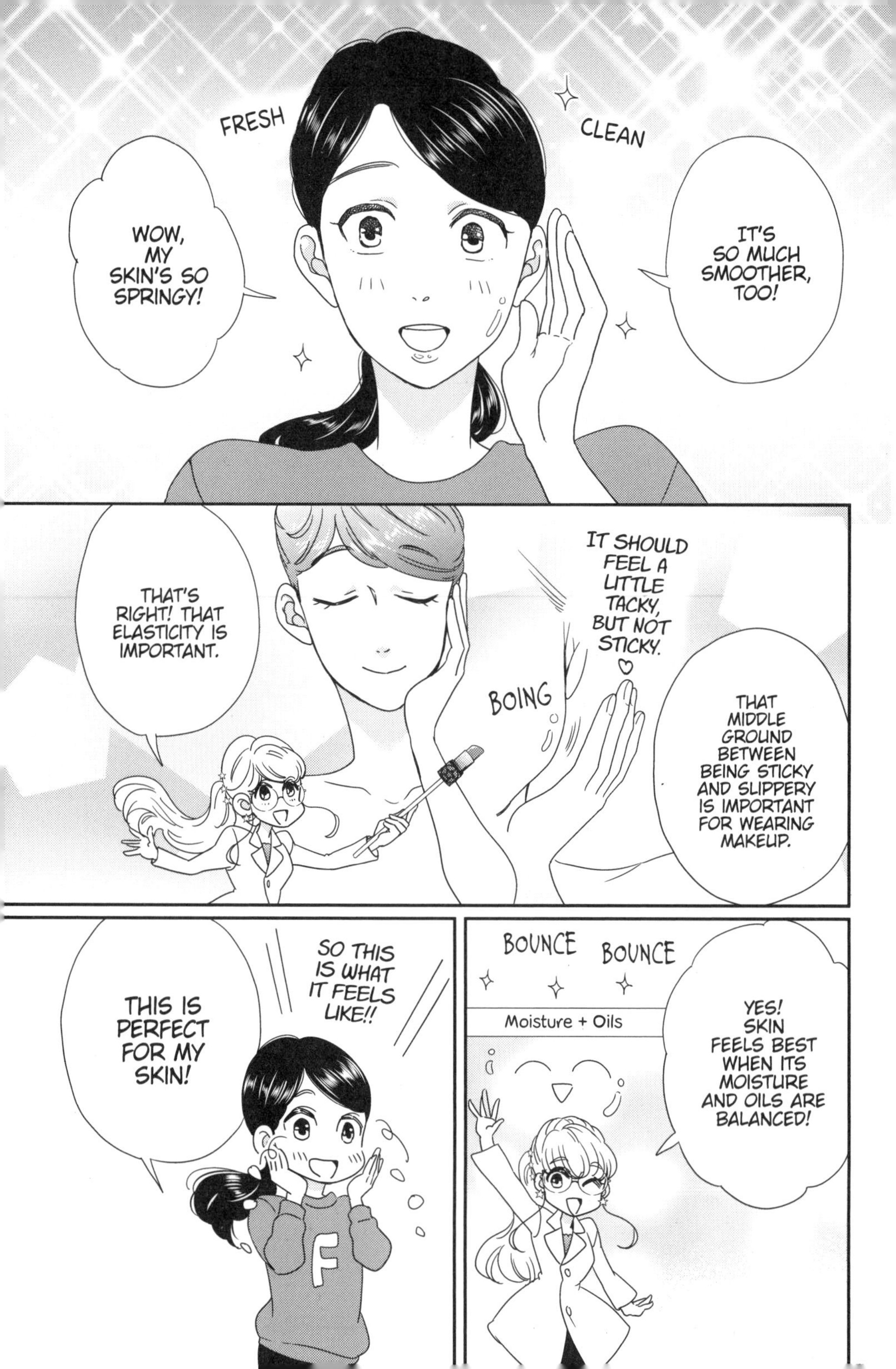
FRESH
CLEAN
WOW, MY SKIN'S SO SPRINGY!
IT'S SO MUCH SMOOTHER, TOO!
THAT'S RIGHT! THAT ELASTICITY IS IMPORTANT.
IT SHOULD FEEL A LITTLE TACKY, BUT NOT STICKY.
BOING
THAT MIDDLE GROUND BETWEEN BEING STICKY AND SLIPPERY IS IMPORTANT FOR WEARING MAKEUP.
THIS IS PERFECT FOR MY SKIN!
SO THIS IS WHAT IT FEELS LIKE!!
BOUNCE
BOUNCE
Moisture + Oils
YES! SKIN FEELS BEST WHEN ITS MOISTURE AND OILS ARE BALANCED!
F

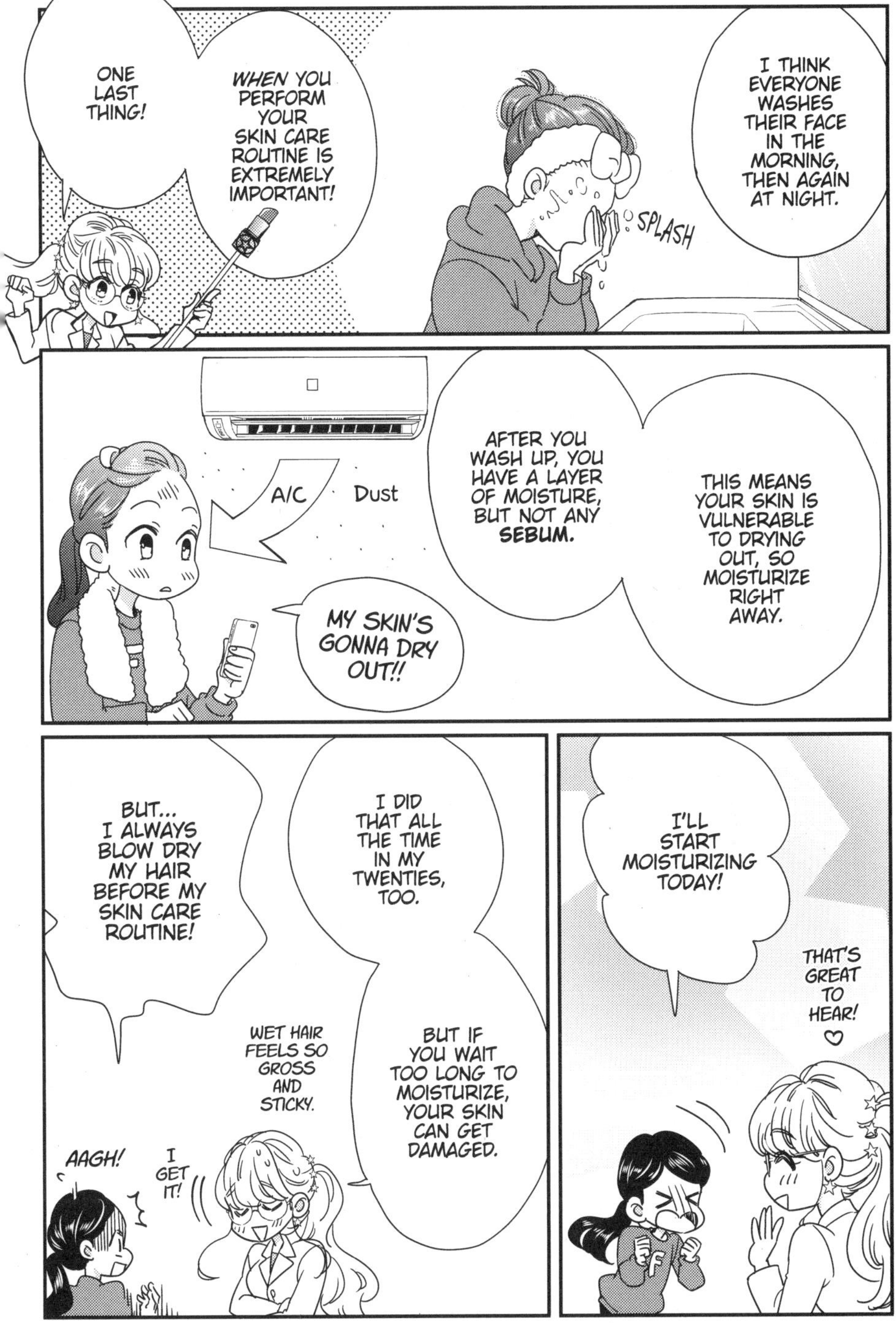
ONE LAST THING!
WHEN YOU PERFORM YOUR SKIN CARE ROUTINE IS EXTREMELY IMPORTANT!
I THINK EVERYONE WASHES THEIR FACE IN THE MORNING, THEN AGAIN AT NIGHT.
SPLASH
A/C
Dust
AFTER YOU WASH UP, YOU HAVE A LAYER OF MOISTURE, BUT NOT ANY **SEBUM.**
THIS MEANS YOUR SKIN IS VULNERABLE TO DRYING OUT, SO MOISTURIZE RIGHT AWAY.
MY SKIN'S GONNA DRY OUT!!
BUT... I ALWAYS BLOW DRY MY HAIR BEFORE MY SKIN CARE ROUTINE!
I DID THAT ALL THE TIME IN MY TWENTIES, TOO.
WET HAIR FEELS SO GROSS AND STICKY.
BUT IF YOU WAIT TOO LONG TO MOISTURIZE, YOUR SKIN CAN GET DAMAGED.
AAGH!
I GET IT!
I'LL START MOISTURIZING TODAY!
THAT'S GREAT TO HEAR! ♡

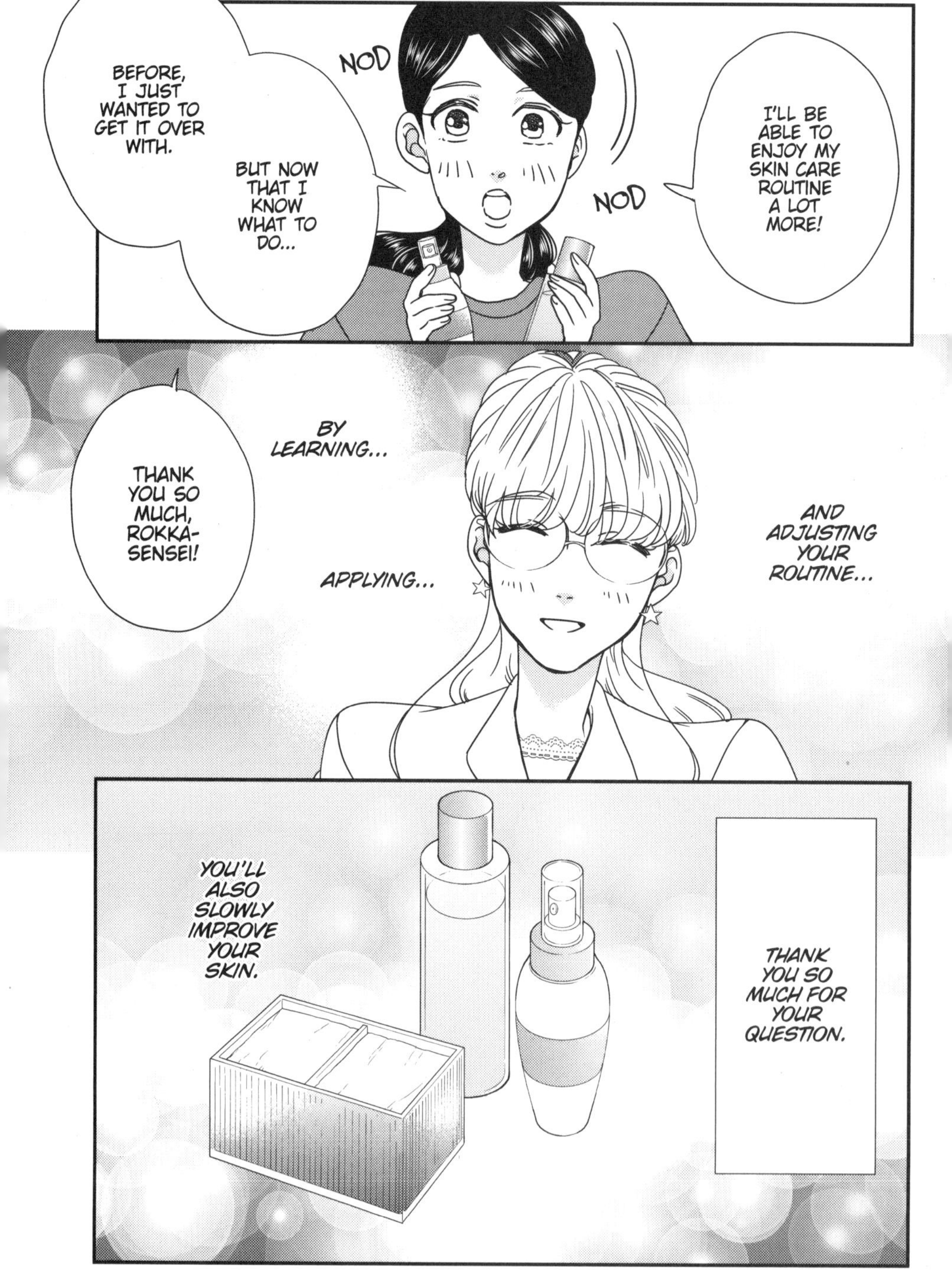
BEFORE, I JUST WANTED TO GET IT OVER WITH.
BUT NOW THAT I KNOW WHAT TO DO...
NOD
NOD
I'LL BE ABLE TO ENJOY MY SKIN CARE ROUTINE A LOT MORE!
THANK YOU SO MUCH, ROKKA-SENSEI!
BY LEARNING...
APPLYING...
AND ADJUSTING YOUR ROUTINE...
YOU'LL ALSO SLOWLY IMPROVE YOUR SKIN.
THANK YOU SO MUCH FOR YOUR QUESTION.

Lesson 11: How to Deal with Pesky Pores

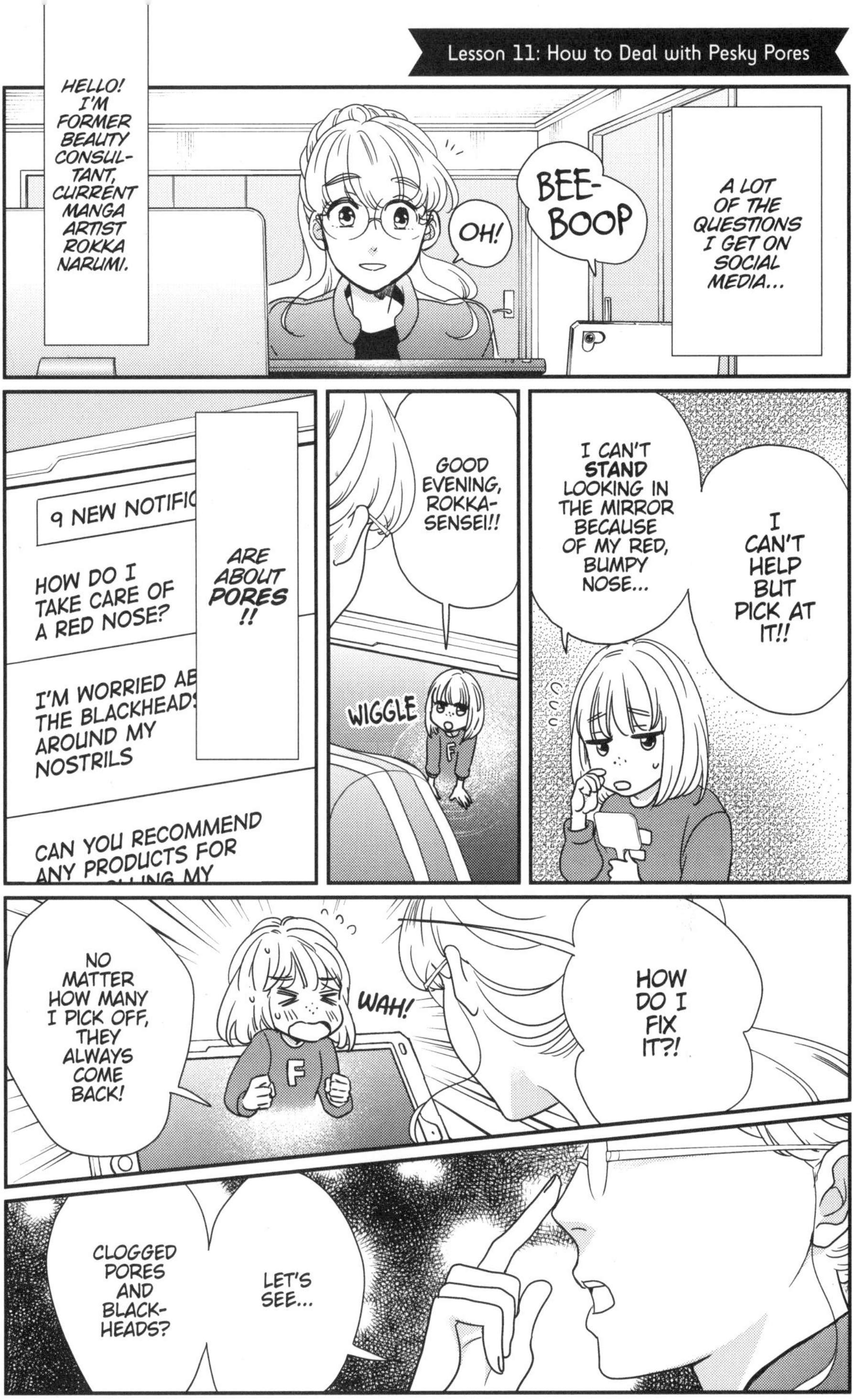

HELLO! I'M FORMER BEAUTY CONSUL-TANT, CURRENT MANGA ARTIST ROKKA NARUMI.
OH!
BEE-BOOP
A LOT OF THE QUESTIONS I GET ON SOCIAL MEDIA...
9 NEW NOTIFIC
HOW DO I TAKE CARE OF A RED NOSE?
I'M WORRIED AB
THE BLACKHEADS
AROUND MY NOSTRILS
CAN YOU RECOMMEND ANY PRODUCTS FOR
ARE ABOUT PORES!!
GOOD EVENING, ROKKA-SENSEI!!
WIGGLE
I CAN'T STAND LOOKING IN THE MIRROR BECAUSE OF MY RED, BUMPY NOSE...
I CAN'T HELP BUT PICK AT IT!!
NO MATTER HOW MANY I PICK OFF, THEY ALWAYS COME BACK!
WAH!
HOW DO I FIX IT?!
CLOGGED PORES AND BLACK-HEADS?
LET'S SEE...

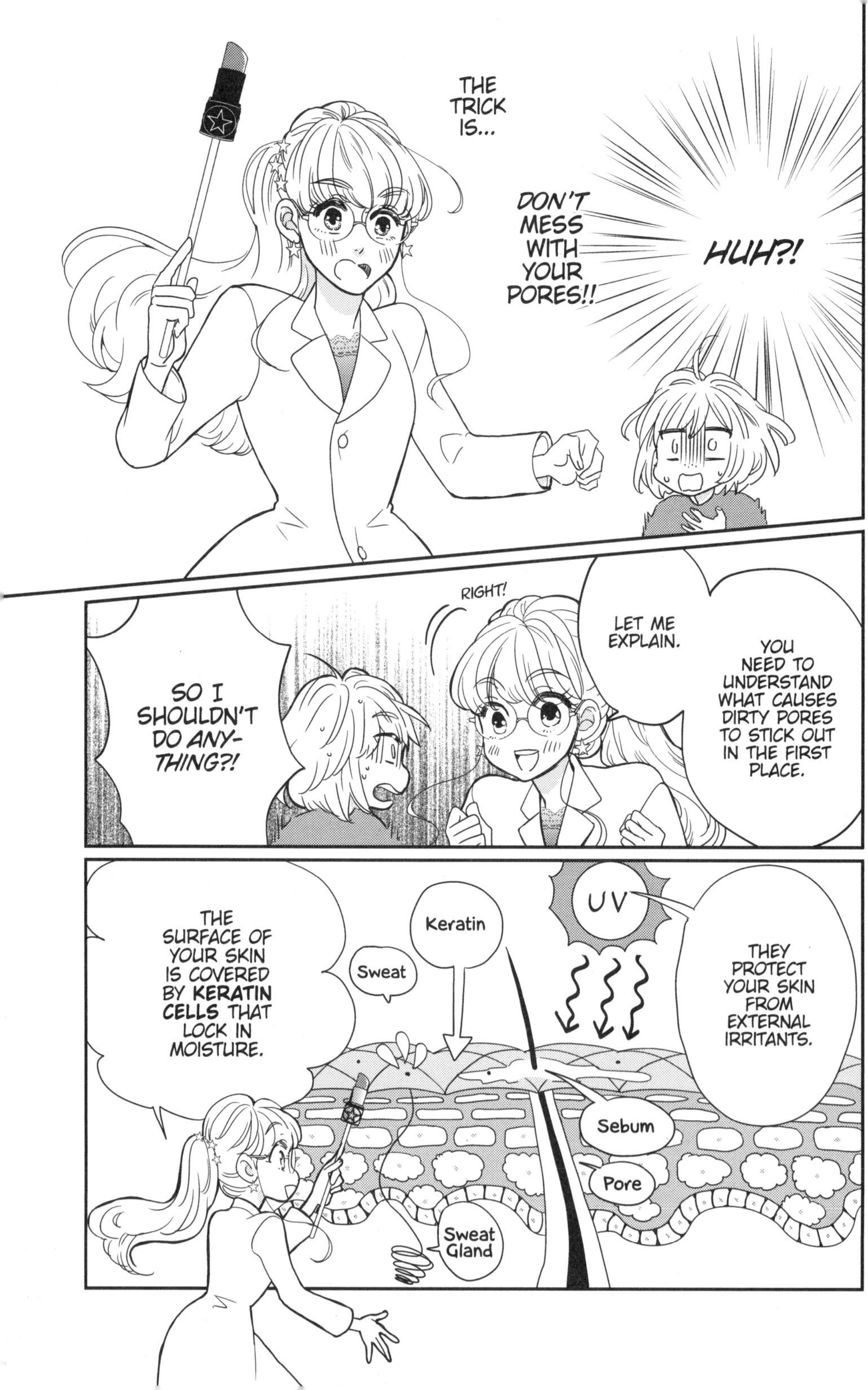
THE TRICK IS...
DON'T MESS WITH YOUR PORES!!
HUH?!
LET ME EXPLAIN.
YOU NEED TO UNDERSTAND WHAT CAUSES DIRTY PORES TO STICK OUT IN THE FIRST PLACE.
RIGHT!
SO I SHOULDN'T DO ANY-THING?!
UV
THEY PROTECT YOUR SKIN FROM EXTERNAL IRRITANTS.
Keratin
Sweat
THE SURFACE OF YOUR SKIN IS COVERED BY KERATIN CELLS THAT LOCK IN MOISTURE.
Sebum
Pore
Sweat Gland

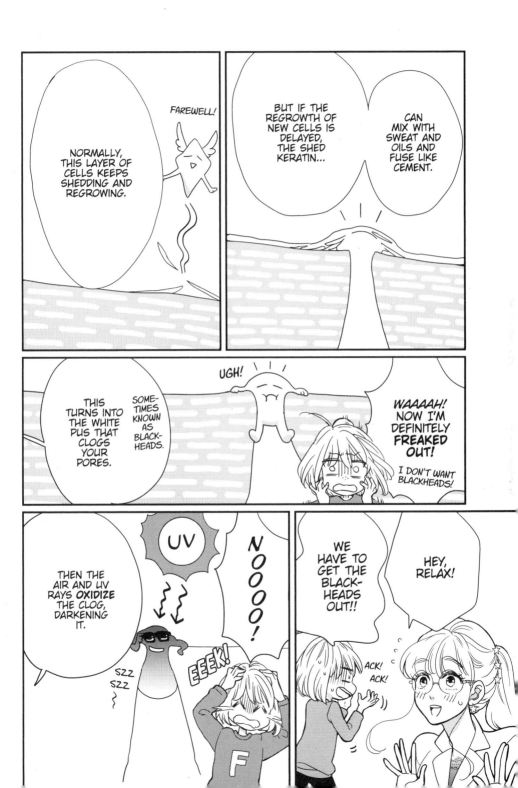

NORMALLY, THIS LAYER OF CELLS KEEPS SHEDDING AND REGROWING.

FAREWELL!

BUT IF THE REGROWTH OF NEW CELLS IS DELAYED, THE SHED KERATIN...

CAN MIX WITH SWEAT AND OILS AND FUSE LIKE CEMENT.

THIS TURNS INTO THE WHITE PUS THAT CLOGS YOUR PORES.

SOME-TIMES KNOWN AS BLACK-HEADS.

UGH!

WAAAAH! NOW I'M DEFINITELY **FREAKED OUT!**

I DON'T WANT BLACKHEADS!

THEN THE AIR AND UV RAYS **OXIDIZE** THE CLOG, DARKENING IT.

UV

N0000!

EEEK!

SZZ SZZ

WE HAVE TO GET THE BLACK-HEADS OUT!!

HEY, RELAX!

ACK! ACK!

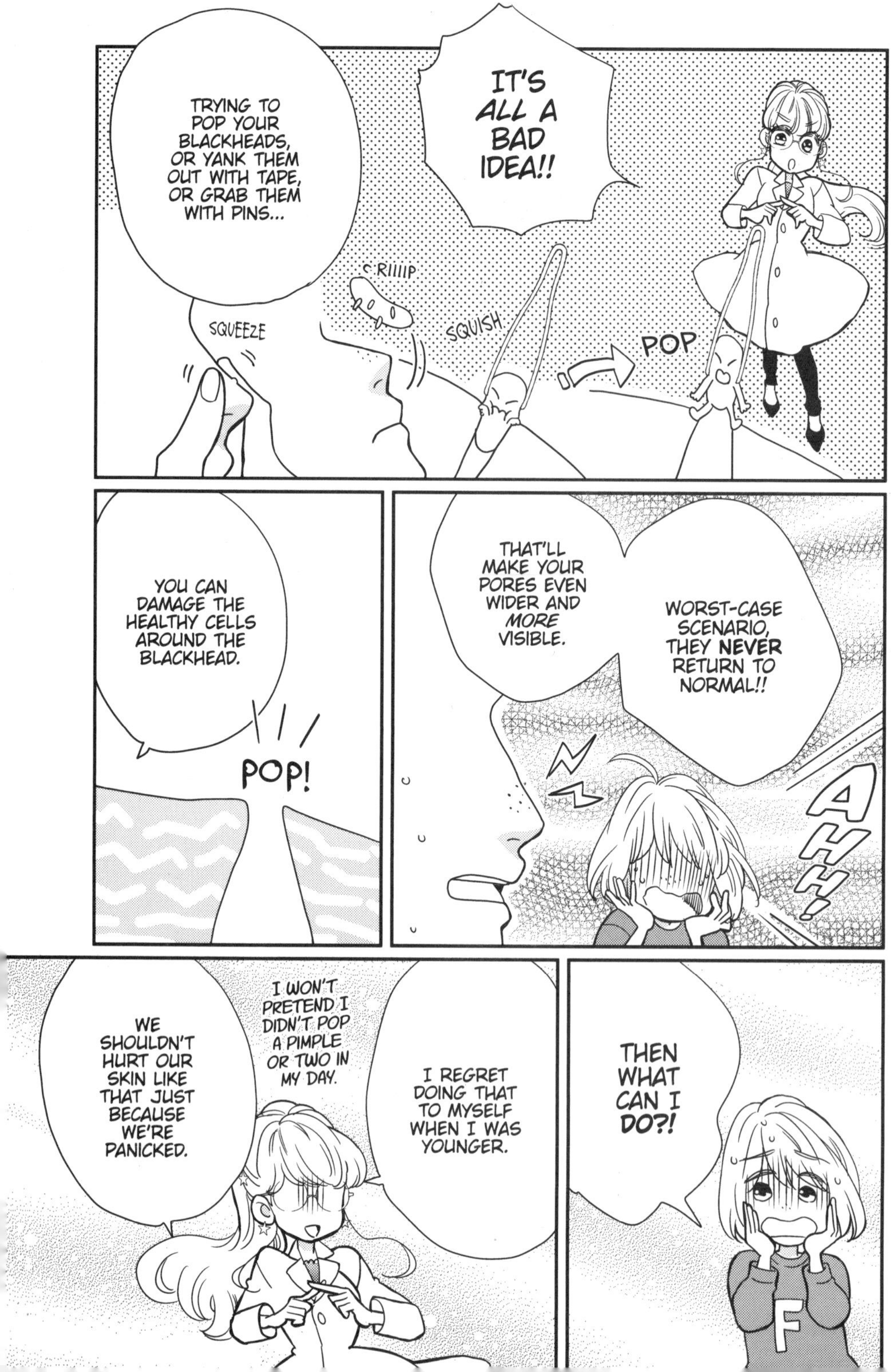
TRYING TO POP YOUR BLACKHEADS, OR YANK THEM OUT WITH TAPE, OR GRAB THEM WITH PINS...
IT'S ALL A BAD IDEA!!
SQUEEZE
RIIIIP
SQUISH
POP
YOU CAN DAMAGE THE HEALTHY CELLS AROUND THE BLACKHEAD.
POP!
THAT'LL MAKE YOUR PORES EVEN WIDER AND MORE VISIBLE.
WORST-CASE SCENARIO, THEY NEVER RETURN TO NORMAL!!
AHHH!
WE SHOULDN'T HURT OUR SKIN LIKE THAT JUST BECAUSE WE'RE PANICKED.
I WON'T PRETEND I DIDN'T POP A PIMPLE OR TWO IN MY DAY.
I REGRET DOING THAT TO MYSELF WHEN I WAS YOUNGER.
THEN WHAT CAN I DO?!
F

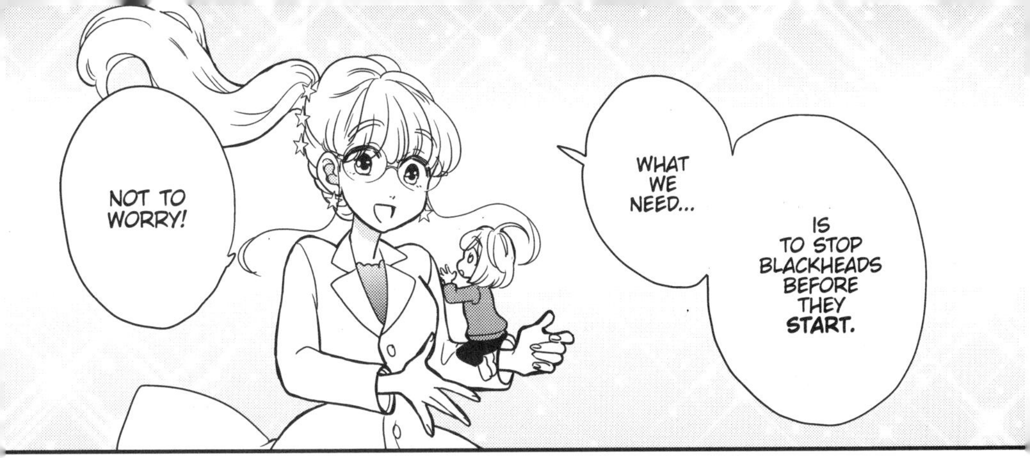
NOT TO WORRY!
WHAT WE NEED...
IS TO STOP BLACKHEADS BEFORE THEY START.

Stopping Clogged Pores the Rokka Way

1. Wash your face twice a day, maximum, working up a good lather each time. Only wash for forty-five seconds each time. (See lessons seven and eight.)
2. Do **not** touch your clogged pores. Do not pluck or pick or pop them.
3. Use foundation and base makeup that is easy to wash off.
4. Support your skin's natural regeneration.
5. Keep your skin nice and soft. Clogged pores are more likely when it's deprived of moisture.

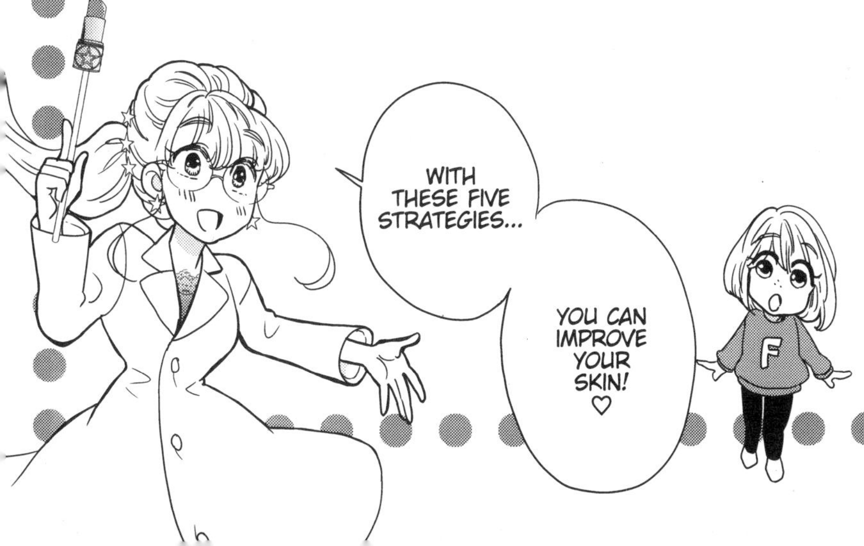
WITH THESE FIVE STRATEGIES...
YOU CAN IMPROVE YOUR SKIN! ♡

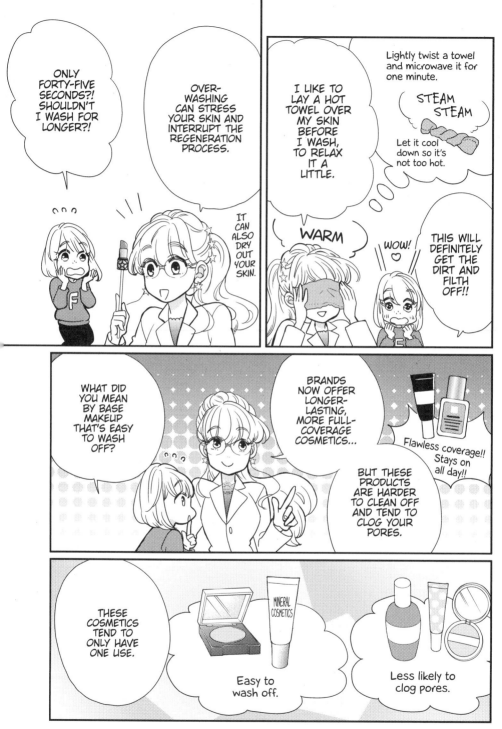

ONLY FORTY-FIVE SECONDS?! SHOULDN'T I WASH FOR LONGER?!

OVER-WASHING CAN STRESS YOUR SKIN AND INTERRUPT THE REGENERATION PROCESS.

IT CAN ALSO DRY OUT YOUR SKIN.

I LIKE TO LAY A HOT TOWEL OVER MY SKIN BEFORE I WASH, TO RELAX IT A LITTLE.

Lightly twist a towel and microwave it for one minute.

STEAM STEAM

Let it cool down so it's not too hot.

WARM

WOW! ♡

THIS WILL DEFINITELY GET THE DIRT AND FILTH OFF!!

WHAT DID YOU MEAN BY BASE MAKEUP THAT'S EASY TO WASH OFF?

BRANDS NOW OFFER LONGER-LASTING, MORE FULL-COVERAGE COSMETICS...

Flawless coverage!! Stays on all day!!

BUT THESE PRODUCTS ARE HARDER TO CLEAN OFF AND TEND TO CLOG YOUR PORES.

THESE COSMETICS TEND TO ONLY HAVE ONE USE.

MINERAL COSMETICS

Easy to wash off.

Less likely to clog pores.

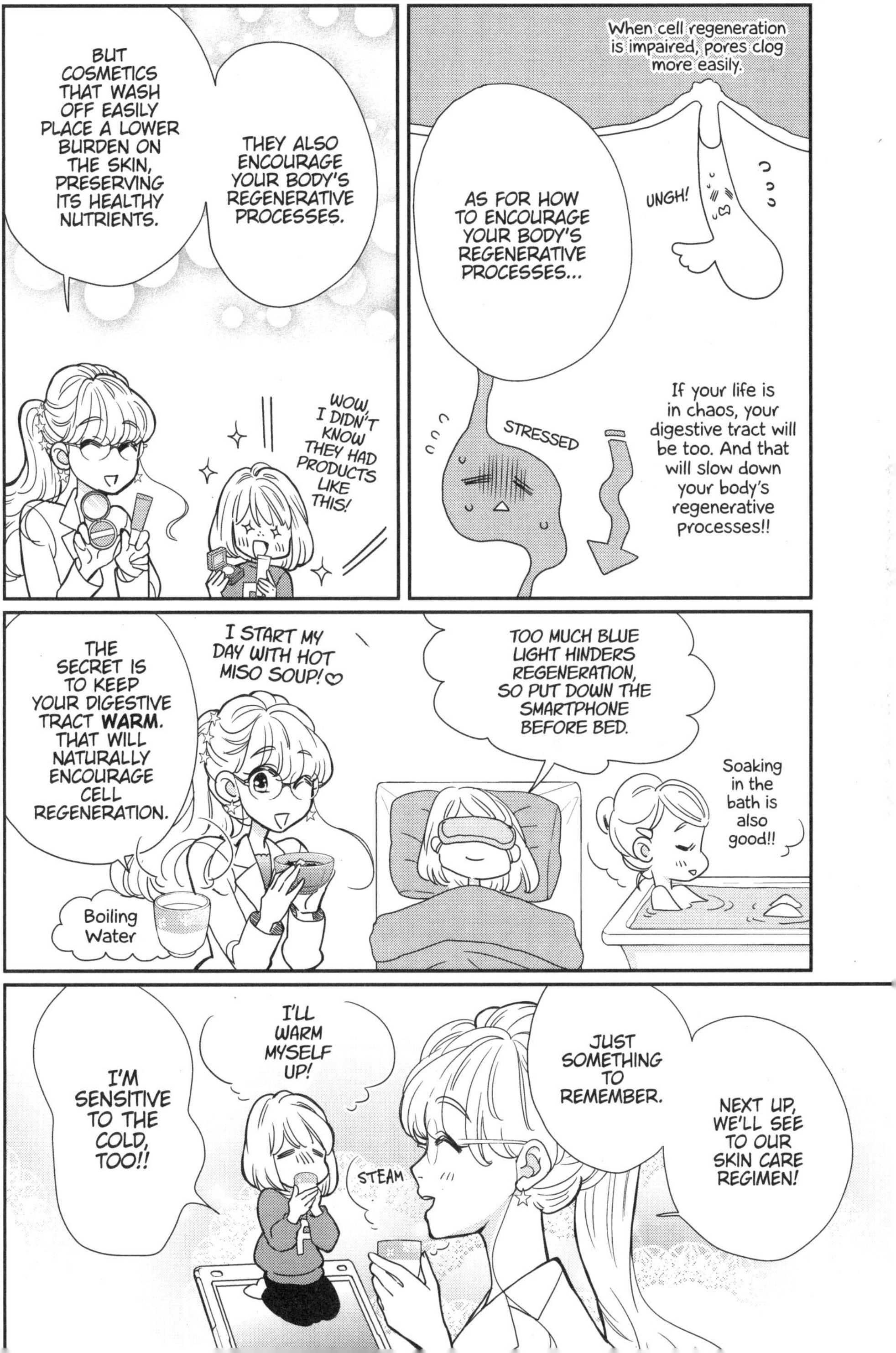

BUT COSMETICS THAT WASH OFF EASILY PLACE A LOWER BURDEN ON THE SKIN, PRESERVING ITS HEALTHY NUTRIENTS.
THEY ALSO ENCOURAGE YOUR BODY'S REGENERATIVE PROCESSES.
WOW, I DIDN'T KNOW THEY HAD PRODUCTS LIKE THIS!
When cell regeneration is impaired, pores clog more easily.
UNGH!
AS FOR HOW TO ENCOURAGE YOUR BODY'S REGENERATIVE PROCESSES...
STRESSED
If your life is in chaos, your digestive tract will be too. And that will slow down your body's regenerative processes!!
THE SECRET IS TO KEEP YOUR DIGESTIVE TRACT WARM. THAT WILL NATURALLY ENCOURAGE CELL REGENERATION.
I START MY DAY WITH HOT MISO SOUP!
Boiling Water
TOO MUCH BLUE LIGHT HINDERS REGENERATION, SO PUT DOWN THE SMARTPHONE BEFORE BED.
Soaking in the bath is also good!!
I'M SENSITIVE TO THE COLD, TOO!!
I'LL WARM MYSELF UP!
STEAM
JUST SOMETHING TO REMEMBER.
NEXT UP, WE'LL SEE TO OUR SKIN CARE REGIMEN!

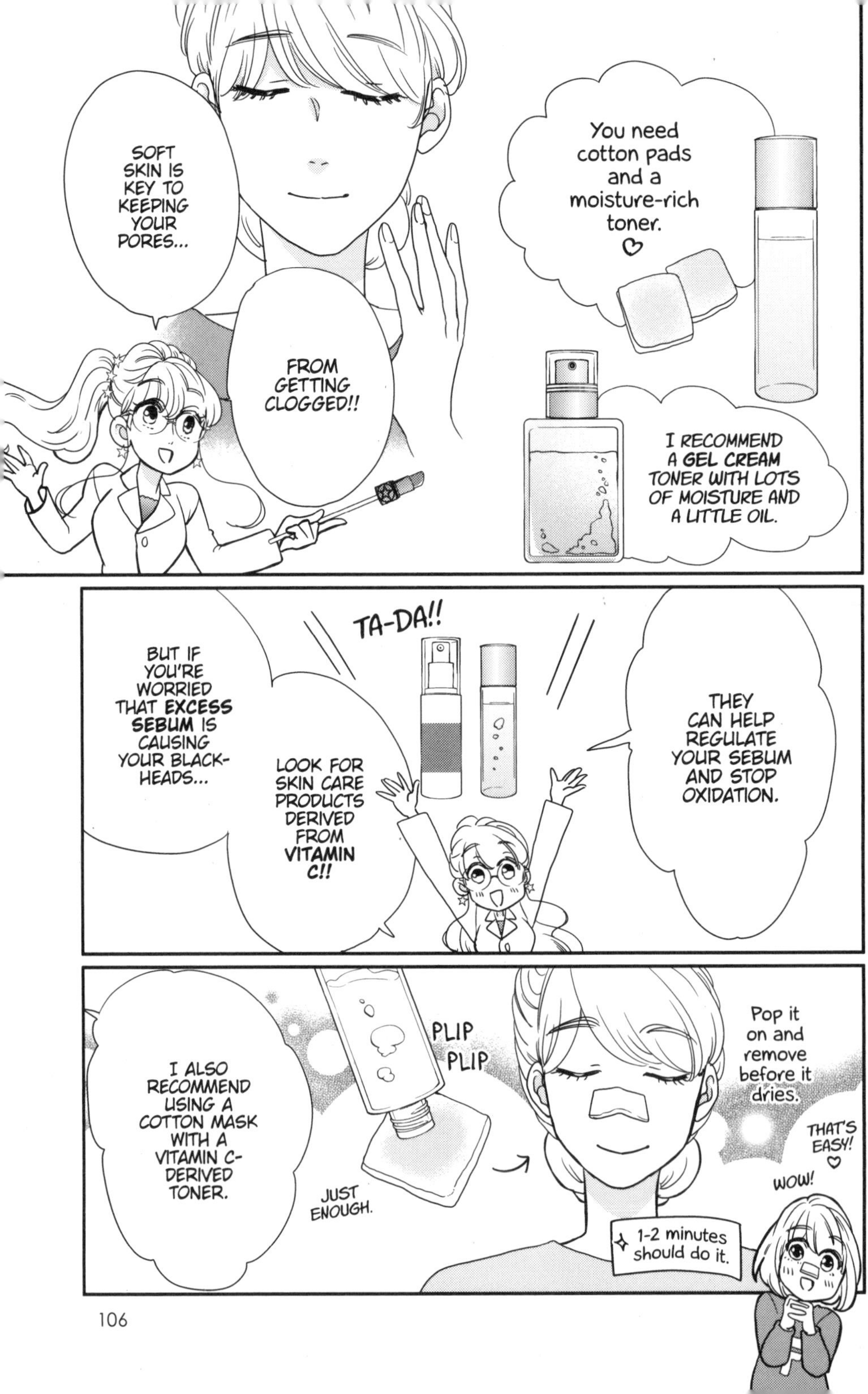
SOFT SKIN IS KEY TO KEEPING YOUR PORES...
FROM GETTING CLOGGED!!
You need cotton pads and a moisture-rich toner. ♡
I RECOMMEND A **GEL CREAM** TONER WITH LOTS OF MOISTURE AND A LITTLE OIL.
BUT IF YOU'RE WORRIED THAT **EXCESS SEBUM** IS CAUSING YOUR BLACK-HEADS...
LOOK FOR SKIN CARE PRODUCTS DERIVED FROM **VITAMIN C!!**
TA-DA!!
THEY CAN HELP REGULATE YOUR SEBUM AND STOP OXIDATION.
I ALSO RECOMMEND USING A COTTON MASK WITH A VITAMIN C-DERIVED TONER.
PLIP PLIP
JUST ENOUGH.
Pop it on and remove before it dries.
1-2 minutes should do it.
THAT'S EASY! ♡
WOW!

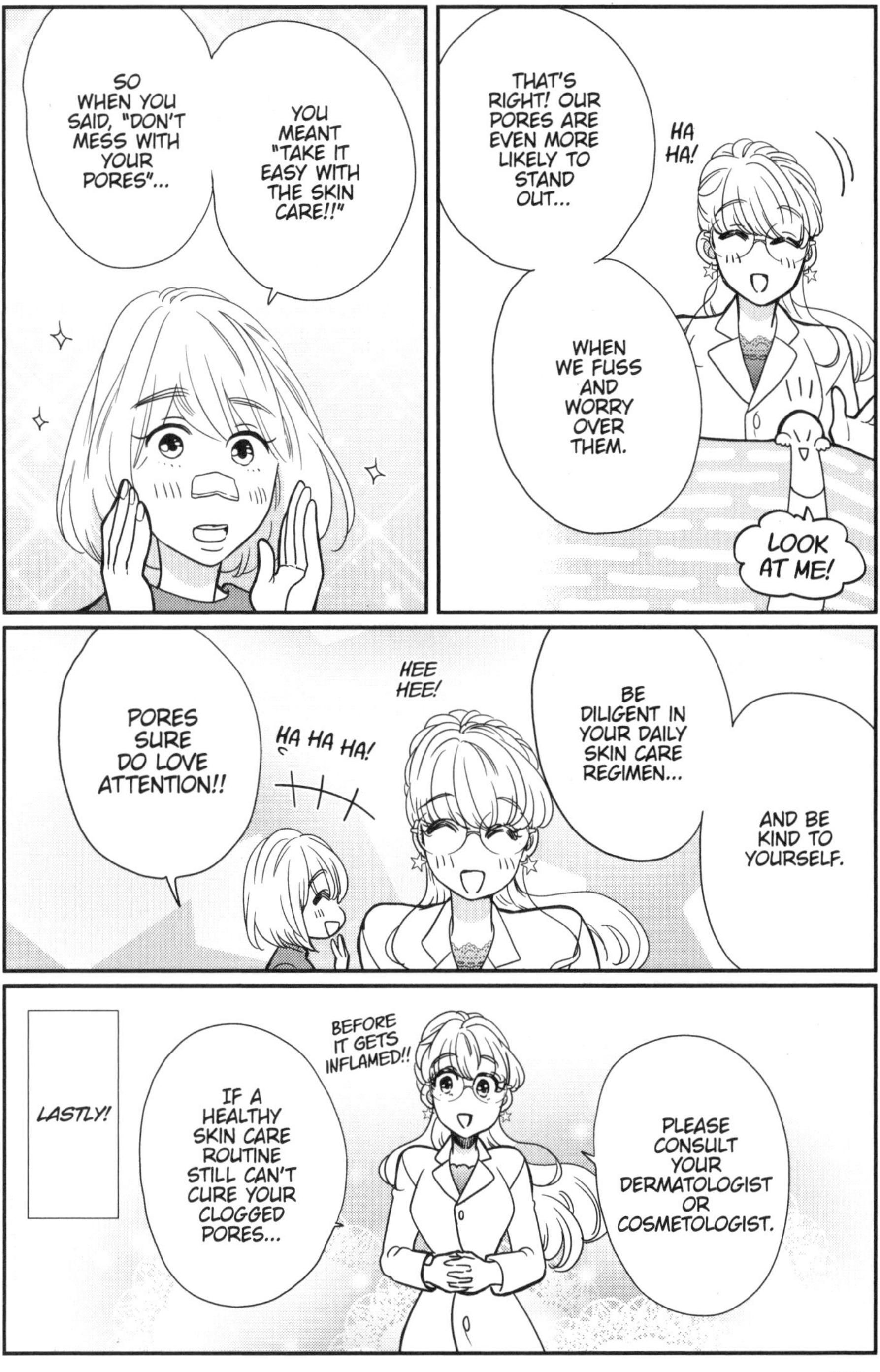
SO WHEN YOU SAID, "DON'T MESS WITH YOUR PORES"...
YOU MEANT "TAKE IT EASY WITH THE SKIN CARE!!"
THAT'S RIGHT! OUR PORES ARE EVEN MORE LIKELY TO STAND OUT...
HA HA!
WHEN WE FUSS AND WORRY OVER THEM.
LOOK AT ME!
PORES SURE DO LOVE ATTENTION!!
HA HA HA!
HEE HEE!
BE DILIGENT IN YOUR DAILY SKIN CARE REGIMEN...
AND BE KIND TO YOURSELF.
LASTLY!
IF A HEALTHY SKIN CARE ROUTINE STILL CAN'T CURE YOUR CLOGGED PORES...
BEFORE IT GETS INFLAMED!!
PLEASE CONSULT YOUR DERMATOLOGIST OR COSMETOLOGIST.

Let's Ask Rokka-Sensei!

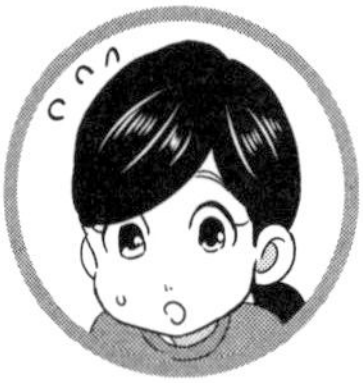

Q. I'm young, but I'm worried about the eventual signs of aging. What sort of skin care regimen should I start now to protect my skin?

A. You can certainly use some anti-aging products if you want, but the most important thing is to continue your skin care regimen. Pay attention to the products you use and apply the correct amount.

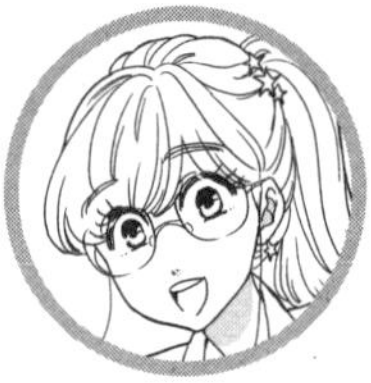

Lesson 12: Eye Makeup for Beginners ①

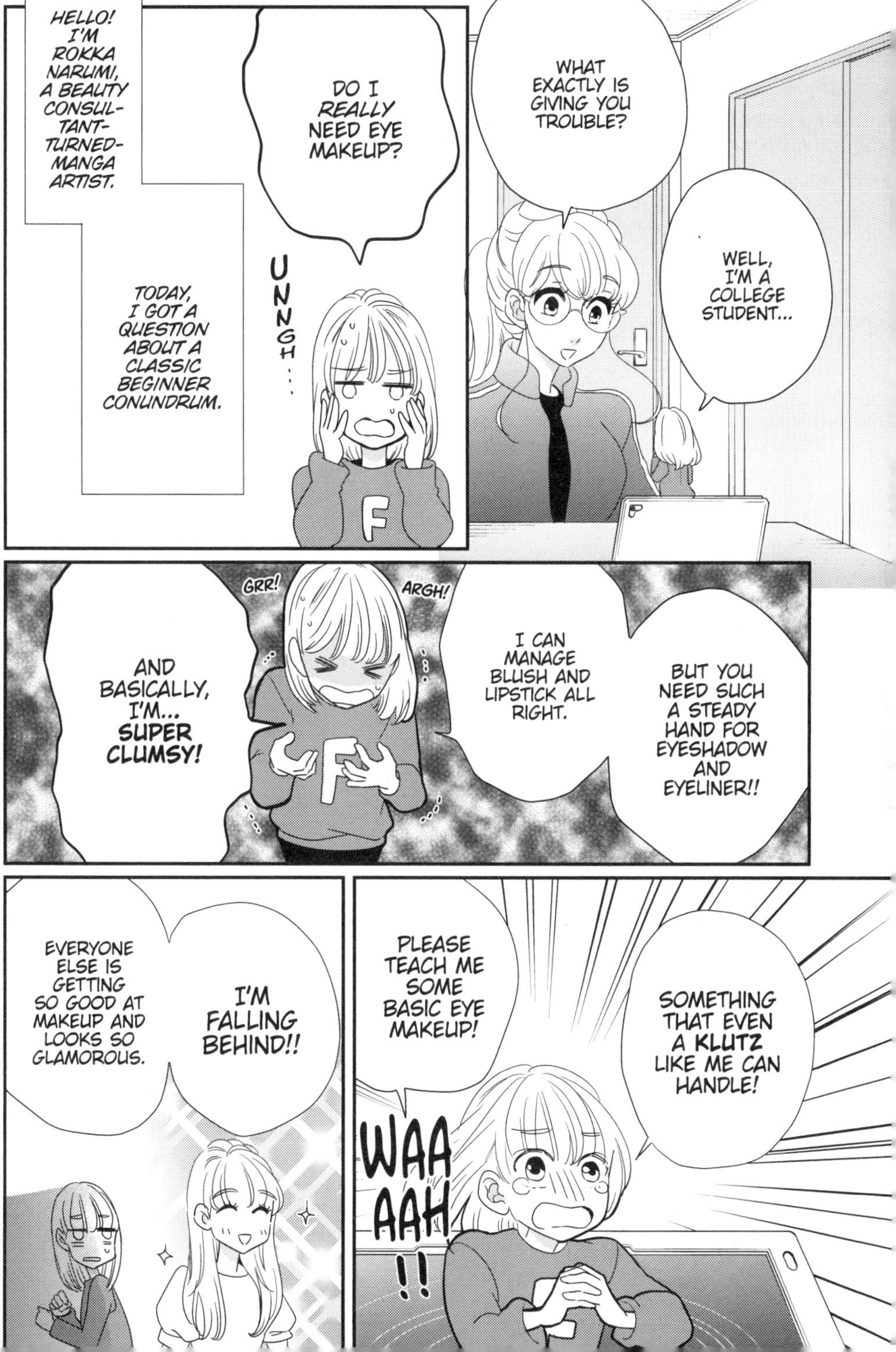

HELLO! I'M ROKKA NARUMI, A BEAUTY CONSUL-TANT-TURNED-MANGA ARTIST.
TODAY, I GOT A QUESTION ABOUT A CLASSIC BEGINNER CONUNDRUM.
DO I REALLY NEED EYE MAKEUP?
UNNGH...
WHAT EXACTLY IS GIVING YOU TROUBLE?
WELL, I'M A COLLEGE STUDENT...
AND BASICALLY, I'M... SUPER CLUMSY!
GRR!
ARGH!
I CAN MANAGE BLUSH AND LIPSTICK ALL RIGHT.
BUT YOU NEED SUCH A STEADY HAND FOR EYESHADOW AND EYELINER!!
EVERYONE ELSE IS GETTING SO GOOD AT MAKEUP AND LOOKS SO GLAMOROUS.
I'M FALLING BEHIND!!
PLEASE TEACH ME SOME BASIC EYE MAKEUP!
SOMETHING THAT EVEN A KLUTZ LIKE ME CAN HANDLE!
WAAAAH!!

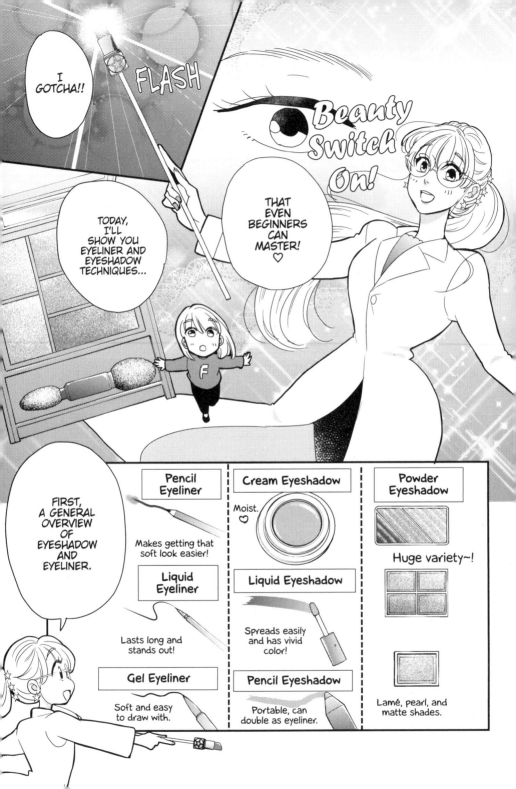

I GOTCHA!!

FLASH

Beauty Switch On!

TODAY, I'LL SHOW YOU EYELINER AND EYESHADOW TECHNIQUES...

THAT EVEN BEGINNERS CAN MASTER! ♡

FIRST, A GENERAL OVERVIEW OF EYESHADOW AND EYELINER.

Pencil Eyeliner	**Cream Eyeshadow**	**Powder Eyeshadow**
Makes getting that soft look easier!	Moist. ♡	Huge variety~!
Liquid Eyeliner	**Liquid Eyeshadow**	
Lasts long and stands out!	Spreads easily and has vivid color!	
Gel Eyeliner	**Pencil Eyeshadow**	Lamé, pearl, and matte shades.
Soft and easy to draw with.	Portable, can double as eyeliner.	

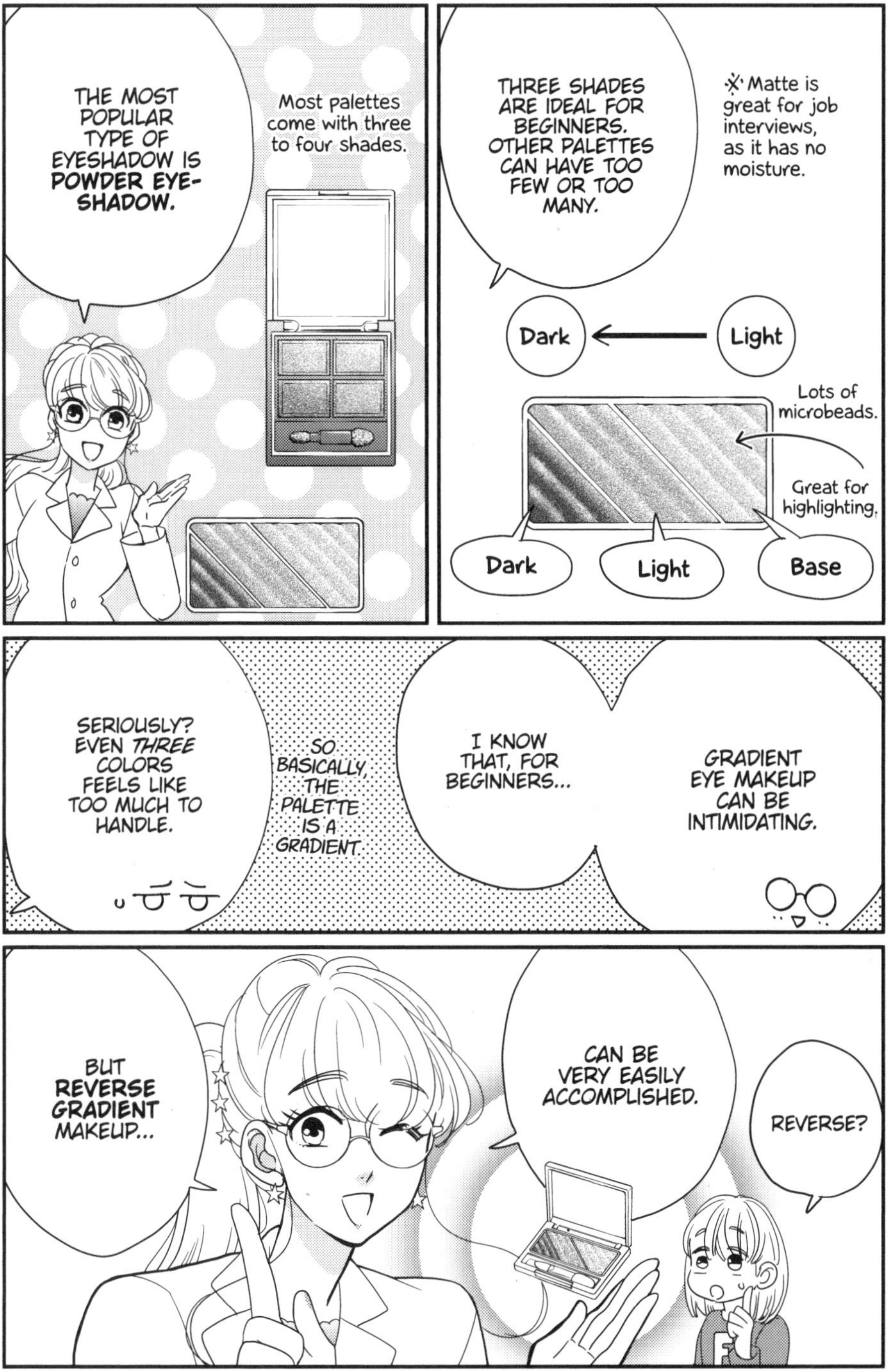
THE MOST POPULAR TYPE OF EYESHADOW IS POWDER EYE-SHADOW.
Most palettes come with three to four shades.
THREE SHADES ARE IDEAL FOR BEGINNERS. OTHER PALETTES CAN HAVE TOO FEW OR TOO MANY.
※ Matte is great for job interviews, as it has no moisture.
Dark
Light
Lots of microbeads.
Great for highlighting.
Dark
Light
Base
SERIOUSLY? EVEN THREE COLORS FEELS LIKE TOO MUCH TO HANDLE.
SO BASICALLY, THE PALETTE IS A GRADIENT.
I KNOW THAT, FOR BEGINNERS...
GRADIENT EYE MAKEUP CAN BE INTIMIDATING.
BUT REVERSE GRADIENT MAKEUP...
CAN BE VERY EASILY ACCOMPLISHED.
REVERSE?

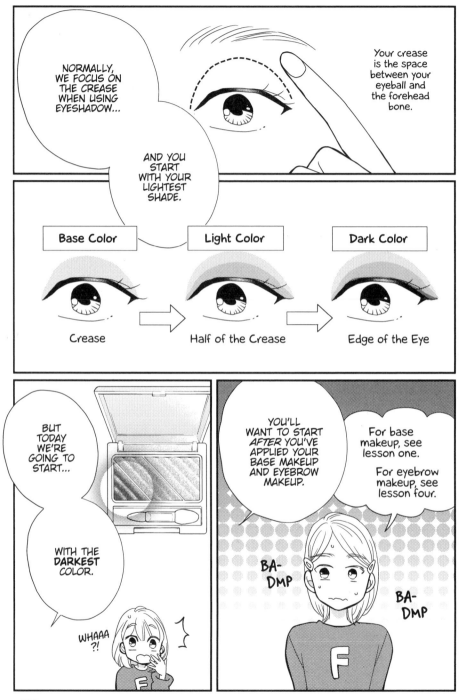

NORMALLY, WE FOCUS ON THE CREASE WHEN USING EYESHADOW...

Your crease is the space between your eyeball and the forehead bone.

AND YOU START WITH YOUR LIGHTEST SHADE.

Base Color

Light Color

Dark Color

Crease

Half of the Crease

Edge of the Eye

BUT TODAY WE'RE GOING TO START...

WITH THE **DARKEST** COLOR.

WHAAA ?!

YOU'LL WANT TO START *AFTER* YOU'VE APPLIED YOUR BASE MAKEUP AND EYEBROW MAKEUP.

For base makeup, see lesson one.

For eyebrow makeup, see lesson four.

BA-DMP

BA-DMP

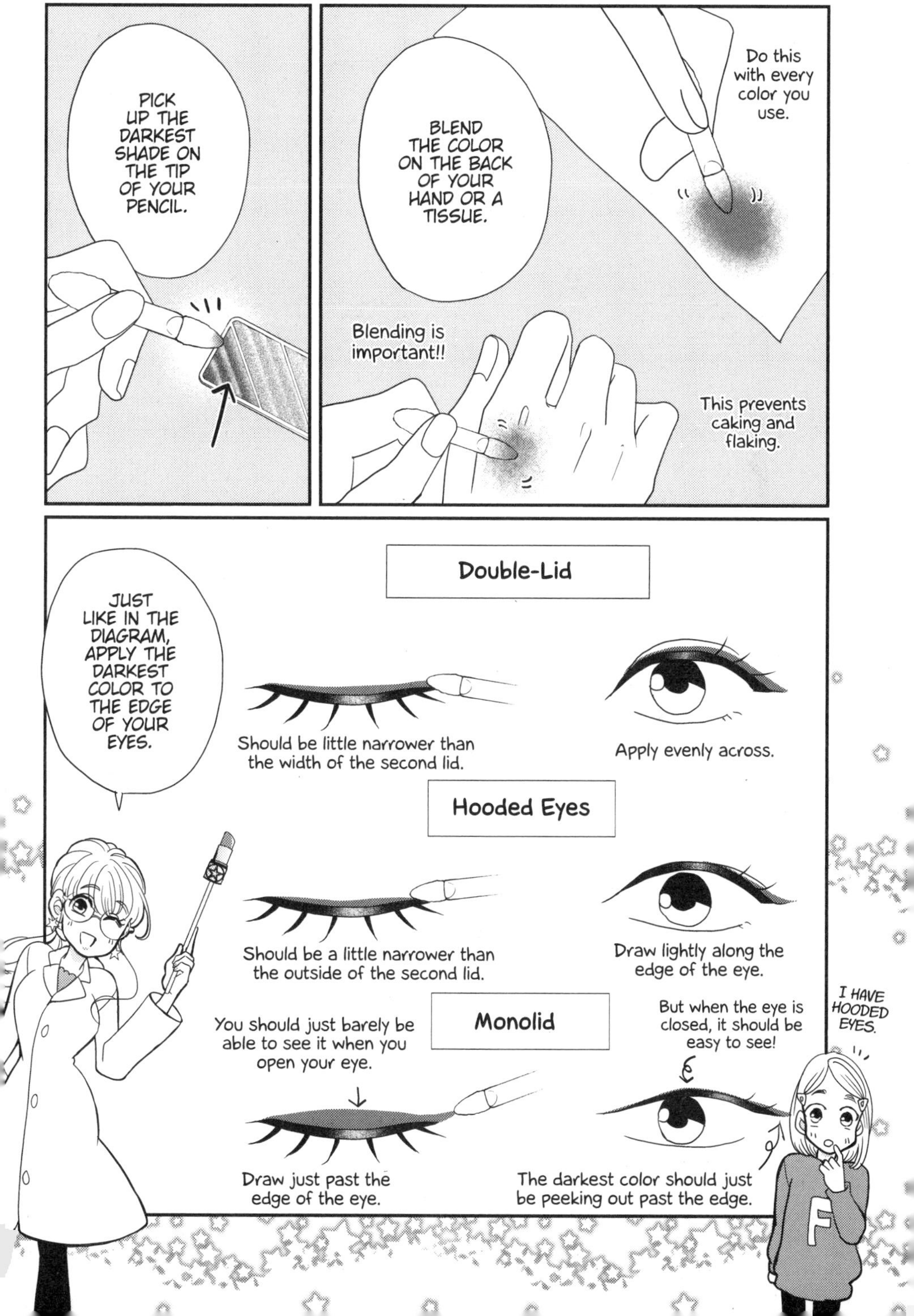

PICK UP THE DARKEST SHADE ON THE TIP OF YOUR PENCIL.
BLEND THE COLOR ON THE BACK OF YOUR HAND OR A TISSUE.
Do this with every color you use.
Blending is important!!
This prevents caking and flaking.
JUST LIKE IN THE DIAGRAM, APPLY THE DARKEST COLOR TO THE EDGE OF YOUR EYES.
Double-Lid
Should be little narrower than the width of the second lid.
Apply evenly across.
Hooded Eyes
Should be a little narrower than the outside of the second lid.
Draw lightly along the edge of the eye.
Monolid
You should just barely be able to see it when you open your eye.
But when the eye is closed, it should be easy to see!
I HAVE HOODED EYES.
Draw just past the edge of the eye.
The darkest color should just be peeking out past the edge.
F

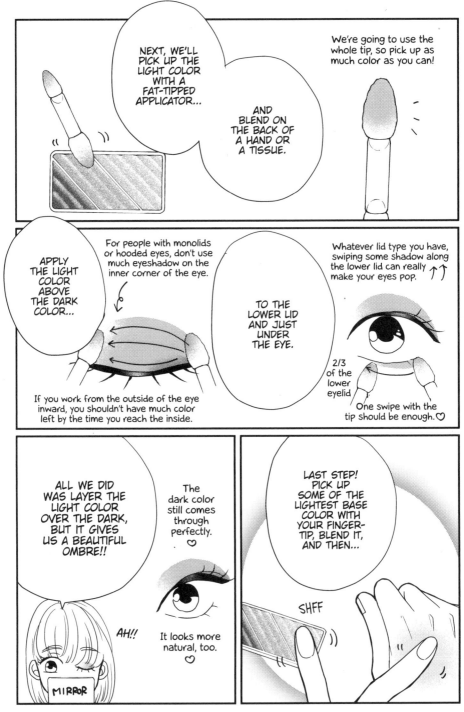

NEXT, WE'LL PICK UP THE LIGHT COLOR WITH A FAT-TIPPED APPLICATOR...

AND BLEND ON THE BACK OF A HAND OR A TISSUE.

We're going to use the whole tip, so pick up as much color as you can!

APPLY THE LIGHT COLOR ABOVE THE DARK COLOR...

For people with monolids or hooded eyes, don't use much eyeshadow on the inner corner of the eye.

If you work from the outside of the eye inward, you shouldn't have much color left by the time you reach the inside.

TO THE LOWER LID AND JUST UNDER THE EYE.

Whatever lid type you have, swiping some shadow along the lower lid can really make your eyes pop.

2/3 of the lower eyelid

One swipe with the tip should be enough. ♡

ALL WE DID WAS LAYER THE LIGHT COLOR OVER THE DARK, BUT IT GIVES US A BEAUTIFUL OMBRE!!

The dark color still comes through perfectly. ♡

AH!!

It looks more natural, too. ♡

MIRROR

LAST STEP! PICK UP SOME OF THE LIGHTEST BASE COLOR WITH YOUR FINGER-TIP, BLEND IT, AND THEN...

SHFF

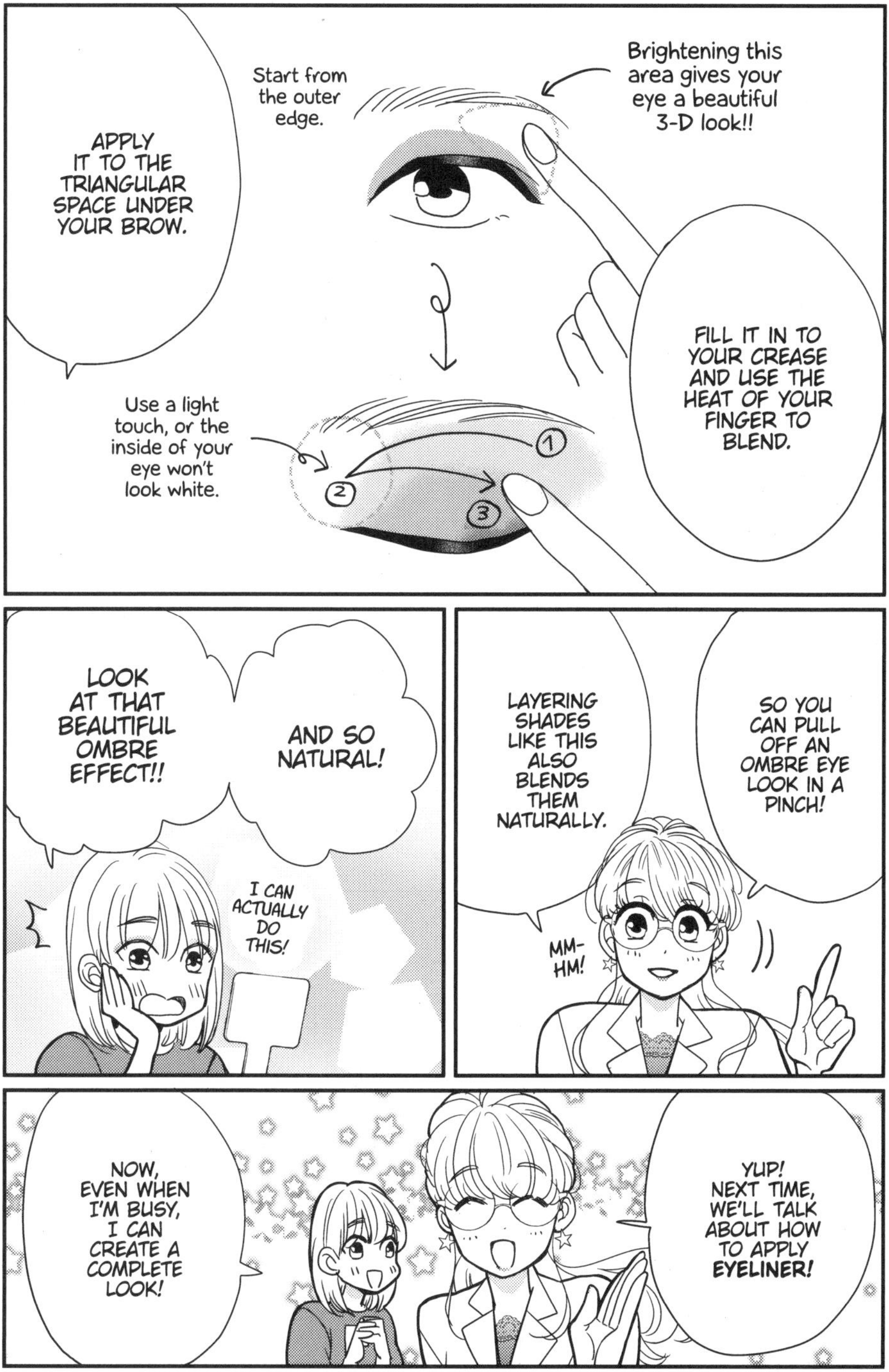
APPLY IT TO THE TRIANGULAR SPACE UNDER YOUR BROW.
Start from the outer edge.
Brightening this area gives your eye a beautiful 3-D look!!
FILL IT IN TO YOUR CREASE AND USE THE HEAT OF YOUR FINGER TO BLEND.
Use a light touch, or the inside of your eye won't look white.
1
2
3
LOOK AT THAT BEAUTIFUL OMBRE EFFECT!!
AND SO NATURAL!
I CAN ACTUALLY DO THIS!
LAYERING SHADES LIKE THIS ALSO BLENDS THEM NATURALLY.
SO YOU CAN PULL OFF AN OMBRE EYE LOOK IN A PINCH!
MM-HM!
NOW, EVEN WHEN I'M BUSY, I CAN CREATE A COMPLETE LOOK!
YUP! NEXT TIME, WE'LL TALK ABOUT HOW TO APPLY **EYELINER!**

Let's Ask Rokka-Sensei!

 Q. A lot of people use their fingers to apply eyeshadow or blush. But some people say it's better to use a brush. Who's right?

A. When you use your finger, your body heat helps to blend the brush or eyeshadow, giving your skin luster and some natural-looking unevenness. On the other hand, using a brush lets you apply product more evenly. I'd say it depends on the look you're going for!

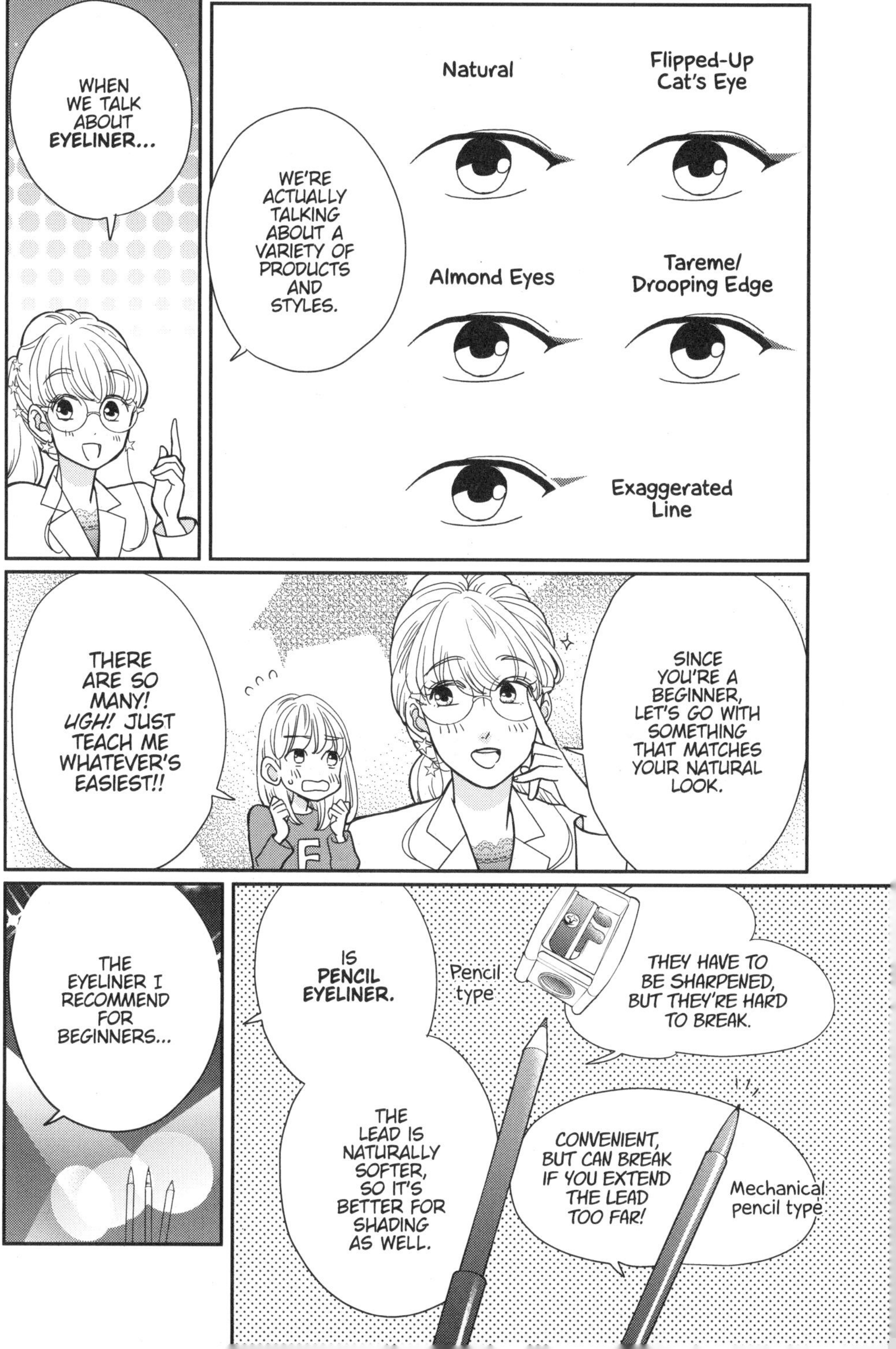
WHEN WE TALK ABOUT **EYELINER...**
WE'RE ACTUALLY TALKING ABOUT A VARIETY OF PRODUCTS AND STYLES.
Natural
Flipped-Up Cat's Eye
Almond Eyes
Tareme/ Drooping Edge
Exaggerated Line
THERE ARE SO MANY! *UGH!* JUST TEACH ME WHATEVER'S EASIEST!!
SINCE YOU'RE A BEGINNER, LET'S GO WITH SOMETHING THAT MATCHES YOUR NATURAL LOOK.
THE EYELINER I RECOMMEND FOR BEGINNERS...
IS **PENCIL EYELINER.**
Pencil type
THEY HAVE TO BE SHARPENED, BUT THEY'RE HARD TO BREAK.
THE LEAD IS NATURALLY SOFTER, SO IT'S BETTER FOR SHADING AS WELL.
CONVENIENT, BUT CAN BREAK IF YOU EXTEND THE LEAD TOO FAR!
Mechanical pencil type

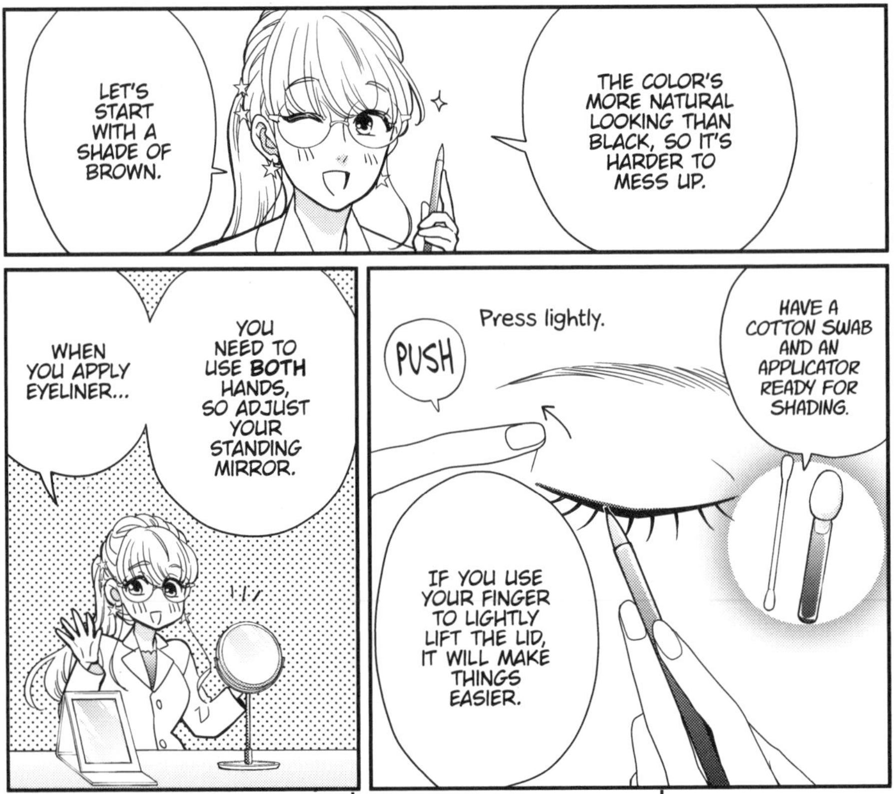
LET'S START WITH A SHADE OF BROWN.
THE COLOR'S MORE NATURAL LOOKING THAN BLACK, SO IT'S HARDER TO MESS UP.
WHEN YOU APPLY EYELINER...
YOU NEED TO USE **BOTH** HANDS, SO ADJUST YOUR STANDING MIRROR.
Press lightly.
PUSH
IF YOU USE YOUR FINGER TO LIGHTLY LIFT THE LID, IT WILL MAKE THINGS EASIER.
HAVE A COTTON SWAB AND AN APPLICATOR READY FOR SHADING.

NATURAL EYELINES FOR EACH EYE TYPE

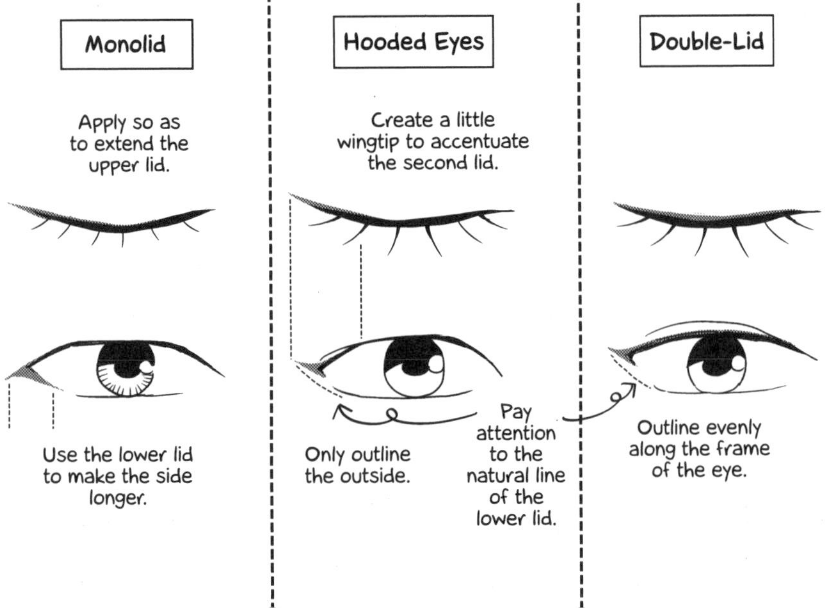
Monolid
Apply so as to extend the upper lid.
Use the lower lid to make the side longer.
Hooded Eyes
Create a little wingtip to accentuate the second lid.
Only outline the outside.
Pay attention to the natural line of the lower lid.
Double-Lid
Outline evenly along the frame of the eye.

AS YOU APPLY YOUR EYELINER, KEEP IN MIND... THE **SHAPE** THAT YOU'RE GOING FOR.

Interior

Exterior

FIRST, APPLY LINER TO THE EDGE OF THE UPPER LID.

DRAW FROM JUST PAST THE OUTER EDGE OF THE EYE AND WORK INWARD.

Don't try to draw one continuous line. You'll need to use a series of short lines.

NEXT, WORK FROM THE INSIDE CORNER OF THE EYE TOWARD THE CENTER.

※People with hooded eyes and monolids don't need to line the innermost corner.

THEN WE FINISH WITH THE CENTER OF THE UPPER LID.

Fill in by going left-to-right.

☆Important!
Open your eyes periodically to check your progress.

BLINK ☆ BLINK ☆

NOW WE'VE FINISHED A BASIC EYELINE!

OH! SO WE APPLY WITH SEVERAL SMALLER LINES, RATHER THAN ONE LONG LINE!

SO THE LINES AREN'T MESSY!

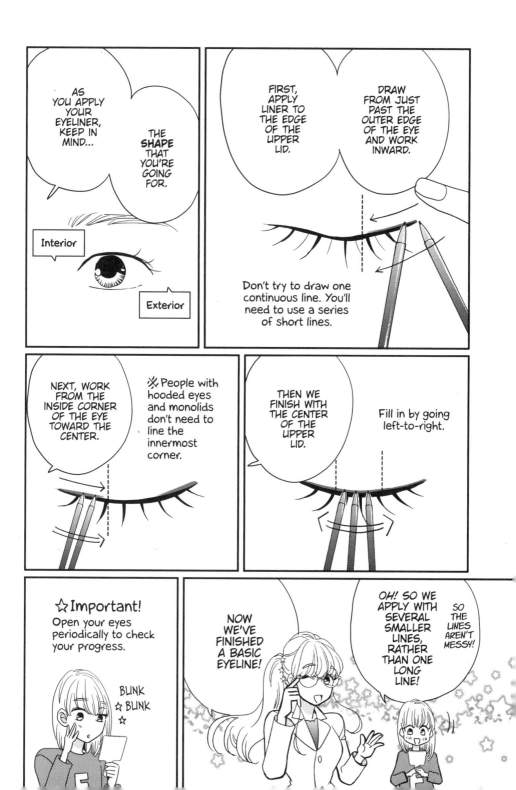

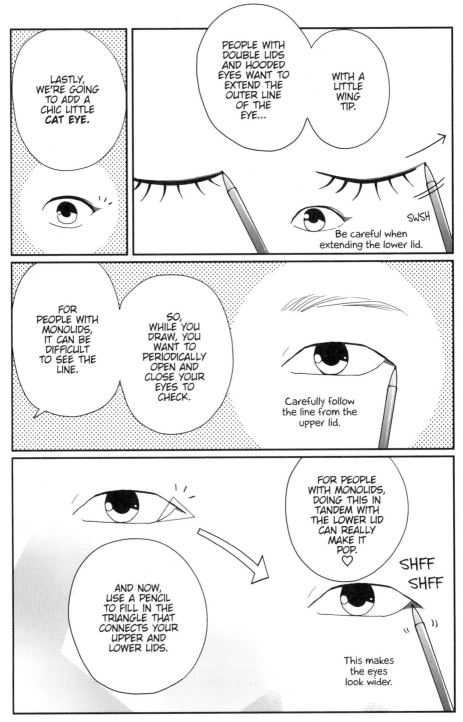

LASTLY, WE'RE GOING TO ADD A CHIC LITTLE **CAT EYE.**

PEOPLE WITH DOUBLE LIDS AND HOODED EYES WANT TO EXTEND THE OUTER LINE OF THE EYE...

WITH A LITTLE WING TIP.

SWSH

Be careful when extending the lower lid.

FOR PEOPLE WITH MONOLIDS, IT CAN BE DIFFICULT TO SEE THE LINE.

SO, WHILE YOU DRAW, YOU WANT TO PERIODICALLY OPEN AND CLOSE YOUR EYES TO CHECK.

Carefully follow the line from the upper lid.

FOR PEOPLE WITH MONOLIDS, DOING THIS IN TANDEM WITH THE LOWER LID CAN REALLY MAKE IT POP. ♡

AND NOW, USE A PENCIL TO FILL IN THE TRIANGLE THAT CONNECTS YOUR UPPER AND LOWER LIDS.

SHFF SHFF

This makes the eyes look wider.

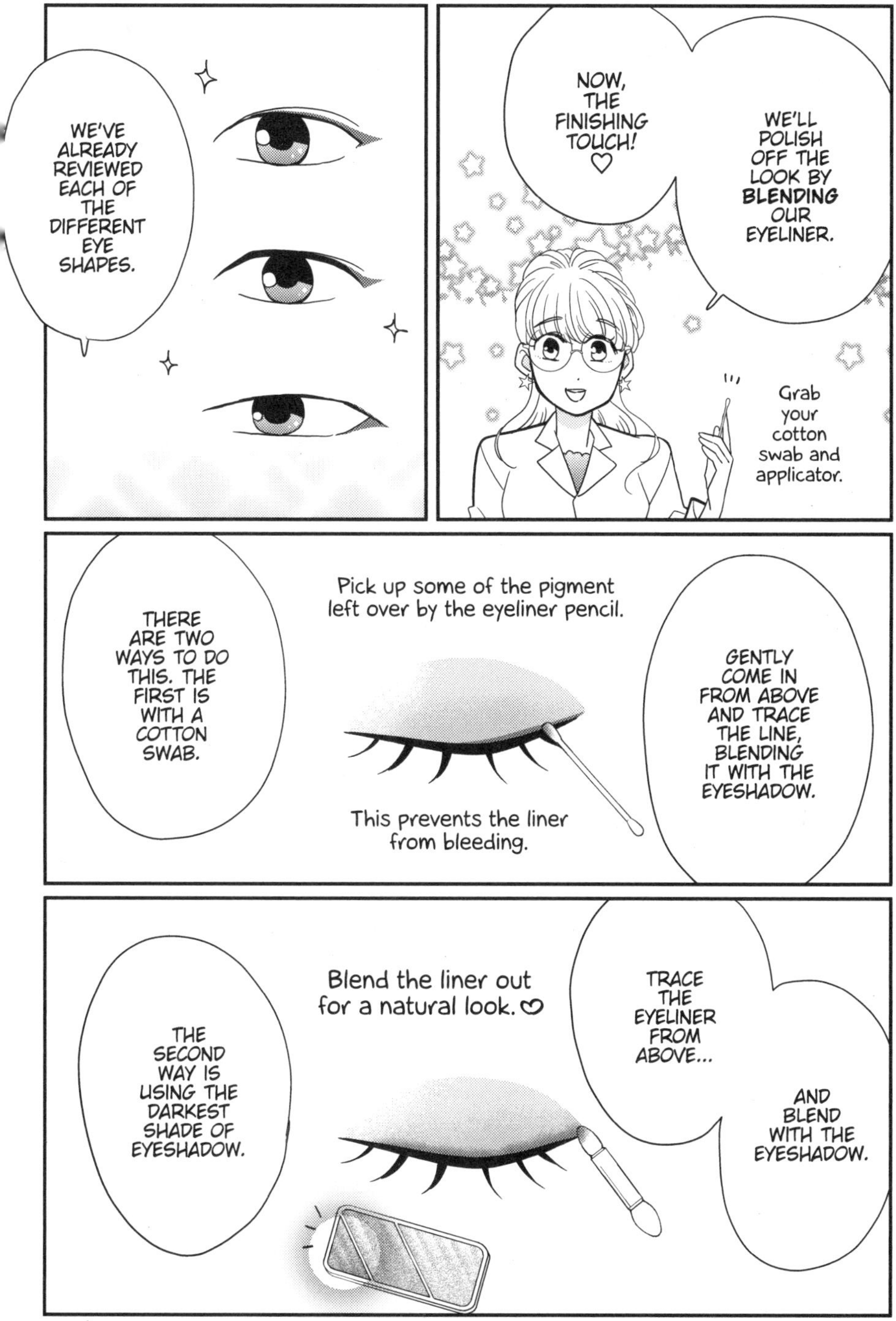

WE'VE ALREADY REVIEWED EACH OF THE DIFFERENT EYE SHAPES.
NOW, THE FINISHING TOUCH! ♡
WE'LL POLISH OFF THE LOOK BY **BLENDING** OUR EYELINER.
Grab your cotton swab and applicator.
THERE ARE TWO WAYS TO DO THIS. THE FIRST IS WITH A COTTON SWAB.
Pick up some of the pigment left over by the eyeliner pencil.
This prevents the liner from bleeding.
GENTLY COME IN FROM ABOVE AND TRACE THE LINE, BLENDING IT WITH THE EYESHADOW.
THE SECOND WAY IS USING THE DARKEST SHADE OF EYESHADOW.
Blend the liner out for a natural look. ♡
TRACE THE EYELINER FROM ABOVE...
AND BLEND WITH THE EYESHADOW.

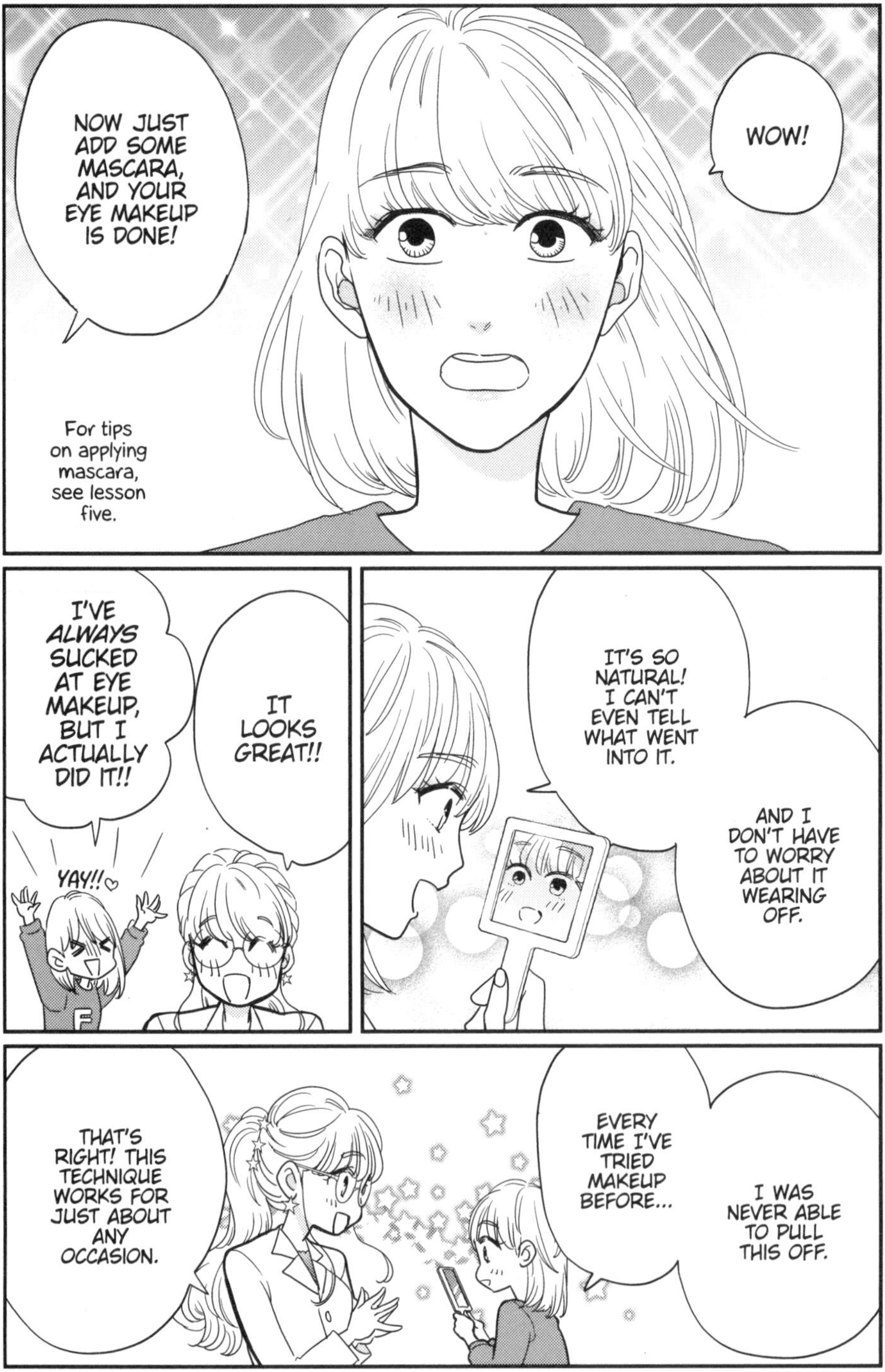
NOW JUST ADD SOME MASCARA, AND YOUR EYE MAKEUP IS DONE!
WOW!
For tips on applying mascara, see lesson five.
I'VE ALWAYS SUCKED AT EYE MAKEUP, BUT I ACTUALLY DID IT!!
YAY!!♡
IT LOOKS GREAT!!
IT'S SO NATURAL! I CAN'T EVEN TELL WHAT WENT INTO IT.
AND I DON'T HAVE TO WORRY ABOUT IT WEARING OFF.
THAT'S RIGHT! THIS TECHNIQUE WORKS FOR JUST ABOUT ANY OCCASION.
EVERY TIME I'VE TRIED MAKEUP BEFORE...
I WAS NEVER ABLE TO PULL THIS OFF.

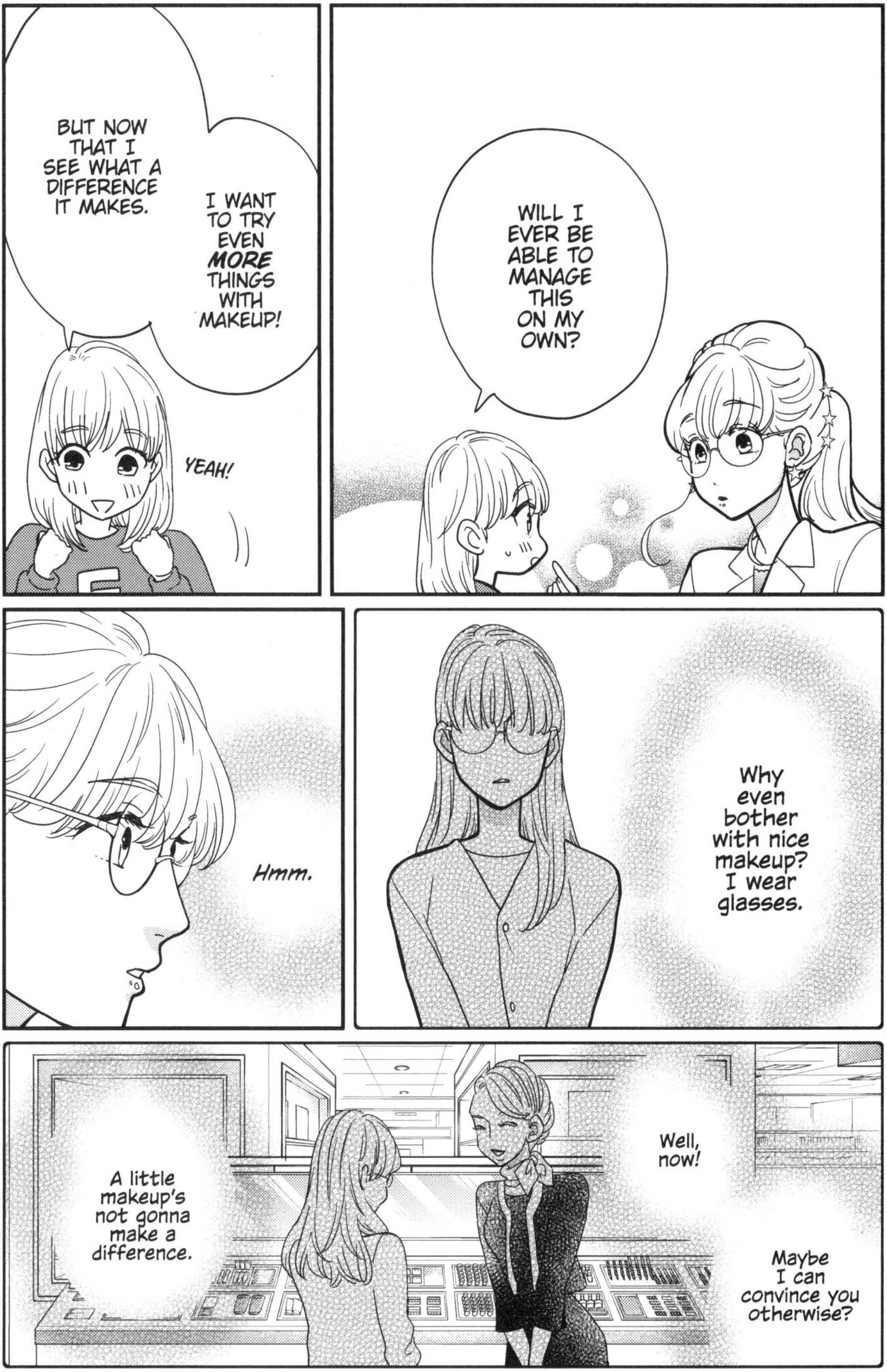

BUT NOW THAT I SEE WHAT A DIFFERENCE IT MAKES.
I WANT TO TRY EVEN MORE THINGS WITH MAKEUP!
YEAH!
WILL I EVER BE ABLE TO MANAGE THIS ON MY OWN?
Hmm.
Why even bother with nice makeup? I wear glasses.
A little makeup's not gonna make a difference.
Well, now!
Maybe I can convince you otherwise?

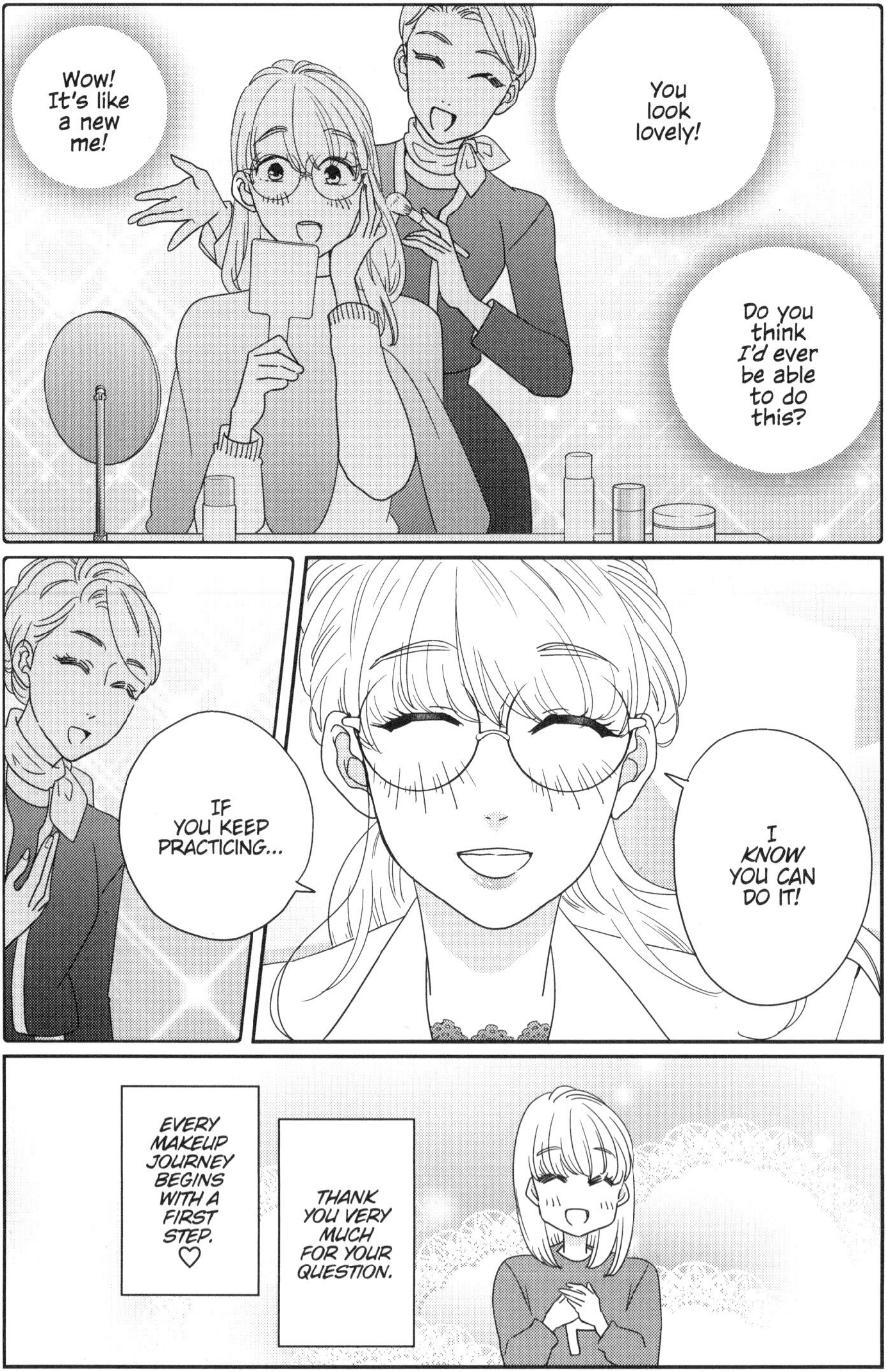

Wow! It's like a new me!
You look lovely!
Do you think *I'd* ever be able to do this?
IF YOU KEEP PRACTICING...
I *KNOW* YOU CAN DO IT!
EVERY MAKEUP JOURNEY BEGINS WITH A FIRST STEP. ♡
THANK YOU VERY MUCH FOR YOUR QUESTION.

Lesson 14: Concealer for Beginners

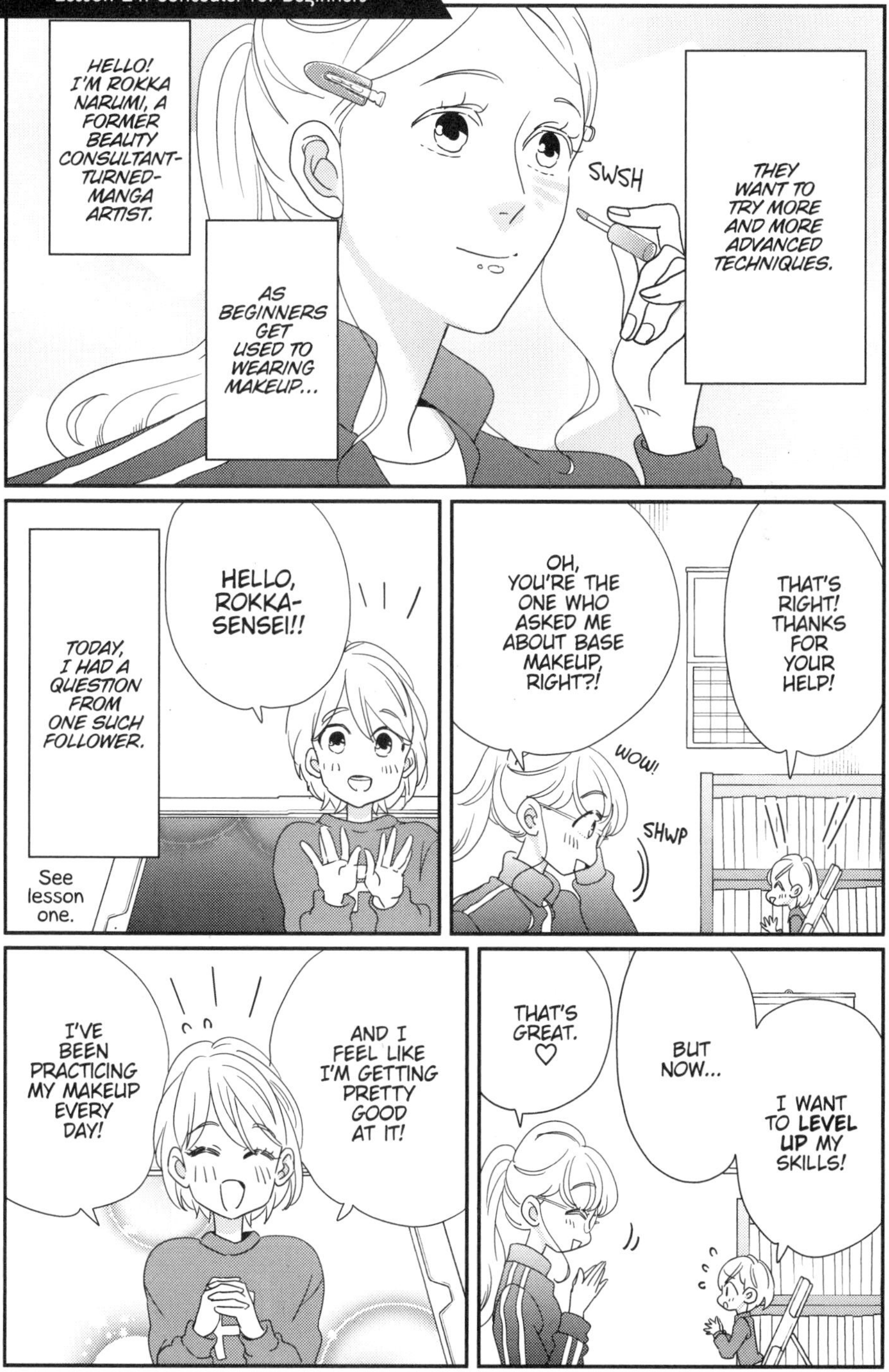
HELLO! I'M ROKKA NARUMI, A FORMER BEAUTY CONSULTANT-TURNED-MANGA ARTIST.
AS BEGINNERS GET USED TO WEARING MAKEUP...
SWSH
THEY WANT TO TRY MORE AND MORE ADVANCED TECHNIQUES.
TODAY, I HAD A QUESTION FROM ONE SUCH FOLLOWER.
See lesson one.
HELLO, ROKKA-SENSEI!!
OH, YOU'RE THE ONE WHO ASKED ME ABOUT BASE MAKEUP, RIGHT?!
WOW!
SHWP
THAT'S RIGHT! THANKS FOR YOUR HELP!
I'VE BEEN PRACTICING MY MAKEUP EVERY DAY!
AND I FEEL LIKE I'M GETTING PRETTY GOOD AT IT!
THAT'S GREAT. ♡
BUT NOW...
I WANT TO **LEVEL UP** MY SKILLS!

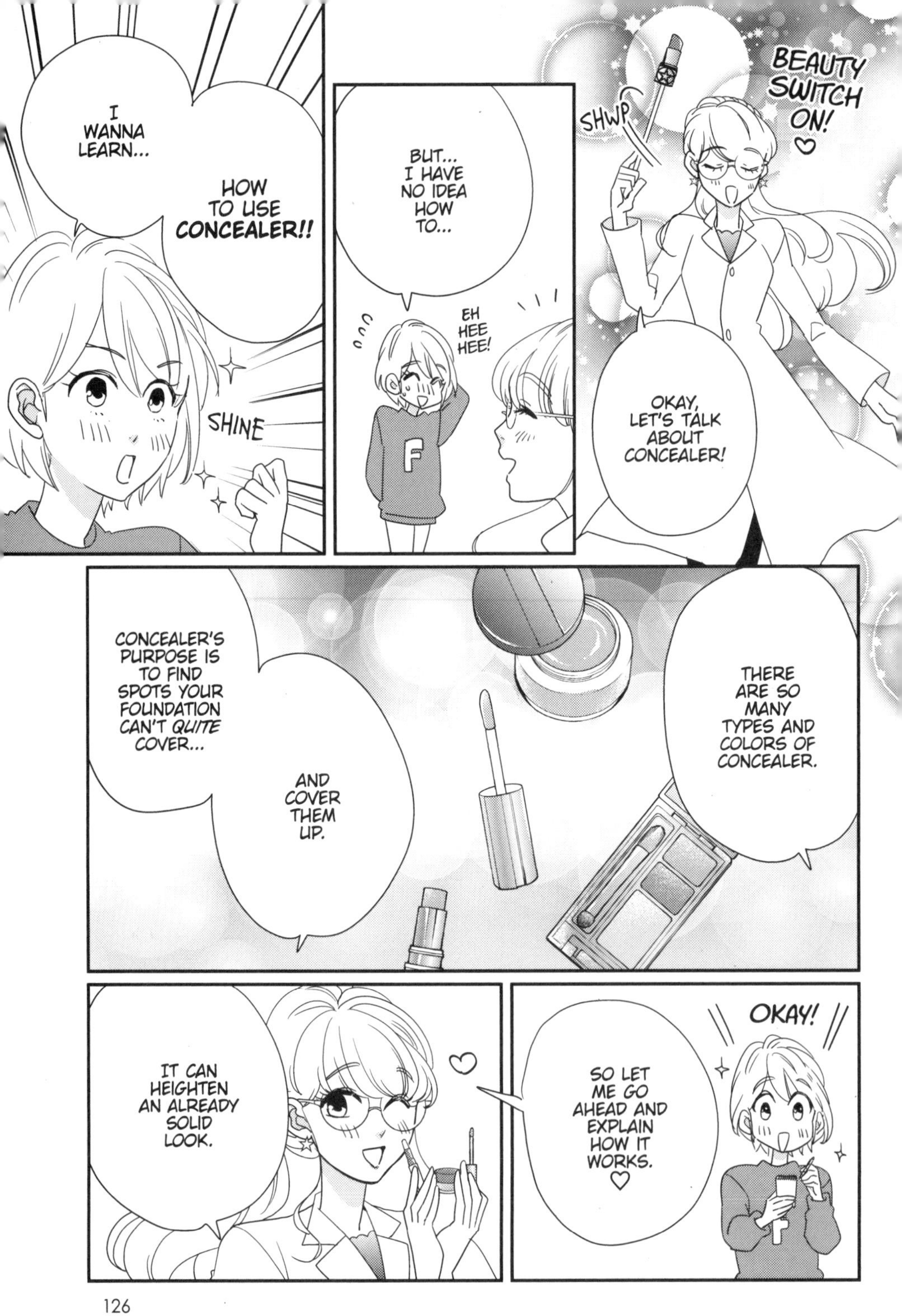
I WANNA LEARN...
HOW TO USE CONCEALER!!
SHINE
BUT... I HAVE NO IDEA HOW TO...
EH HEE HEE!
BEAUTY SWITCH ON!
SHWP
OKAY, LET'S TALK ABOUT CONCEALER!
CONCEALER'S PURPOSE IS TO FIND SPOTS YOUR FOUNDATION CAN'T QUITE COVER...
AND COVER THEM UP.
THERE ARE SO MANY TYPES AND COLORS OF CONCEALER.
IT CAN HEIGHTEN AN ALREADY SOLID LOOK.
SO LET ME GO AHEAD AND EXPLAIN HOW IT WORKS.
OKAY!

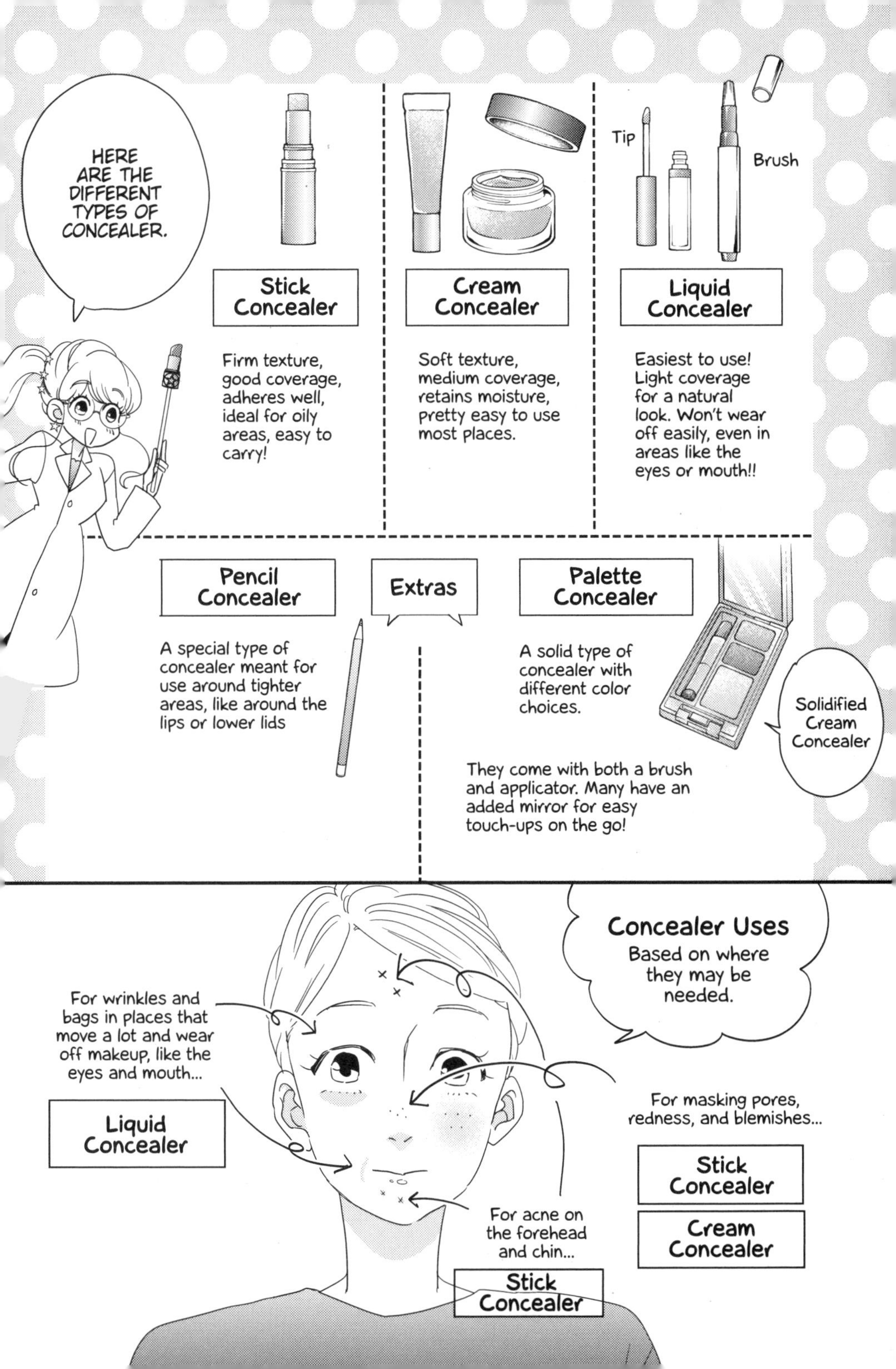

HERE ARE THE DIFFERENT TYPES OF CONCEALER.
Stick Concealer
Firm texture, good coverage, adheres well, ideal for oily areas, easy to carry!
Cream Concealer
Soft texture, medium coverage, retains moisture, pretty easy to use most places.
Tip
Brush
Liquid Concealer
Easiest to use! Light coverage for a natural look. Won't wear off easily, even in areas like the eyes or mouth!!
Extras
Pencil Concealer
A special type of concealer meant for use around tighter areas, like around the lips or lower lids
Palette Concealer
A solid type of concealer with different color choices.
Solidified Cream Concealer
They come with both a brush and applicator. Many have an added mirror for easy touch-ups on the go!
Concealer Uses
Based on where they may be needed.
For wrinkles and bags in places that move a lot and wear off makeup, like the eyes and mouth...
Liquid Concealer
For masking pores, redness, and blemishes...
Stick Concealer
Cream Concealer
For acne on the forehead and chin...
Stick Concealer

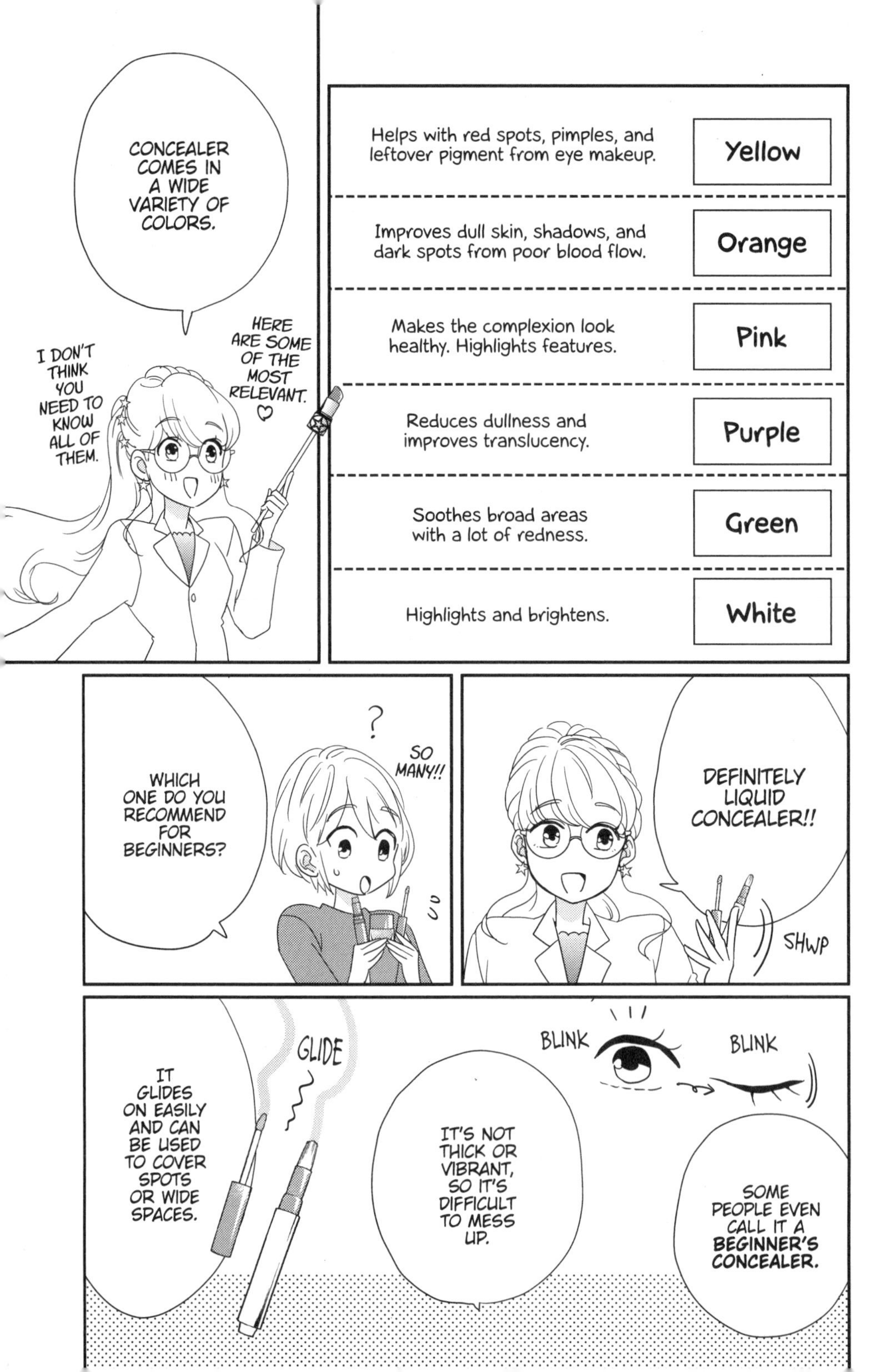
CONCEALER COMES IN A WIDE VARIETY OF COLORS.
HERE ARE SOME OF THE MOST RELEVANT. ♡
I DON'T THINK YOU NEED TO KNOW ALL OF THEM.
WHICH ONE DO YOU RECOMMEND FOR BEGINNERS?
?
SO MANY!!
DEFINITELY LIQUID CONCEALER!!
SHWP
GLIDE
IT GLIDES ON EASILY AND CAN BE USED TO COVER SPOTS OR WIDE SPACES.
IT'S NOT THICK OR VIBRANT, SO IT'S DIFFICULT TO MESS UP.
BLINK
BLINK
SOME PEOPLE EVEN CALL IT A BEGINNER'S CONCEALER.

Helps with red spots, pimples, and leftover pigment from eye makeup.	Yellow
Improves dull skin, shadows, and dark spots from poor blood flow.	Orange
Makes the complexion look healthy. Highlights features.	Pink
Reduces dullness and improves translucency.	Purple
Soothes broad areas with a lot of redness.	Green
Highlights and brightens.	White

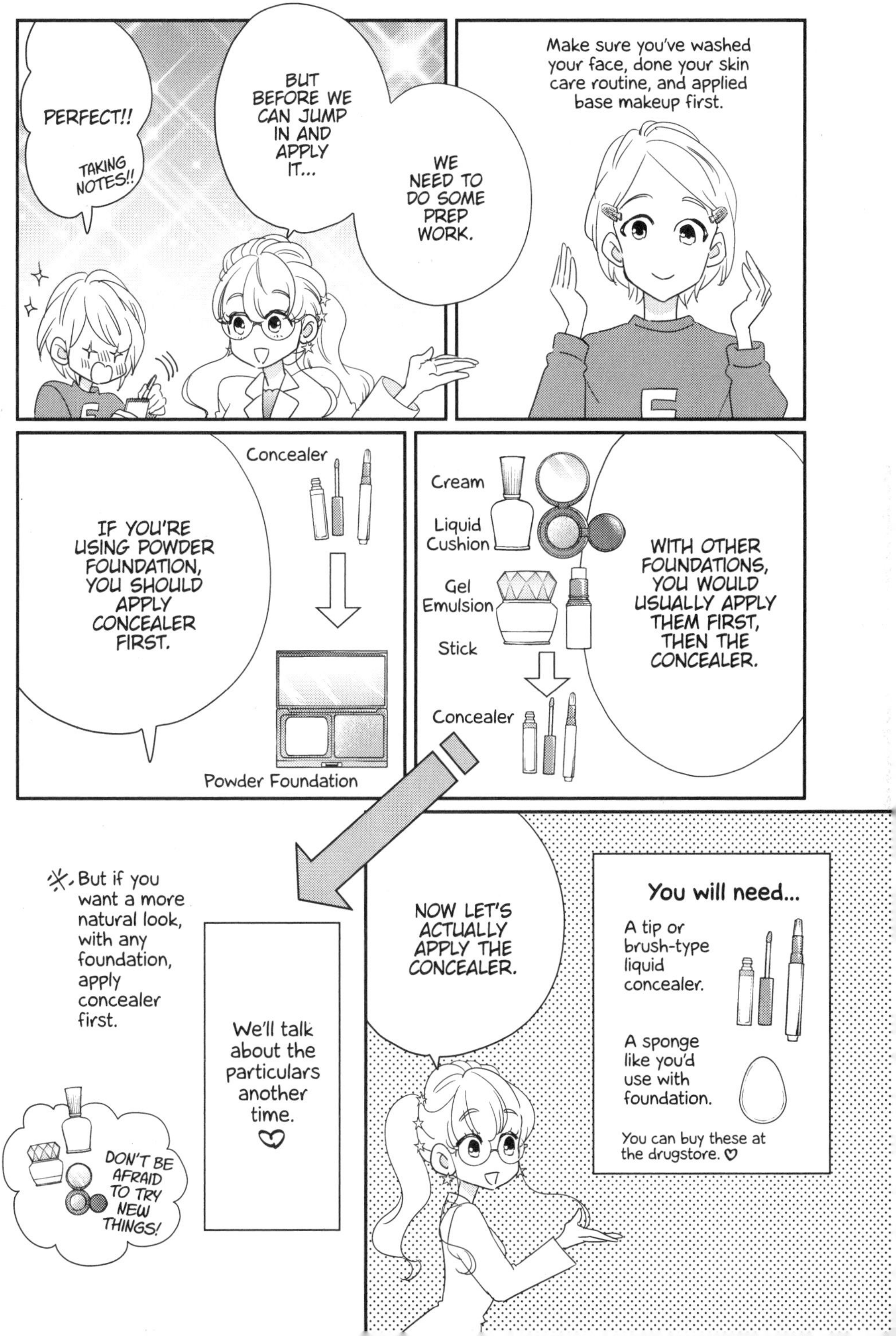
PERFECT!!
TAKING NOTES!!
BUT BEFORE WE CAN JUMP IN AND APPLY IT...
WE NEED TO DO SOME PREP WORK.
Make sure you've washed your face, done your skin care routine, and applied base makeup first.
IF YOU'RE USING POWDER FOUNDATION, YOU SHOULD APPLY CONCEALER FIRST.
Concealer
Powder Foundation
Cream
Liquid
Cushion
Gel
Emulsion
Stick
Concealer
WITH OTHER FOUNDATIONS, YOU WOULD USUALLY APPLY THEM FIRST, THEN THE CONCEALER.
※. But if you want a more natural look, with any foundation, apply concealer first.
We'll talk about the particulars another time. ♡
DON'T BE AFRAID TO TRY NEW THINGS!
NOW LET'S ACTUALLY APPLY THE CONCEALER.
You will need...
A tip or brush-type liquid concealer.
A sponge like you'd use with foundation.
You can buy these at the drugstore. ♡

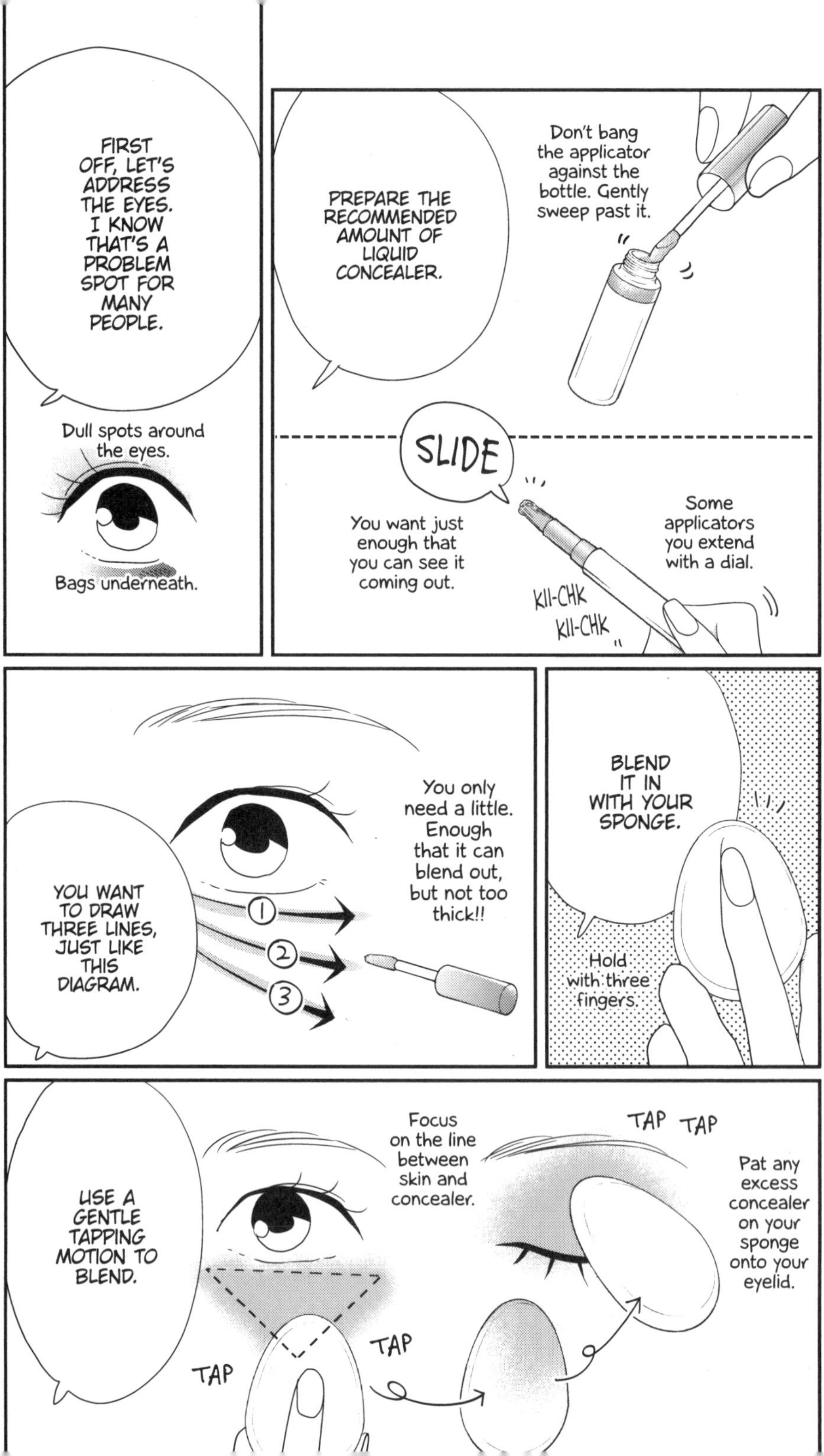

FIRST OFF, LET'S ADDRESS THE EYES. I KNOW THAT'S A PROBLEM SPOT FOR MANY PEOPLE.
Dull spots around the eyes.
Bags underneath.
PREPARE THE RECOMMENDED AMOUNT OF LIQUID CONCEALER.
Don't bang the applicator against the bottle. Gently sweep past it.
SLIDE
You want just enough that you can see it coming out.
Some applicators you extend with a dial.
KII-CHK KII-CHK
YOU WANT TO DRAW THREE LINES, JUST LIKE THIS DIAGRAM.
1
2
3
You only need a little. Enough that it can blend out, but not too thick!!
BLEND IT IN WITH YOUR SPONGE.
Hold with three fingers.
USE A GENTLE TAPPING MOTION TO BLEND.
Focus on the line between skin and concealer.
TAP TAP
Pat any excess concealer on your sponge onto your eyelid.
TAP
TAP

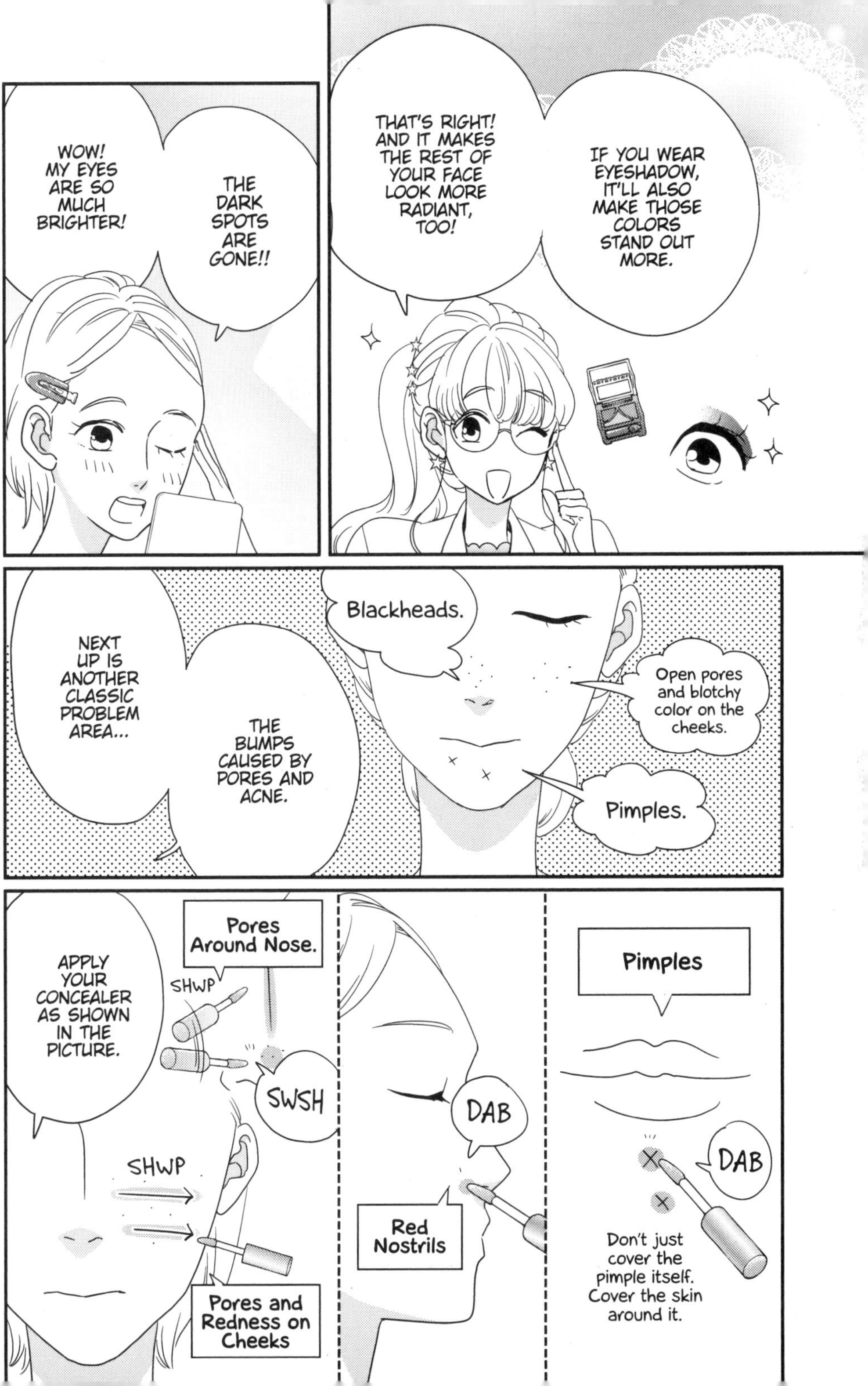
WOW! MY EYES ARE SO MUCH BRIGHTER!
THE DARK SPOTS ARE GONE!!
THAT'S RIGHT! AND IT MAKES THE REST OF YOUR FACE LOOK MORE RADIANT, TOO!
IF YOU WEAR EYESHADOW, IT'LL ALSO MAKE THOSE COLORS STAND OUT MORE.
NEXT UP IS ANOTHER CLASSIC PROBLEM AREA...
THE BUMPS CAUSED BY PORES AND ACNE.
Blackheads.
Open pores and blotchy color on the cheeks.
Pimples.
APPLY YOUR CONCEALER AS SHOWN IN THE PICTURE.
Pores Around Nose.
SHWP
SWSH
SHWP
Pores and Redness on Cheeks
DAB
Red Nostrils
Pimples
DAB
Don't just cover the pimple itself. Cover the skin around it.

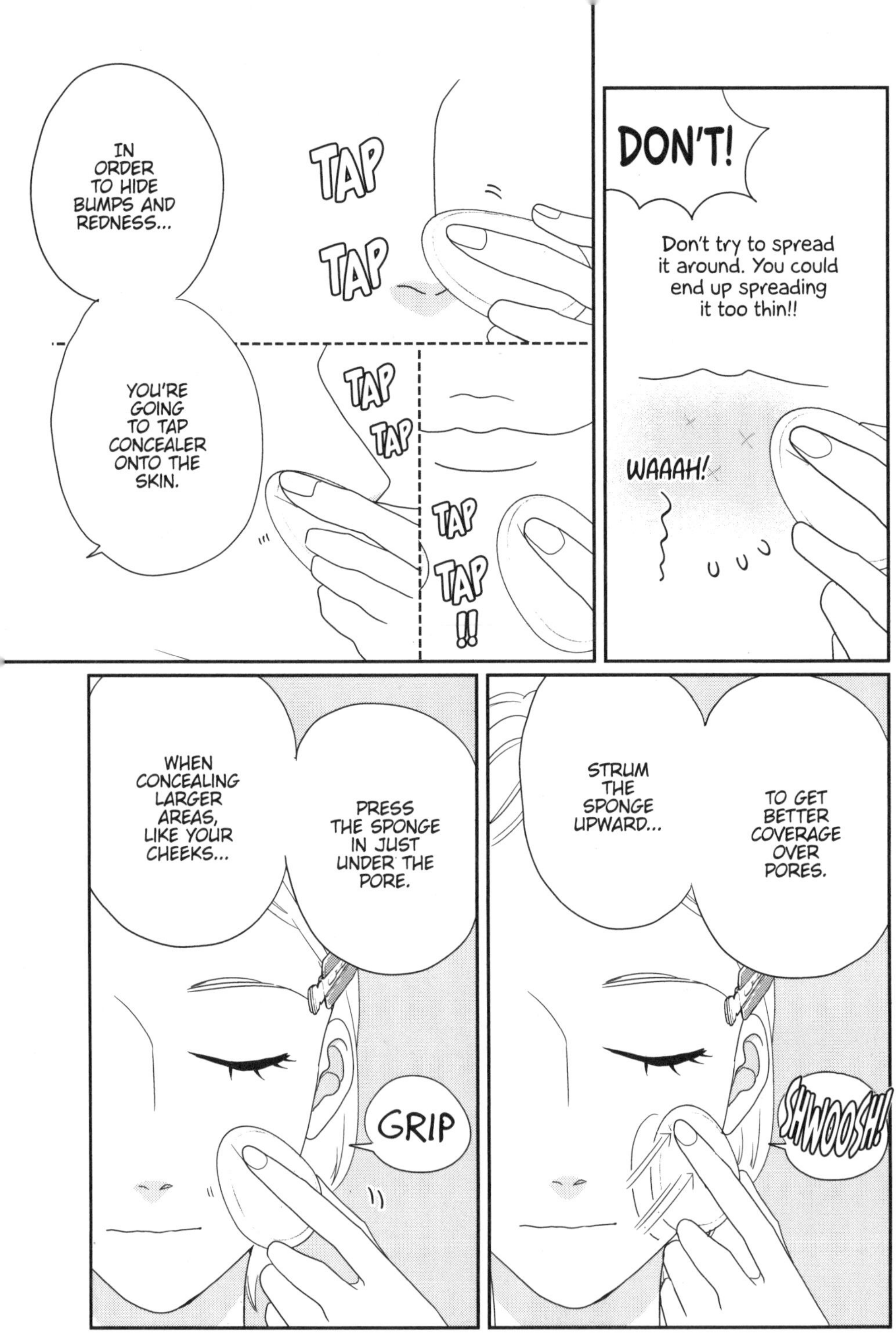

IN ORDER TO HIDE BUMPS AND REDNESS...
TAP
TAP
YOU'RE GOING TO TAP CONCEALER ONTO THE SKIN.
TAP
TAP
TAP
TAP!!
DON'T!
Don't try to spread it around. You could end up spreading it too thin!!
WAAAH!
WHEN CONCEALING LARGER AREAS, LIKE YOUR CHEEKS...
PRESS THE SPONGE IN JUST UNDER THE PORE.
GRIP
STRUM THE SPONGE UPWARD...
TO GET BETTER COVERAGE OVER PORES.
SHWOOSH!

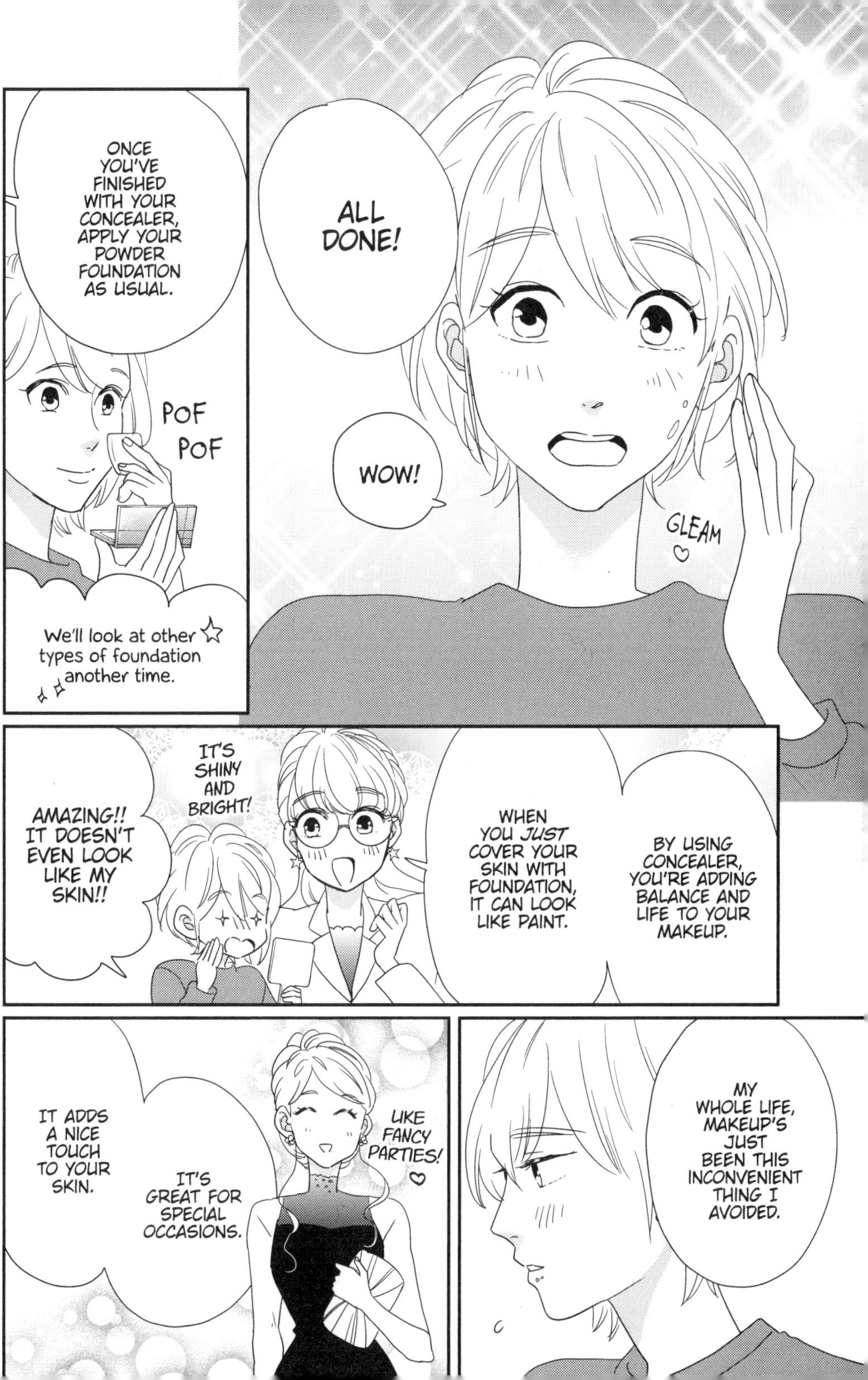
ONCE YOU'VE FINISHED WITH YOUR CONCEALER, APPLY YOUR POWDER FOUNDATION AS USUAL.
POF POF
We'll look at other types of foundation another time.
ALL DONE!
WOW!
GLEAM
AMAZING!! IT DOESN'T EVEN LOOK LIKE MY SKIN!!
IT'S SHINY AND BRIGHT!
WHEN YOU *JUST* COVER YOUR SKIN WITH FOUNDATION, IT CAN LOOK LIKE PAINT.
BY USING CONCEALER, YOU'RE ADDING BALANCE AND LIFE TO YOUR MAKEUP.
IT ADDS A NICE TOUCH TO YOUR SKIN.
IT'S GREAT FOR SPECIAL OCCASIONS.
LIKE FANCY PARTIES!
MY WHOLE LIFE, MAKEUP'S JUST BEEN THIS INCONVENIENT THING I AVOIDED.

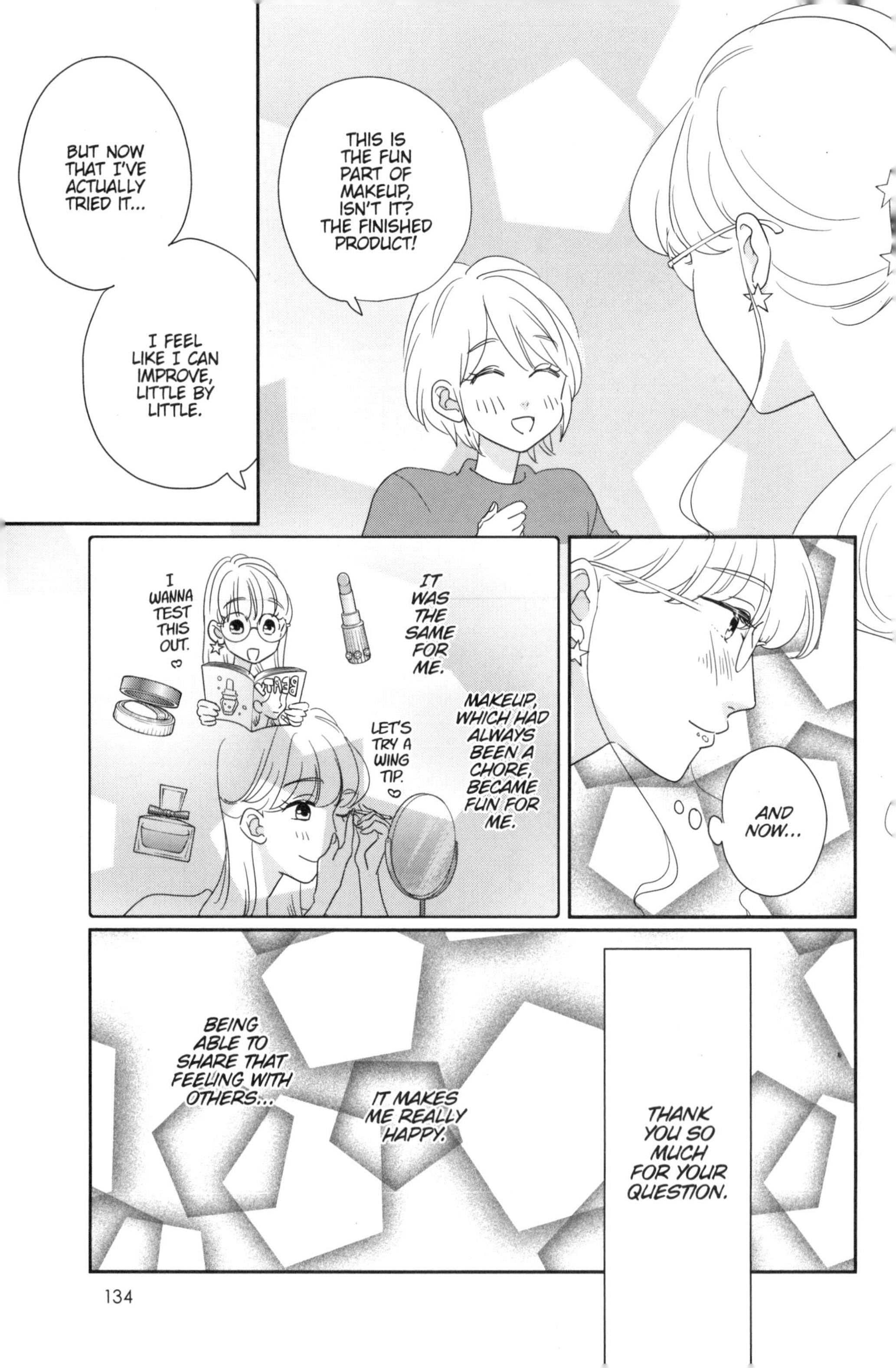

THIS IS THE FUN PART OF MAKEUP, ISN'T IT? THE FINISHED PRODUCT!
BUT NOW THAT I'VE ACTUALLY TRIED IT...
I FEEL LIKE I CAN IMPROVE, LITTLE BY LITTLE.
IT WAS THE SAME FOR ME.
I WANNA TEST THIS OUT.
LET'S TRY A WING TIP.
MAKEUP, WHICH HAD ALWAYS BEEN A CHORE, BECAME FUN FOR ME.
AND NOW...
BEING ABLE TO SHARE THAT FEELING WITH OTHERS...
IT MAKES ME REALLY HAPPY.
THANK YOU SO MUCH FOR YOUR QUESTION.

Afterword

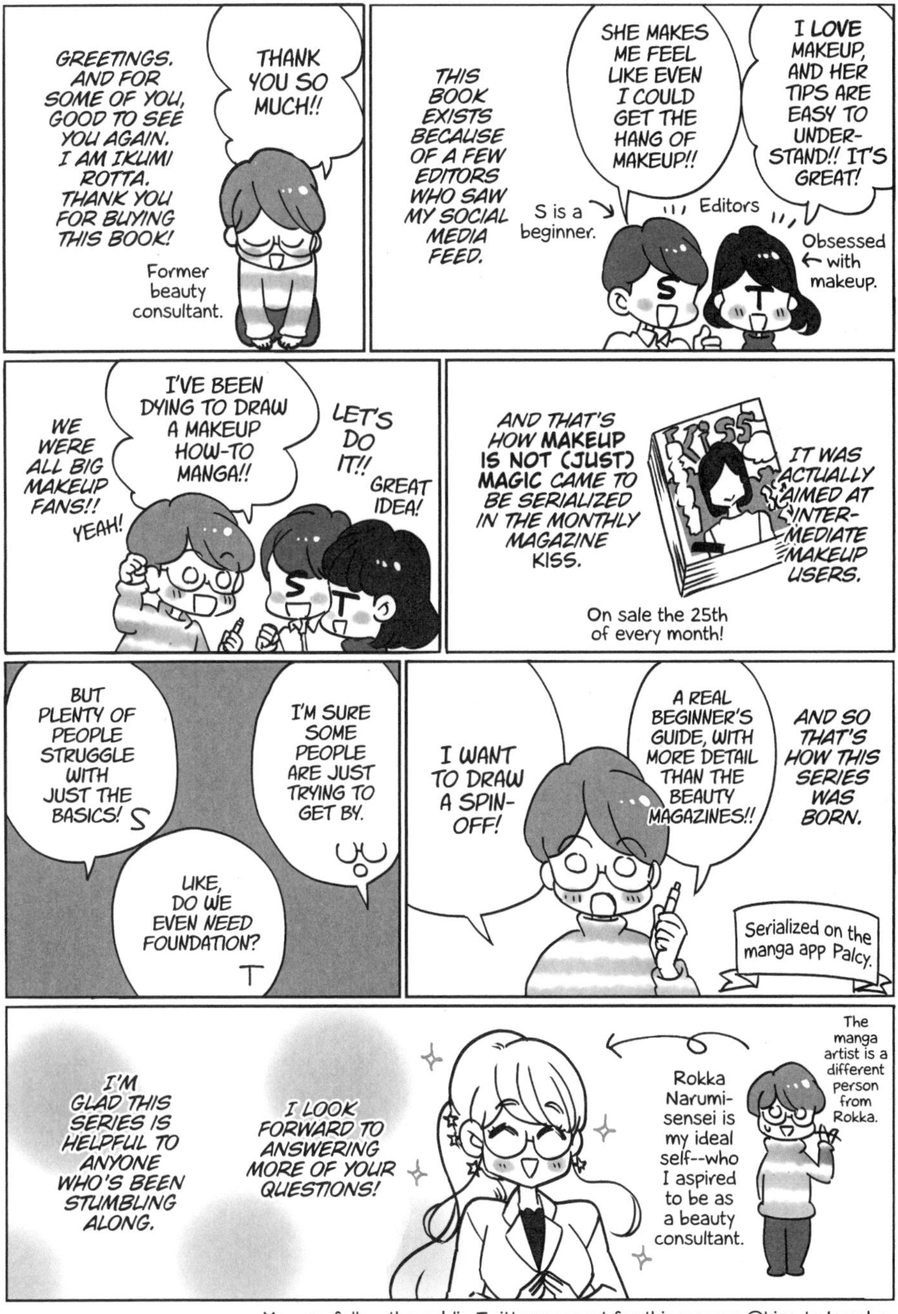

GREETINGS. AND FOR SOME OF YOU, GOOD TO SEE YOU AGAIN. I AM IKUMI ROTTA. THANK YOU FOR BUYING THIS BOOK!
THANK YOU SO MUCH!!
Former beauty consultant.
THIS BOOK EXISTS BECAUSE OF A FEW EDITORS WHO SAW MY SOCIAL MEDIA FEED.
SHE MAKES ME FEEL LIKE EVEN I COULD GET THE HANG OF MAKEUP!!
I LOVE MAKEUP, AND HER TIPS ARE EASY TO UNDER-STAND!! IT'S GREAT!
S is a beginner.
Editors
Obsessed with makeup.
S
T
WE WERE ALL BIG MAKEUP FANS!!
I'VE BEEN DYING TO DRAW A MAKEUP HOW-TO MANGA!!
LET'S DO IT!!
YEAH!
GREAT IDEA!
S
T
AND THAT'S HOW MAKEUP IS NOT (JUST) MAGIC CAME TO BE SERIALIZED IN THE MONTHLY MAGAZINE KISS.
IT WAS ACTUALLY AIMED AT INTER-MEDIATE MAKEUP USERS.
On sale the 25th of every month!
BUT PLENTY OF PEOPLE STRUGGLE WITH JUST THE BASICS!
S
I'M SURE SOME PEOPLE ARE JUST TRYING TO GET BY.
LIKE, DO WE EVEN NEED FOUNDATION?
T
I WANT TO DRAW A SPIN-OFF!
A REAL BEGINNER'S GUIDE, WITH MORE DETAIL THAN THE BEAUTY MAGAZINES!!
AND SO THAT'S HOW THIS SERIES WAS BORN.
Serialized on the manga app Palcy.
I'M GLAD THIS SERIES IS HELPFUL TO ANYONE WHO'S BEEN STUMBLING ALONG.
I LOOK FORWARD TO ANSWERING MORE OF YOUR QUESTIONS!
Rokka Narumi-sensei is my ideal self--who I aspired to be as a beauty consultant.
The manga artist is a different person from Rokka.

You can follow the public Twitter account for this manga: @kiss_tadamaho

SEVEN SEAS ENTERTAINMENT PRESENTS

Makeup is Not (just) *Magic*

A Manga Guide to
Cosmetics and
Skin Care

written and illustrated by IKUMI ROTTA

TRANSLATION
Amber Tamosaitis

ADAPTATION
Marykate Jasper

LETTERING AND RETOUCH
Karis Page

COVER DESIGN
Nicky Lim

PROOFREADER
Kurestin Armada

EDITOR
Shannon Fay

PREPRESS TECHNICIAN
Rhiannon Rasmussen-Silverstein

PRODUCTION MANAGER
Lissa Pattillo

MANAGING EDITOR
Julie Davis

ASSOCIATE PUBLISHER
Adam Arnold

PUBLISHER
Jason DeAngelis

MAKEUP IS NOT (JUST) MAGIC:
A MANGA GUIDE TO COSMETICS AND SKIN CARE
© Rotta Ikumi 2019
First published in Japan in 2019 by Kodansha Ltd., Tokyo.
Publication rights for this English edition arranged through Kodansha
Ltd., Tokyo.

Seven Seas press and purchase enquiries can be sent to Marketing
Manager Lianne Sentar at press@gomanga.com. Information regarding
the distribution and purchase of digital editions is available from Digital
Manager CK Russell at digital@gomanga.com.

Seven Seas and the Seven Seas logo are trademarks of
Seven Seas Entertainment. All rights reserved.

ISBN: 978-1-64505-446-7

Printed in Canada

First Printing: May 2020

10 9 8 7 6 5 4 3 2 1

References:
· *Japan Cosmetics Test Class 1 Measures Textbook*, Sayaka Konishi (2016).
· *Japan Cosmetics Test Class 2 and 3 Measures Textbook*, Sayaka Konishi (2016).
Supervised by the Japan Cosmetics Certification Association, Shufunotomosha.